THE ANTICHRIST LEGEND

AMERICAN ACADEMY OF RELIGION
TEXTS AND TRANSLATIONS SERIES

Edited by

Terry Godlove
Hofstra University

Number 24
THE ANTICHRIST LEGEND
A Chapter in Christian and Jewish Folklore

W. BOUSSET
Translated by A. H. Keane
Introduction by D. Frankfurter

THE ANTICHRIST LEGEND
A Chapter in Christian and Jewish Folklore

W. BOUSSET
Translated by A. H. Keane
Introduction by D. Frankfurter

Scholars Press
Atlanta, Georgia

THE ANTICHRIST LEGEND

A Chapter in Christian and Jewish Folklore

W. BOUSSET
Translated by A. H. Keane
Introduction by D. Frankfurter

Copyright ©1999 by the American Academy of Religion

Library of Congress Cataloging in Publication Data

Bousset, Wilhelm, 1865–1920.
    The antichrist legend : a chapter in Christian and Jewish folklore / W. Bousset ; translated by A. H. Keane ; introduction by D. Frankfurter.
       p.   cm. — (Texts and translations series ; no. 24)
    Originally published: London ; Hutchinson, 1896.
    Includes bibliographical references and index.
    ISBN 0-7885-0541-6 (paper : alk. paper)
    1. Antichrist—History of doctrines. I. Title. II. Series:
Texts and translations series (American Academy of Religion) ; no. 24.
BT985.B7 1999
236—dc21   99-12981
                              CIP

Printed in the United States of America
on acid-free paper

TABLE OF CONTENTS.

Publisher's Note: This volume is reprinted with permission from the AMS Press edition of 1979, which itself was a reprint of the English translation of *The Antichrist Legend* as first published (London: Hutchinson, 1896). The new Introduction by David Frankfurter is set apart from the original text in a pagination format of "*iii," etc. This format maintains the integrity of the pagination in the original text and assures the continuing usefulness of the original index.

INTRODUCTION.

THE STUDY OF ESCHATOLOGY.

T HEN another portent appeared in heaven: a great red dragon,
with seven heads and ten horns, and seven diadems on his
heads. His tail swept down a third of the stars of heaven and threw
them to the earth. . . . And war broke out in heaven; Michael and his
angels fought against the dragon. . . . The great dragon was thrown
down, that ancient serpent, who is called the Devil and Satan, the
deceiver of the whole world—he was thrown down to the earth, and
his angels were thrown down with him. [Rev 12:3-4, 7, 9 NRSV]

Whether read aloud or portrayed in image, as in the famous woodcuts of Albrecht Dürer, this description has the
singular capacity to challenge an audience not only to imagine but to *identify* the dragon. Everything in it suggests
that "more" is going on: extraneous but portentous details
like heads and horns, for example; clues in names (Devil,
Satan); the unclarity of time (Once-upon-a-time? Now?
Soon?); and the illusion of the battle's finality. Thus opens
the vortex of apocalyptic symbolism: a world of conspiracy,

calculation, circular reasoning, and preparation for the end
into which both groups and individuals, believers and, more
recently, scholars have been drawn for more than two
millennia.

What draws scholars to the topic is the sheer imagination
of end-time scenarios and their power in mobilizing prophets, sects, and mass-religions. We are fascinated as well by
that tendency among believers to linger obsessively over
details and numbers, to seek with all conviction a precise
reading of time, events, people. Our curiosity is drawn to
that balance that arises between social structure and what
we might call the eschatological consciousness, as well as
to those rationalizing instincts that perpetually impel believers to put imminence off and balance the raw charisma
of immediate change with the need for order and program.

As a scholarly pursuit, the study of end-time beliefs has
roots in post-Enlightenment culture, which simultaneously
required that religious belief-systems be subject to systematic analysis and created a kind of longing for the irrational, the Dionysiac, in its most extreme and overwhelming
forms. And the symbols of eschatology, whether biblical,
Zoroastrian, Norse, or Mayan, are nothing if not overwhelming. Wilhelm Bousset was among the first to study eschatology according to the most systematic analysis of the era;
but he was followed by a steady river of scholarship that
has lasted much of this century: R. H. Charles' *Eschatology* (1899; 2nd ed. 1913), Mircea Eliade's *The Myth of the
Eternal Return* (first, French ed. 1949), the rise to domi-
nance of Albert Schweitzer's model of an eschatologically-

oriented Jesus, detailed research on extra-canonical Jewish and Christian books that surpass in imagination even the Book of Revelation, and now, as we near the turn of the millennium (according to the exoteric calendar never taken seriously by true millennialists), an *Encyclopedia of Apocalypticism* that surveys the entire western tradition in all its strangeness and power (McGinn, Collins, and Stein, eds., 1998).

WILHELM BOUSSET AND THE HISTORY-OF-RELIGION SCHOOL.

Born to a devout Protestant family in 1865, Johann Franz Wilhelm Bousset studied at Leipzig, then Göttingen, where he assumed a professorship in New Testament in 1896. With the combined intellectual forces of Albert Eichhorn, Wilhelm Rede, Hermann Gunkel, Ernst Troeltsch, and Bousset, Göttingen was to become the center of the "History-of-Religion School [*religionsgeschichtliche Schule*]," a consortium of scholars devoted to bringing the full battery of critical methods—literary, historical, social-scientific, folkloric—upon the study of early Christianity and its scriptures (See Lüdemann/Schroder 1987). Gunkel described their enterprise as

. . . a history of religion without breaches or window-dressing, carried out according to the strict rules of the rest of the discipline of history; it is a history of religion which shows the intricate picture of a religion as it stands in inmost connection to the political, cultural and social milieux; it shows how religious ideas originate, how they grapple and unite among themselves, how the stuff of religion is transferred from one generation to the next, continually altered and bearing new ideas. [*Reden und Aufsätze* (Göttingen: Vanden-hoeck & Ruprecht, 1913), vi, tr. Chapman 57].

Underlying their methodology, however, lay a peculiar mixture of quasi-mystical Protestantism, anti-dogmatism and theological rationalism, and more than a hint of anti-Catholicism (Chapman 1993; Smith 1990, ch. 1). Through scientific method, the Göttingen scholars believed, the historical influence of established Religion, its myths and scriptures, could be scrutinized and broken, and people could then return to a more interior and individualized experience of Christianity—or of the Holy itself, as Rudolf Otto would later carry the idea.

The Antichrist Legend, published in 1895, arises naturally from the *religionsgeschichtliche* enterprise in its most exciting aspect: to study religion not through its official, intellectual, dogmatic media, but through the strange subterranean currents that perpetually rise up in ritual and enthusiastic piety. In Bousset's words,

one looks at the broad stream of the religious life which flows along a different bed from which we had previously imagined; it flows along the bed of moods and fantasies, of experiences and events of the most primitive kind which are often difficult to control. [Bousset, "Die Religionsgeschichte und das neue Testament," *Theologische Rundschau* 7 (1904):271, tr. Chapman 56]

In dwelling on one of the central *dramatis personae* of the ancient Jewish and Christian apocalyptic imagination, moreover, Bousset reflects the *religionsgeschichtliche*

Schule's radical new focus on apocalypticism itself as the essential dynamic in the genesis of Christianity. Jesus and his followers emerged out of a storm of fantastic end-time speculation and otherworldly prophets; and, for Bousset and his colleagues, Antichrist beliefs fairly epitomized that storm. At the same time, *The Antichrist Legend* demonstrates the power of historical, textual, and folkloric research to demystify one of the great dogmas of Protestant and Catholic institutions alike. And here in particular Bousset reflects two more basic sentiments in turn-of-the-century European academic culture.

First, the reader can detect the excitement of discovery—in particular, of the mythological antecedents of biblical ideas, evident in the tablets and art excavated in the Near East. Bousset's colleague Hermann Gunkel was at the same time proposing that the mythical chaos dragons (Tiamat, Leviathan, Yam) appearing repeatedly in various ancient near eastern texts represented an archetype of sorts, which in turn lay behind the "ancient serpent" in Revelation 12 (quoted above). The Göttingen scholars, and even more their British Orientalist followers, like Bousset's translator Keane and the subsequent "Pan Babylonian" and "Myth-Ritual" Schools, began to direct their search for the nature of biblical symbols towards distant antiquity, even (as Keane proposes) prehistoric culture and its ecology. With texts like the *Enuma Elish* and, later, the tablets from Ugarit, one could practice an "archaeology of symbols" much like the archaeology of cities, following motifs and ideas back through layers to original formulations in far more primitive times. If their sense of the historical transmission of these symbols and ideas was vague—one winces at Bousset's notion of a "secret oral tradition" (7)—these scholars forged ahead with the enthusiastic conviction that an obscure apocalyptic symbol's true character was to be found not in its later, scriptural manifestation but in its more full-blown exposition in ancient, myth-dominated times.

The second attitude that emerges in *The Antichrist Legend* concerns those scholars and interpreters who either preceded or remained on the outside of the *religionsgeschichtliche Schule* and held onto traditional ecclesiastical (or even uncritically apocalyptic) perspectives on history and scripture. Bousset's subtle disdain for dogmatic traditionalists could hardly be surprising at this period of post-enlightenment scholarship on religion and the Bible. "In a period of secularization," one historian has noted, the Göttingen scholars' enthusiasm for tracing biblical images to ancient near eastern mythology "supported the conviction that the Old Testament—which for so long had been the revealed Word of God—was just a collection of stories, borrowed in part from other nations, and must be treated like any other 'literature'" (De Vries 70). And in thus giving ancient myths interpretive authority over scripture like the Book of Revelation, Gunkel, Bousset, Keane, and others were also reflecting a lingering resentment towards the use of apocalyptic scripture to interpret current events *eisegetically*—reading present realities (world wars, cruel monarchs) *into* scripture without regard for the sense of the passage itself. For Bousset and the *religions-geschichtliche Schule,* this crude form of confessional interpretation flew in the face of the great advances that historical criticism offered.

Now, in the contemporary American religious landscape, we may be familiar with Hal Lindsay, Scoville Bible commentaries, prophecy seminars, and the establishment of Adventism; but critical biblical scholarship pays their interpretations of prophecy little heed. Thus we may find it difficult to recapture the deep irrita-tion that preachers of "realized prophecy" caused scholars like Bousset at the turn of the century. Then, as now, the Book of Revelation represented for many believers a potential script for the outcome of any war, the unveiling of any world-leader; but critical scholarship (and secularization itself) had not then influenced the broader culture of Bible-followers enough to be a match for this kind of interpretation. Thus turn-of-the-century biblical scholars of an empirical, modernist bent sought actively to remove scripture from service as key to history and incitement to irrational activity.

One sees Bousset's explicit rejection of eisegetical, "realized" interpretations of the Antichrist image both in this book (10) and in his subsequent (1924) entry on the same topic for Hastings' *Encyclopedia of Religion and Ethics* (581; see also Schmidt 97-98). Ironically, when the noted scholar of ancient apocalyptic texts R. H. Charles sought to revise Bousset's Antichrist theory for his own commentary on the Book of Revelation, he once again took Antichrist as some trans-historical, monolithic truth to be applied to current history: "in regard to the present war, it is difficult to determine whether the Kaiser or his people can advance the best claims to the title of modern Antichrist"(2:87).

ANTICHRIST AND ESCHATOLOGICAL ADVERSARIES.

With this complex and even polemical background in mind, we might more easily understand Bousset's more glaring errors in assembling an "Antichrist Legend" as products of the time. The first systematic layout of an Antichrist "legend," the work of the second-century Latin church father Hippolytus, conjured a monolithic figure, a singular representative of eschatological evil whose reality was more important than the particular (and often conflicting) details and texts from which he was extrapolated. Bousset's opponents, the Revelation-eisegetes—those who applied the text to contemporary events—inherited this same confessional tendency towards a monolithic Antichrist; and so also Bousset assumed that all the vivid and various details he so voluminously documented in this book revolved around one basic idea: a figure of monstrous, trans-historical evil. Indeed, such diverse texts as 2 Thessalonians, the Book of Revelation, 1 and 2 John, and the Gospel of Matthew, chapter 24, are, for Bousset, mere outcrops of an underlying legend, which might be mixed and matched like so many puzzle-pieces. The notion that this underlying legend could have stemmed from the ancient chaos-dragon of Near Eastern lore whom all creator gods had to slay in order to establish order in the universe, as Gunkel proposed, would thus have represented a natural move for the times: monolithic symbols like Antichrist for these scholars must have monolithic heritages—like ancient creation mythology. Consequently, Bousset depended inordinately upon texts that actually *describe* a great supernatural adversary in dragon-like imagery—as in the Book of Revelation's twelfth chapter—and on later patristic depictions of a monstrous Antichrist (143-53). In fact, Revelation's seven-headed dragon is a quite distinct figure from other "Antichrist" refractions: the same book's tyrannical "beast" (ch. 13), the *pseudochristoi* of the gospels (Mk 13:22 & par.), or the multiple *antichristoi* appearing in the Epistles of John.

Today, in our own era of radical nominalism, in which every generalization is eventually exploded into discrete cultural, historical, or textual particulars, Bousset's actual conclusions have little historical value. "Antichrist" beliefs, if we can speak of such a genus of eschatological motif, must be understood in the context of the individual authors who coin them. And yet Bousset's contribution still carries much value. At the very least, the book is a gold-mine of eschatological tableaux as they developed through the medieval period. One might, to be sure, want to check the latest editions and translations—and the publication of obscure early Christian literature of the sort Bousset surveys has multiplied to a staggering degree over the last half-century with series like the *Corpus Scriptorum Christianorum*

Orientalium and the *Corpus Christianorum, Series Apocryphorum.* But Bousset provides a convenient overview of the immense and quite imaginative eschatological fantasy-world of late antique, Byzantine, and early medieval ecclesiastical writers.

The Antichrist Legend also makes some important methodological points that are useful to consider historically. In broadest terms, Bousset argues that the religious conceptualization of evil has a history, and that one should at least recognize a long sequence of traditions, albeit different, that go back to early antiquity. One must, we know now, be primarily attentive to immediate cultural worlds to understand the meaning of a symbol of evil; and yet the power of that symbol derives partly from a *lineage* of traditions of symbolizing, personifying, and articulating evil in intimate terms. Whereas for Gunkel and Bousset this history may have consisted in an unwavering body of lore passed down through cultures, for us it may have a more abstract connotation, highlighting perhaps an author's ways of indicating that "this" evil is of a character transcending history.

For Bousset the very recognition of the history behind the symbol would *correct* the popular interpretation of eschatological adversaries as the Bible's unique attempt to warn contemporary mankind. Together with Gunkel's *Schöpfung und Chaos, The Antichrist Legend* was supposed to prove the antiquity of the human preoccupation with identifying evil and dispense with the uniqueness of the biblical revelations. Bousset himself carried this thesis further, illustrating the symbols' historical *proclivity* to attract current global misfortunes, political or theological rivals, or opponents of any stripe. That is, if people were imagining Antichrist to be a European leader in Bousset's day, then they were likewise labelling the Pope in Martin Luther's time and the Roman imperium in the days of the Book of Revelation. For us, on the other hand, to acknowledge that the symbolism of evil and the rhetoric of conceptualizing religious opposition both *depend* on tradition, a sense of the archaic, provides a useful corrective against reading every apocalyptic symbol as a banal allegory for events and persons of a particular period. The point, we should realize, is not that the dragon of Revelation 12 or the beast of Revelation 13 or the Lawless One of 2 Thessalonians 2 represents one emperor or another in the time of the early Christian authors, but that each figure is a monstrous conglomerate of evil, deceit, rivalry, and arrogance, and that this monstrousness, not the human forms and nefarious political acts, constitutes the figure's "true nature." There is an allusion to "history," to be sure, but "history" is only the puppet theatre for the actions of far greater powers. "Our struggle is *not* against enemies of blood and flesh," warns one first-century Greek Christian, "but against the rulers, against the authorities, against the cosmic powers of this present darkness, against the spiritual forces of evil in the heavenly places" (Eph 6:12). Too much scholarly focus on the historical tyrants in authors' midsts may obscure the larger, more paranoid point they seek to make.

NEW QUESTIONS AND DIRECTIONS.

Studies of the Antichrist idea since Bousset have worked gradually towards the historicizing and dismantling of the category in the monolithic, ahistorical sense in which Bousset assembled it. R. H. Charles (1920, 2:76-87) distinguished a Satanic "Beliar myth" from an anthropomorphic "Antichrist myth" and a quasi-historical "Nero *redivivus*" legend, and he proposed stages for their entanglement over the course of the first century C.E. A. Yarbro Collins (1976) showed that the symbols of evil in the Book of Revelation, at least, have little to do with "Antichrists," although much to do with ancient combat myths and with traditions of Nero *redivivus* (and they do cluster in basic opposition to the multiform Christ of the Book of Revelation). Gregory Jenks (1991) traced the origin of an "Antichrist myth," apparently consolidated during the third century C.E., to a Jewish image of the "Endtyrant," which had developed through various encounters with horrific Gentile rulers. Jenks but nuanced the progressive, teleological explanation of "Antichrist" beliefs that Charles had initiated: the Jewish and early Christian texts, although wildly diverse in their images of eschatological adversaries, represented no more than milestones on the way to *the* "Antichrist myth." Consequently L. J. Lietaert Peerbolte (1996) examined these texts on their own terms—1 and 2 John, 2 Thessalonians, Revelation, *Ascension of Isaiah, Apocalypse of Peter,* and others, all among the most vivid and passionate attempts at conceptualizing eschatological evil—in order to trace what patterns may have influenced the construction of these "Antichrist proof-texts.

What Lietaert Peerbolte found poses an interesting corrective to the kind of grand scope that makes Bousset so captivating. First, each text seems to emanate from a preexisting *but discrete* world of speculation and biblical exegesis. Secondly, the overwhelming concern in the earliest Christian documents is not, as many have assumed, with evil "Endtyrants" and Nero-types (as he shows to be the interest of contemporaneous Jewish documents) but rather with false prophets and teachings. Thirdly, the earliest Christian images of ultimate, personified evil pertain not to an eventual or imminent eschaton but to the immediate time of the writer: it is the urgency of current rivalries that elicits such demonization, not casual speculation on the end of the world. The individual worlds of these Antichrist proof-texts are thus at a considerable remove from the Antichrist legend, which, we may now say, began with Hippolytus's second-century treatise on the topic: not with distant antiquity nor with the first mention of the Greek word *antichristos* in 1 Jn 2:18.

But if the scholarship on eschatological adversaries and the personification of evil must now distinguish sharply between traditions pre- (and extra-) Hippolytus and traditions post-Hippolytus, such work remains of great interest in the contemporary field of History of Religions—and of some importance as well, since popular attempts to identify Antichrist in history have continued at a gallop throughout the twentieth century. Bernard McGinn (1994) has discussed the history of the post-Hippolytus Antichrist legend as an alternative demonology to the all-too-invisible Satan: the man-devil Antichrist mirrors the man-god Christ and is thus somehow more tangible in the historical world and in the imbroglios of human community. At the same time, Boyer (1992), O'Leary (1994), and Fuller (1995) have all analyzed the past century and a half of American Christian eschatologies, invariably revolving around the identification of Antichrist. It is perhaps especially in this area that Bousset's deepest mission is being furthered: the eisegetes, the confessional eschatologists, become data in their own right, not simply the retrograde opponents of Revelation scholars.

One way of looking at this kind of literature that has been less apparent in the studies of Antichrist's "origins" begins precisely with the observation, reaffirmed by Lietaert Peerbolte, that what motivated the earliest conceptualizations of eschatological adversaries in the Christian movement (and, significantly, also among the Qumran sectarians) was anxiety about false charismatic leadership (Frankfurter 1993). In apocalyptic sects led primarily by prophetic leaders, believers' overwhelming need for *precision* in preparing for their new millennial status is only exacerbated by their need for precision in discerning true from false *leadership* and *teachings*. In a world in which everything is stated with conviction the ambiguity of truth amounts to a crisis, and differences—as the sociologist Georg Simmel once pointed out—need to be sharpened according to the starkest cosmic polarities. In a world consumed with "unveiling" the secret supernatural design of these latter days, true and false leadership must signify the militant intervention of angelic or demonic forces: thus the apostle Paul's demonizing rhetoric in 2 Corinthians (11:13-15) and that of the Johannine Epistles (1 Jn 4:1-6; 2 Jn 7). Some texts conjure an eschatological adversary as a way of negotiating more ambiguous rivalries: 2 Thessalonians 2:3-11 sharpens the nature of a conflict expressed more vaguely in 1:6-9, while the third-century prophetic tract *Apocalypse of Elijah* turns to the signs of the "Lawless One" immediately after denouncing rival teachers.

It is when this latter author turns to physiognomic and thaumaturgical signs by which the Adversary might be known that we discover how precision—the imagination and collection of details—can provide a hedge against uncertainty and ambiguity, crises that could and repeatedly did rip sectarian communities apart: "By this you will *know* that he is the Lawless One!" assures the *Apocalypse of Elijah* (3:18). The list, the physiognomy, the demonological nomenclature (the choice of "Lawless One" or "antichrist" or "beast"), like the apocalyptic timetable, had more than speculative value for apocalyptic communities; they had functional value, creating a sense of coherence in an incoherent world. The traditions of eschatological adversaries were indeed a dimension of demonology, one that arose in and served apocalyptic sects preoccupied with the authority of charismatic leaders. As often as such traditions became spiritualized or banally politicized through history, they also repeatedly fired and polarized apocalyptic sects in their internecine disputes. As we bring *The Antichrist Legend* into the twenty-first century we would do well to acknowledge this social context for the symbolizing of the eschatological adversary, which Bousset altogether neglected, for we are dealing here with a symbol of forceful dimensions even without the scales, heads, and sweeping tail.

BIBLIOGRAPHY.

Bousset, Wilhelm

    1924   "Antichrist." *Encyclopedia of Religion and Ethics,* vol. 1, pp. 578-81. Ed. James Hastings. New York: Scribners.

Boyer, Paul

    1992   *When Time Shall Be No More.* Cambridge: Harvard University Press.

Chapman, Mark D.

    1993   "Religion, Ethics and the History of Religion School." *Scottish Journal of Theology* 46:43-78.

Charles, R. H.

    1920   *A Critical and Exegetical Commentary on the Revelation of St. John* 1-2. Edinburgh: T. & T. Clark.

    1913   *Eschatology: The Doctrine of a Future Life in Israel, Judaism and Christianity.* 2nd ed., London: A. & C. Black. Repr. ed., New York: Schocken, 1963.

de Vries, Jan.

    1977   *Perspectives in the History of Religions.* Tr. by Kees W. Bolle. Berkeley: University of California Press.

Eliade, Mircea
   1965   *The Myth of the Eternal Return, or Cosmos and History.* Princeton: Princeton University Press.

Frankfurter, David
   1993   *Elijah in Upper Egypt: The Apocalypse of Elijah and Early Egyptian Christianity.* Minneapolis: Fortress.

Fuller, Robert
   1995   *Naming the Antichrist: The History of An American Obsession.* New York: Oxford.

Gunkel, Hermann
   1895   *Schöpfung und Chaos in Urzeit und Enzeit: Eine religionsgeschichtliche Untersuchung über Gen 1 und Ap Joh 12.* Göttingen: Vandenhoeck und Ruprecht.

Jenks, Gregory C.
   1991   *The Origins and Early Development of the Antichrist Myth.* Berlin and New York: De Gruyter.

Lietaert Peerbolte, L. J.
   1996   *The Antecedents of Antichrist: A Traditio—Historical Study of the Earliest Christian Views on Eschatological Opponents.* Leiden: E. J. Brill.

Lüdemann, Gerd, and Schroder, Martin
   1987   *Die Religionsgeschichtliche Schule in Gottingen: eine Dokumentation.* Gottingen: Vandenhoeck & Ruprecht, 1987.

McGinn, Bernard
   1994   *Antichrist: Two Thousand Years of the Human Fascination with Evil.* San Francisco: HarperCollins.

McGinn, Bernard; Collins, John J.; and Stein, Stephen, eds.
    1998   *Encyclopedia of Apocalypticism.* 3 vols. New York: Continuum.

O'Leary, Stephen
    1994   *Arguing the Apocalypse: A Theory of Millennial Rhetoric.* New York: Oxford University Press.

Schmidt, Johann Michael
    1981   "Bousset, Wilhelm (1865-1920)." *Theologische Realenzyklopdie,* vol. 7, pp.97-101. Berlin: De Gruyter.

Smith, Jonathan Z.
    1990   *Drudgery Divine: On the Comparison of Early Christianities and the Religions of Late Antiquity.* Chicago: University of Chicago Press.

Yarbro Collins, Adela
    1975   *The Combat Myth in the Book of Revelation.* Missoula MT: Scholars Press.

DAVID FRANKFURTER

TABLE OF CONTENTS.

PART II.

HISTORY OF THE ANTICHRIST LEGEND.

CHAPTER IX.

CHAPTER X.

CHAPTER XI.

CHAPTER XII.

AUTHOR'S PREFACE.

I CANNOT better introduce the present treatise than by a remark appended by Gutschmid to his critique of Zezschwitz' work *On Roman Imperialism of German Nationality* : " The whole of this apocalyptic literature, extending on the one hand from the Book of Daniel, or even from the Old Testament Prophets, and on the other from the Cymæan Sibyl, in an all but unbroken chain, down to the time of Capistrano and the capture of Constantinople by the Turks, has hitherto been strangely neglected by historians. Yet it would be difficult to mention any other manifestation of popular thought in which was at all to the same extent directly reflected the impression produced by historical events on contemporary generations, on their ideas, hopes, and fears." * I may here add that in this work I have been unable to offer more than an indispensable preliminary essay on the subject to which Gutschmid draws attention. I trust, however, still

---

* *Kleine Schriften*, V. 505.

to find time and strength for a comprehensive treatment of the eschatology of the Christian Church. Meanwhile the sketch, such as it is, may perhaps serve to stimulate the efforts of other workers in this endlessly entangled and almost limitless field of literature, and thus promote its study and bring fresh materials to light.

I may further remark that in the list of authorities referred to the editions of all quoted works are given together with an indication of the way the quotations are made. The reader is therefore requested to consult this list wherever the quotations may not be intelligible.

WILHELM BOUSSET.

GÖTTINGEN,
   June, 1895.

PROLOGUE TO THE ENGLISH EDITION.

ORIGIN OF THE BABYLONIAN DRAGON MYTH.

IT may be safely affirmed that no popular myth can compare with that of the Antichrist legend in general interest, widespread diffusion, and persistence, from a hoar antiquity down to the present time. In the present work, which deals mainly with the early Christian and mediæval aspects of the subject, no attempt is made to trace the origin of the saga much farther back than about the dawn of the new era. But the author leaves no doubt on the mind of the reader that he regards it not merely as a pre-Christian tradition quite independent of the New Testament writings, but as prior even to the oldest of the Old Testament records themselves. From many passages it is evident that he is in full accord with Gunkel, whose canons of interpretation he adopts, and whose views regarding the ultimate Babylonian source of the myth he implicitly accepts, though of course not in all their details. Thus Gunkel's reference of the mystic number 666 to the "primeval monster" (p. 11) is for obvious reasons rightly rejected, and a complete reconstruction of the old Babylonian legend by the aid of S. John's Revelation is declared to be opposed to all evidence, and consequently to be "nothing more than a piece of pure fancy work."

But on the other hand it is clearly implied that the Antichrist legend is nothing less than a later anthropomorphic transformation of the Babylonian Dragon myth, which is "doubtless one of the earliest evolved by primitive man" (p. 13). And although Gunkel may have exaggerated the influence of this legend on the New Testament writers, he is none the less declared to have done a real service by following up the after-effects of the Dragon myth "to its last echoes in the New Testament" (p. 13).

My own attention was first attracted to this subject by the stimulating writings of Mr. Andrew Lang, and I was struck in a special manner by the theory, now almost become an axiom amongst folklorists, that the elucidation of the widely diffused mythologies of cultured peoples is to be sought, not in later "solar myths" or in literary influences of any kind, but rather in the beliefs and traditions of our ruder forefathers, of uncultured peoples, and possibly of primitive man himself.

This theory, it seems to me, receives a brilliant confirmation from the early history of the legend under consideration—a legend which may without exaggeration be said to link together some of the very oldest reminiscences of struggling humanity with its aspirations for a better future (the Millennium) and its forebodings of the final consummation (the Last Judgment). At least this much may be said, that Gunkel's views regarding the evolution of the Antichrist legend from the Dragon myth have been greatly strengthened by the results of recent studies in the hitherto almost unexplored field of early Babylonian folklore.

In Mr. Th. G. Pinches' *Religious Ideas of the Babylonians* we plainly see how the myth of Tiamat, "the Dragon of Chaos," prevalent amongst the Akkadian founders of Babylon and by them transmitted to the later Assyrian Semites, is the very first and oldest element in the current mythologies of those ancient peoples. At the same time this primeval dragon presents so many features in common with the dragon of Revelation, as well as of the independent Antichrist legend, that the descent of one from the other can scarcely any longer be denied. All the more readily may the identification be accepted, when such obvious connecting links are afforded as may be drawn from the Books of Daniel and of Enoch, and even from many passages in the prophets and other earlier biblical writings. The parallelism between dragon and serpent is too close to need discussion, while the intimate association of the Hebrew writers with their Assyrian kinsfolk is attested by such common popular names as Marduka (Mardochai), Shama'-îlu (Samuel), Ishmê-îlu (Ishmael), Mutu-sha-îli (Methusael), Gamal-îli (Gamaliel), and many others.

Ninip, the deity who, according to the Tell-el-Amarna tablets, was worshipped at Jerusalem before the advent of the Israelites, seems to have been identified with many gods, amongst others with Bêl mâtāti, " Lord of the Lands," this, as Mr. Pinches tells us (p. 17), being one of the titles of Merodach. But Merodach himself (Amar-uduk, " Brightness of the Day ") was the chief deity of the Babylonian pantheon, though not the father or the oldest of the gods. In fact he was originally only the son of Êa or Aê, king of the underworld, and acquired the place of eminence by his triumph over Mummu-Tiamat, the Dragon of Chaos, who is not distinguishable from the Kirbish-Tiawat associated with the " Bel and the Dragon " myth. In the Semitic account of the creation this Tiamat or Tiawat (both words meaning the " sea ") is represented as presiding over the waste of waters in a time of disorder and confusion prior to the creation of Lahmu and Lahamu, of Anshar and Kishar, of Anu and the other gods of the heavens and the earth.

Then comes a period of strife between the primordial chaos and the established order. Tiawat rises in rebellion against the gods, and arms herself (she is always represented as a female monster, the prototype of the scarlet woman of Babylon) with formidable weapons for the struggle. " I have collected un-rivalled weapons—the great serpents are hostile (they war on her side)—sharp-toothed also, and I have made them relentless. I have filled their bodies with poison like blood. I have clothed dreadful monsters with terrors—fearful things I have set up and left on high—scorpion-men, fish-men—wielding weapons, ruthless, fearless in battle," and so on, in strains that recall the descriptions of the combatants in the Old English poem of Beowulf.

In the first encounters the gods are worsted ; Anu, god of the heavens, avails not ; Eâ himself trembles and, in prosaic language, runs away. Then there appears to be a gathering of the gods, in which Eâ's son, Merodach, boldly offers to come to the rescue. He also arms himself for the fight with formidable weapons, with spear, bow, and arrows ; he flashes lightning before him, fills his body with darting flames ; and sets his net to catch and entangle the evil one. She cries out in her rage, utters spells and charms, but is overthrown, and Chaos being thus ended, Merodach orders the world anew, and in gratitude for his great deeds he is proclaimed king of the gods. And the Assyrian text goes on :

As he tirelessly thwarted Kirbish-Tiawat,
Let his name be Nibiru, seizer of Kirbish-Tiawat.
May he restrain the paths of the stars of heaven.
Like sheep let him pasture the gods, all of them.
May he imprison the sea [*tiawat*], may he remove and
    store up its treasure,
For the men to come, in days advanced (*ib.*, p. 6).

But if all this goes a long way to connect the Antichrist legend with the Babylonian Dragon myth, it may still be asked with Herr Bousset, though in another and a wider sense, " Whence this whole cycle of thought ? " (p. 24) ; whence the Babylonian myth itself ? Here we are reminded by folklorists that man invents little. He borrows, modifies, recasts, freely adapts the legacies of preceding ages to the ever-shifting environment, to his own immediate surroundings. The apocalyptic writers themselves, we are here told, do not create or invent their materials. "They of course modify here and there ; but their function consists essentially in adaptation, not in invention—in application to the times, not in fresh creations " (p. 6). Hence it may be inferred that, as neither the Christians nor the Jews invented their dragon, but borrowed it from the Babylonians, so did the Babylonians in their turn borrow it from some still earlier source.

But the Dragon myth was the property, not merely of the later Assyrians, but of their far more ancient Akkadian (and Sumerian) precursors, as shown by the above-given Akkadian interpretation of the name Merodach, "Brightness of the Day." Now the Akkadians were beyond all question the first civilised inhabitants of Mesopotamia, although it need not be supposed that they entered this region already in the possession of an advanced culture. It is obvious enough that they may have themselves developed this advanced culture on the spot, as their Egyptian contemporaries certainly did in the Nile valley. But however this be, whether the Akkadians were civilised or savage intruders in the Lower Euphrates valley, we have no knowledge of any possible earlier culture prior, for instance, to the foundation of their city of Lagash (Tell-Loh), which its discoverer, M. de Sarzec, assigns to about 4000 B.C., or, say, 6000 years ago. Thus nothing is known to stand between these presumably Mongolo-Túrki settlers in Chaldæa and primitive man himself. Consequently their dragon, if borrowed, could only have been borrowed from the men of the Stone Ages.

It is evident that these rude prehistoric peoples could not be credited with the invention of such an anthropomorphic conception as that here in question. Nor is it necessary to suppose that they did invent it. In my *Ethnology* (Part II., chap. x.) I advance grounds for believing that Pleistocene man may well have

b

reached the Mesopotamian plains both from South Asia and from North Africa ; and Professor Flinders Petrie's recent explorations in Upper Egypt prove that men of the Old Stone Age were already settled in that region at a time when " the Nile still rolled down as a vast torrent fifty times its present volume at the latter age of palæolithic man."

What was the condition of the Euphrates and Tigris basins at that remote epoch and for long generations afterwards ? We know that there was no Shatt el-Arab in the comparatively recent Akkadian times, when the Persian Gulf penetrated much farther inland than at present, and when Lagash itself may have almost been a seaport. At that time the twin rivers entered the head of the gulf through independent channels ; and what a vast volume they rolled down during the floods may be inferred from Mr. D. G. Hogarth's description of the Euphrates, which, during the melting of the snows, is even still, in its upper reaches, " a fuller, broader Rhine, rushing six miles an hour between towering banks which had weathered to fantastic pinnacles, and displaying a hundred metres' breadth of turbid flood, boiling in mid-stream over sunken rocks " (*A Wandering Scholar in the Levant*).

Lower down the estuaries were infested by huge crocodiles, which may well have been over thirty feet long, like their plesiosaurian and ichthyosaurian precursors. Even now the Gangetic gavial reaches twenty-five feet, and the crocodiles in many tropical

African rivers range from twenty to thirty, while a water-camoodi measured by Mr. E. im Thurn was found to be thirty feet long (*Among the Indians of Guiana,* p. 133). Assuredly the chief difficulties that primitive man had to contend with on first reaching the Lower Mesopotamian plains were the turbulent streams themselves and their voracious saurian fauna. Nor can there be any doubt that the struggle with these relentless foes must have been maintained from age to age throughout the Old and New Stone epochs right into prehistoric times.

Here therefore was a region of all others most likely to have given rise to popular tales of fights with monsters of the deep and with the watery element itself—fights real enough at first, but gradually assuming a fabulous character, according as the actual occurrences faded into mere memories of past contests, of heroic deeds, of dangers overcome. Then the foremost champions engaged in these contests acquired their apotheosis in the minds of a grateful posterity, while the vanquished enemy assumed more and more the form of unearthly monsters and demons hostile to man. Such memories easily passed on from generation to generation until they acquired consistency and permanency in the written records of the cultured Babylonian peoples. The interval between the dawn of Babylonian culture and the last amphibious monster slain by neolithic man cannot have been too long for the oral transmission of such reminiscences from prehistoric to historic times. And thus may the elements of the Dragon myth, without being invented, have been passed on through the Stone Ages to the first civilised inhabitants of Mesopotamia, and later by them handed on to the forefathers of the Israelites, Terah and his son Abram, who " went forth . . . from Ur of the Chaldees to go into the land of Canaan " (Gen. xi. 31). And if not to Terah and Abram, then to their descendants ; for the great extent of Babylonian influences throughout this region during the whole of the period from Abraham to Moses has now been fully revealed by the researches of Akkadian and Assyrian scholars.*

We now begin also to understand the peculiar form assumed by the Semitic account of the creation, which is itself based on earlier Akkadian traditions. Before the dawn of Akkadian (and Sumerian) civilisation all was still chaos and disorder, the chief elements of confusion being the periodical freshets of the Euphrates and Tigris, which were caused by the melting of the snows on the Armenian and Kurdistán highlands, and which produced widespread devastation among the early settlements on the low-lying plains of Chaldæa. Then the next great difficulty that the settlers had to contend with were the saurian inhabitants of these turbulent waters ; so that there could be no peace or progress until the waters were quelled (confined within

* See, amongst others, Professor A. H. Sayce, *Patriarchal Palestine*, 1896.

their banks, and diverted into irrigation canals), and until their presiding genius (the reptile or dragon, "lord of chaos") was overthrown.

In these respects the Mesopotamian rivers must have assumed, in the eyes of the early Akkadian or pre-Akkadian dwellers on their banks, much the same aspect as did the Achelous and other wild torrents to the early Hellenic settlers in Greece. The Achelous, which also had its rise in a mountainous region (Pindus), and which by its recurrent floods spread havoc over the lowlands, had, like the Euphrates, to be vanquished—that is, restrained within its natural bed. Hence it was afterwards fabled to have contended under various forms (man, serpent, bull) with Herakles, a sort of Greek Merodach, a general redresser of wrongs and restorer of order throughout the Hellenic world. Here it is specially noteworthy that when Herakles breaks off one of the bull's horns the vanquished Achelous retires to its bed, and the broken horn is presented to the goddess of Plenty, that is, becomes a cornucopia, emblem of the abundance that follows the subsidence of the flood-waters and their confinement to their natural channel.

So in Babylonia law and order succeed chaos when the gods of heaven and earth are created—that is, when man himself becomes strong enough to contend successfully with the difficulties of his physical environment. But before that time Tiawat (the sea, the Euphrates estuary) ruled supreme, and the dragon

is represented as an aquatic monster aided in the fight
with Merodach by " fish-men," " scorpion-men," and
such-like allies.   Then in the Assyrian text Merodach
himself opens his mouth, and says : " I will confine
Tiawat—I will save you."   Such language, hitherto
misunderstood or given up as hopeless, is now clear
enough.   Tiawat, the waste of waters, cannot be slain;
but it may be " confined " (to its proper channel), and
the people seated on its margin may thus be " saved."
In other words, they may be enabled to sow and reap
their crops in peace, when protected by Merodach's
victory from the periodical inundations, and from the
attacks of the fierce dragon, the huge reptiles coming
up out of the deep, the " great serpents " that are
" hostile " and " sharp-toothed " like Machairodon, or
" sabre-tooth," associated with palæolithic man in
Britain.

After the combat Tiawat is represented as being
divided ; one portion being made into a covering for the
heavens—" the waters above the firmament "—while
the other remained below—" the waters under the
firmament " (Pinches, p. 4).   But the meaning would
rather seem to be, that henceforth the turbulent streams
are brought under better control, the waters on high—
that is, the flood-waters from the uplands—being
regulated by irrigation works, while the others—that
is, the surface waters—subside into their respective
river-beds, where they are confined by dykes and
embankments.   Those who might suppose that this

is a fancy picture should remember that such works were carried out on a vast scale by the ancient Babylonians thousands of years ago. The plains of the Lower Euphrates and Tigris, rendered desolate under Turkish misrule, are intersected by the remains of an intricate system of canalisation covering all the space between the two rivers, and are strewn with the ruins of many great cities, whose inhabitants, numbering many scores of thousands, were supported by the produce of a highly cultivated region which is now an arid waste encumbered by crumbling mounds, stagnant waters, and a few fanatical Arab tent-dwellers.

The scribe who has left to posterity this fragmentary Semitic account of the creation goes on to sing the praises of the legendary hero by whom order was evolved out of chaos : " May he imprison Tiawat ; may he remove and store up its treasures for the men to come, in days advanced, . . . that his land may prosper and he himself have peace." Here again the nature of the great change brought about by Merodach is clearly indicated. Tiawat is once more " imprisoned " (confined), and its treasures are stored up (possibly an allusion to the development of trade and navigation) for the benefit of " the men to come " (future generations) ; the land prospers, and Merodach, now " the lord of the gods," has peace, rests after his triumph over the foes of his people. He receives another title, Zi, " Life," for he is the " life-giver," who " doeth glorious things, God of the good wind, lord of hearing and obeying ; he who causeth glory and plenty to exist, establishing fertility." These continual references to prosperity, abundance, fertility present a most striking parallelism .with the " cornucopia " of the Achelous legend, although it does not follow that one is borrowed from the other. The resemblances may be equally well accounted for, whether we assume one origin, or merely analogous causes for both.

Thus we see that even in many of its details all this legendary matter, saturated as it is with local colouring, carries us back to the primeval conditions under which it grew up and crystallised into later national mythologies. These conditions were here, as elsewhere, the circumstances incident to the struggle of primitive man with his physical surroundings. Thus also the weird story of the Antichrist legend is completed in its three successive phases—from the new era to mediæval times, a millennium (Bousset) ; from Babylonia to the new era, four millenniums (Gunkel) ; from the Stone Ages to Babylonia, as here suggested, many millenniums.

And still a boundless and fascinating field of inquiry is open to folklorists, who may be tempted to follow the endless ramifications of the saga throughout the rich mythologies of the Greeks, Scandinavians, Teutons, and other imaginative peoples. But before plunging into these fathomless depths of speculation they will be wise to carefully study Herr Bousset's judicious remarks on Gunkel's method of interpretation (chap. i.), and remember that in the wide range of comparative mythology "the temptation to yield to fancy flights is all but irresistible" (p. 16).

And here we are forcibly reminded of the reckless way in which certain popular and unscrupulous "expositors" are accustomed to handle such extremely difficult texts as, for instance, the Books of Daniel and Revelation. We all know how the rage for expounding these texts breaks out at intervals, and especially how it has tended to assume the character of a virulent epidemic towards the close of each successive century of the Christian era. Symptoms are not wanting that as the present century approaches its end the intermittent fever will again reach its centennial crisis, and the advertisement columns of the periodical press show that prophecy-mongering about the Antichrist and "the crack of doom" is already "in the air."

A sober, and above all a scholarly, treatment of the subject, such as is here presented to the thoughtful reader, may perhaps be found the best corrective of such disorders. These professional and not always disinterested "latter-day saints and seers" may at least here learn that, "to understand Revelation, we need a fulness of eschatological and mythological knowledge" (p. 17), and that "no one should venture on an exposition of this book without a comprehensive knowledge of all its bearings" (p. 9). These presumptuous charlatans should take warning from the repeated failures of their illustrious predecessors, such as Hippolytus, Irenæus, and other Fathers of the Church, all of whose predictions served only to show how rash it is, even for qualified expositors, to venture into the dangerous field of prophetic interpretation. And they will do well to bear in mind the solemn words of Origen : " Because perhaps amongst the Jews were some persons professing to know about the Last Things either from Holy Writ or from hidden sources, therefore he [Paul] writes warning his disciples to believe no one making such professions " (p. 31).

Lastly, they should clearly understand that the Antichrist legend, connected, as it undoubtedly is, with the Babylonian Dragon myth, if not also with reminiscences of primitive man himself, is far less a biblical subject than a chapter in uninspired folklore, the most persistent, the most widespread, of all popular myths.

A few words will suffice to explain the plan I have adopted in preparing this English edition of Herr Bousset's book. Such changes as have been made affect the arrangement of the subject-matter only—chapters substituted for indicated sections, a clause here and there removed from the text to the notes, a note now and then transferred to the text, and above all the text disencumbered of a large number of Greek and

Latin passages from the documents consulted by the author and by him left untranslated. All these will be found brought together in an Appendix at the end, their place being taken by versions as close as was compatible with English idiom. I have not, however, thought it necessary to print any of these passages more than once, or to reproduce those from the Greek and Latin Scriptures, which are easily accessible to all. By this plan the book is made more generally readable without detriment to its value for serious students, while folklorists unfamiliar with the classical languages will here find, for the first time, placed at their disposal a multiplicity of out-of-the-way texts bearing on the Antichrist legend in all its varied aspects, at least for a period of about a thousand years, from the new era far into mediæval times. The scheme of references is explained in a note at the beginning of each chapter. Several of the Greek and Latin passages, such especially as those from the Sibylline sources, are not only designedly obscure, but are also extremely corrupt. Two or three of these have been given up as hopeless, while I have to thank Mr. Henry Chettle, Head Master of Stationers' School, for his kind assistance in the elucidation of the others. Herr Bousset, who has looked over the proofs, has also favoured me with a German version of the passage from an old Bavarian poem reproduced in English at p. 243. The figure of Bel and the Dragon on the cover has been prepared from a cast taken by

Mr. A. P. Ready from a Babylonian cylinder in the British Museum.

No complete text is anywhere given by Herr Bousset of any particular form of the Antichrist legend, such as might serve the purpose of an object-lesson in enabling the reader to understand the general character of the saga as it exists in extant documents. Through the courtesy of Mr. F. C. Conybeare I am enabled to supply this want by reproducing, at the end of the volume, an old Armenian form of the legend, a translation of which was given by Mr. Conybeare in the *Academy* of October 26th, 1895.

A. H. KEANE.

ARÁM-GÁH,
79, BROADHURST GARDENS, N.W.,
March, 1896.

EXPLANATION

OF THE

REFERENCES TO AUTHORITIES QUOTED IN THE TEXT.

Andr.: Andreas, *Commentary on the Apocalypse*, Sylburg's edition.

Bk. K. : *Book of S. Clement* (Βιβλίον Κλήμεντος), ed. Lagarde, in *Reliquiæ Juris, etc.*, 80 *et seq.*

Cyr. : Cyril of Jerusalem, *Catechetical Lectures* (Κατηχήσεις, 15), in Migne, Vol. XXXIII.

D. A. Gr. : *Greek Apocalypse of Daniel*, ed. Klostermann, *Analecta*, 113 *et seq.* ·

D. A. Arm. : *Armenian Apocalypse of Daniel*, ed. Kalemkiar, *Wiener Zeitschrift*, VI. 127 *et seq.*

Eluc. : *Elucidarium* of Honorius of Autun, III. 10; Migne, Vol. CLXXII., p. 1163.

Ephr. Gr. : *Discourse on the Antichrist* (Λόγος εἰς τὸν Ἀντίχριστον), Assemani, III. 134-143 ; Prologue from W. Meyer's MSS.

Ephr. Syr. : *Discourse on the Consummation* (*Sermo de fine Extermo*), Lamy, III. 187.

Eter. : Eterianus Hugo, *On the Return of the Souls from the Lower Regions* (*Liber de Regressu Animarum ab Inferis*), chaps. xxiv. *et seq.* ; Migne, Vol. CCII., p. 168.

Hild. : Hildegard, *Scivias*, III. 11 ; Migne, Vol. CXCVI., p. 709.

Hipp. : Hippolytus, *Exposition . . . on the Antichrist* (Ἀπόδειξις . . . περὶ τοῦ Ἀντιχρίστου), ed. Lagarde, 1 *et seq.*

J. A. : *Pseudo-Johannine Apocalypse* ; Tischendorf, *Apocalypses Apocryphæ*, lxx.

Joh. Damasc. : S. John of Damascus, *Exposition of the Orthodox Faith* (Ἔκθεσις τῆς ὀρθοδόξου πίστεως), iv. 27.

Lact. : Lactantius, *Institutiones Divinæ*, VII. 10 *et seq.*, ed. Brandt, *Corpus Scriptorum Latinorum*, Vol. XIX.

Mart. : S. Martin of Tours, in Sulpicius Severus, *Dialog.*, II. 14 ; Migne, Vol. XX.

P. A. Æth. : ⎫
P. A. Ar. : ⎬ Ethiopic, Arabic, Syriac Recension of *Clement's Petrine Apocalypse* (*Petri Apostoli Apocalypsis per Clementem*) ; Bratke.
P. A. Syr. : ⎭

Phil. Sol. : Philippus Solitarius, *Dioptra*, III. 10 *et seq.* ; Migne, Vol. CXXVII.

Ps. Chrys. : Pseudo-Chrysostom, *On the Second Coming, etc.* (Εἰς τὴν δευτέραν παρουσίαν, κ. τ. λ.), amongst the works of S. Chrysostom ; Migne, Vol. LXI., p. 776.

Ps. E. : *The Syriac Apocalypse of Ezra* ; Baethgen.

Ps. Ephr. : Pseudo-Ephrem, the Discourse preserved under the name of S. Ephrem ; Caspari, *Briefe und Abhandlungen*, 1890, pp. 208 *et seq.*

Ps. H. : Pseudo-Hippolytus, *On the End of the World* (Περὶ τῆς συντελείας τοῦ κόσμου) ; Lagarde, 92.

Ps. M. : Pseudo-Methodius, *Orthodoxographa* (Greek 93, Latin 100 pp.).

Sib. B. : The Sibylline document included in the works of the Venerable Bede ; Migne, Vol. XC., p. 1183.

Sib. Us. : The Sibyl published by Usinger in his *Forschungen zur Deutschen Geschichte,* X. 621.

Vict. : Victorinus, *Commentary on Revelation* ; ed. de la Bigne, Vol. I. (2nd ed., 1589).

Z. A. : *The Apocalypse of Zephaniah* ; Stern, *Zeitschrift für ägyptische Sprache,* 1886, 115 *et seq.*

Note.—In the English edition most of the abbreviated forms have been extended. The same remark applies to many other forms of reference, which might be unintelligible to any but specialists. Thus Z. K. W. K. L. becomes *Zeitschr. für Kirkliche Wissenschaft und Kirkliches Leben* (p. 84), and so on.

PART I.

THE SOURCES.

CHAPTER I.

INTRODUCTION—METHODS OF INTERPRETATION—RELATIONS TO THE BABYLONIAN DRAGON MYTH.

THE present work was originally undertaken with a view to the explantion and interpretation of some obscure passages in the Revelation of S. John. My inquiries were first turned in this direction by the remarks contained in Isolin's *Comparative Study of Revelation with the Later Syriac Apocalypse attributed to Ezra.** Then my attention was drawn to these remarkable literary problems by Bratke's work on the Arabo-Ethiopic Petrine Apocalypse.

After reading a fellow-worker's treatise on the Apocalypse two years ago, it seemed to me highly probable that at least chap. xi. of the Johannine Apocalypse had its origin in an earlier tradition which might still be recovered. Corrodi's *History of the Millennium* for the first time brought under my notice the writings of S. Ephrem bearing on this subject. Then one branch after another of this astonishingly widespread literature was in due course brought to

---

* This work, however (*Theol. Zeitschrift aus der Schweiz*, 1887), is known to me only by report.

3

light, although I should have still undoubtedly overlooked some important documents but for the help
repeatedly rendered to me by Professors Bonwetsch
and W. Meyer. My thanks are also due to Dr.
Achelis and to Dr. Rahlfs for the assistance kindly
afforded by them on several points occurring in the
course of my investigations. But even so I am
far from claiming any finality for these researches,
many documents from which light might be derived
being still inaccessible to students. However, I have
at least reason to believe that nothing essential has
been overlooked in connection with the current of
tradition on the Antichrist saga in the early Church.
I would, nevertheless, here point out that the later
mediæval history of the saga has only been glanced at
by me, so that here I make no kind of pretence to
thoroughness. I was fain to set this limit to my work
in order not to break down altogether in the attempt
to elucidate the apocalyptic text.

At the same time my researches have thus developed
into something more than a mere aid to the interpretation of Revelation. The interest felt by me in the
spread and influence of the Antichrist legend itself,
once aroused, grew steadily stronger, and thus it came
about that the work has assumed the character of a
contribution to the eschatology of the early Church.
Despite their entangled and fantastic nature, the
records here dealt with in their literary connection
possess at least a great and special charm. In this
literature are simply and directly mirrored the sentiments, the sufferings, hopes, and aspirations of the

masses in times of great political throes and convulsions. The generations pass before our eyes in a
weird, fantastic light, for it is never to be forgotten
that all these whirling and checkered thoughts at one
time throbbed with life ; they excited the popular
imagination more than dogmatic wranglings, and at
least in mediæval times they made history.

Meanwhile I would indulge the hope that my efforts
to unravel the apocalyptic entanglement may yield
no little fruit both directly and above all indirectly.
We have not yet come to an end in the interpretation
of the Apocalypse. Much has doubtless been cleared
up by the historical and critical methods of inquiry.
But these very methods themselves have plunged us
into deep complications and an almost boundless range
of hypotheses. Hence fresh ground must be broken,
fresh processes applied, nay, a thoroughly new method
of investigation will be needed, if the subject is to be
advanced beyond the phase it has now reached. But
the essential point will be to form a clear conception of
the method to be applied. In my studies I have not
failed to notice the law of eschatological tradition
apparent in a whole series of apocalyptic documents.
And precisely herein lies in my opinion the indirect
value of my labours for the interpretation of the
Apocalypse.

It is at this point that the present work comes in
contact with Gunkel's *Creation and Chaos* (*Schöpfung und Chaos*), a work which has already struck out
or indicated new lines of inquiry. In fact a feeling of
gratitude requires that at the very outset I should

state how greatly I have been stimulated and en-
couraged by this work, more especially as regards
the method and the statement of the problem.   I
emphasise this point all the more willingly that, in
respect of the results, I have frequently found myself
in points of detail at variance with the author himself.
In the present connection, however, I am concerned
mainly with the second half of Gunkel's work, where
in proposing an explanation of Revelation, chap. xii.,
he formulates the laws for the interpretation of all
apocalyptic traditions bearing on the Last Days.

Of these laws the most frequent and valuable in my
opinion is that laid down by Gunkel at pp. 252 *et seq.*
Here he suggests that, speaking broadly, the several
apocalyptic writers do not themselves create or invent
their materials, or even merely weave them together
of all sorts of scattered threads.   How could they else
succeed in passing off their fancies for authentic holy
revelations ?   This could be done only by the possession of an unbroken chain of traditions hallowed with
age, so that these seers simply reveal the sacred lore
of primeval times.   They of course modify here and
there; but their function consists essentially in adaptation, not in invention, in application (to the times),
not in fresh creations.   " Such personal activity must
always be taken as confined to those limits within
which the belief of the writer in his own words does
not become impossible " (p. 254).

Naturally this limitation is somewhat vague ; one
apocalyptic writer may be trusted less, another more,
but the limitation exists.   Gunkel's assumption is,

in fact, confirmed by the history of the eschatological literature which I have here surveyed, and which—herein consists its advantage—lies in the clear light of history. Let it not here be objected that the later epochs of Christian apocalyptic literature should not be applied to the laying down of rules for the interpretation of the inspired Revelation of S. John. In the course of the present work it will be shown that the eschatological literature here dealt with still stands in a position of independence in respect of the New Testament, and more especially of the Johannine Apocalypse.

From the following review of a literature spread over a thousand years the clearest evidence will also be afforded of the great persistence of eschatological imagery, which passes on from hand to hand with scarcely a change of form in the course of centuries.

To explain this persistence of legendary eschatological conceptions, Gunkel advances the hypothesis of an esoteric oral tradition, and endeavours to support his assumption by 2 Thessalonians ii., and by passages from the Apocalypse of Ezra (pp. 265, 292). I am now in a position to bring forward proof of such a secret eschatological tradition even for the first centuries of Christianity.

It has been objected to Gunkel that he does not make it sufficiently clear how utterly unconscious the author of Revelation may have been of adopting earlier mythical and eschatological materials, how largely he dealt with unintelligible and half-under- stood eschatological traditions. Although this is repeatedly acknowledged by Gunkel himself, there is still some force in the objection. The contact of Revelation more particularly with the early Babylonian myths—a contact which Gunkel has really proved— is after all frequently limited to some misunderstood borrowings. And on the strength of such contacts it was very venturesome to credit the circles amongst which the Apocalypse grew up with the further know- ledge of a coherent early Babylonian myth, of which no trace is elsewhere to be found. Yet this is what Gunkel attempts to do in his explanation of Revela- tion, chap. xii., and of the numerical riddle in chap. xiii. 18. So much may be admitted without prejudice to the accuracy of the above-mentioned law respecting the persistence of eschatological tradition. If the Book of Revelation is not to be explained, or explained only to a very small extent, by the old Babylonian myth, it may still perhaps find its interpretation in some less remote tradition.

At the same time the potency of early traditions and the possibility of their being still partly understood are not to be underestimated. In fact they can hardly be overrated; in this connection centuries need scarcely be taken into account, and it must be frankly stated that no one has a right to an opinion on this subject who has not earnestly and sedulously studied the traditions of mythical and eschatological records.

But even if the fullest weight be given to the objection urged against Gunkel, and if nothing more than a few scattered fragments of early Babylonian mythology can be detected in Revelation, still the verified relations must be regarded as something more than mere literary "curiosities." They might even afford a sure means of distinguishing in the interpretation of this book between the material handed down by tradition and that special to the apocalyptic writer. And in such discrimination lies the whole art of sound exegesis for all apocalyptic writings. Everything depends on clearly distinguishing between the traditional and what is peculiar to each document.

Gunkel's work may accordingly be regarded as the starting-point of a new method of interpretation of Revelation. To the study of contemporary history and of textual criticism is superadded that of traditional history, by which both are controlled but not superseded, as might appear from occasional passages in Gunkel's work.

The method of textual criticism so much in vogue at present will certainly have to greatly modify its pretensions; an end must once for all be put to the reckless use of the knife, and critics must henceforth refrain from laying rude hands on original documents. As is rightly urged by Gunkel, all attempts at verbal criticism must be preceded by a far more accurate knowledge of the logical connection of all available materials. A few exegetic remarks on the Johannine Apocalypse, such as every one fancies himself capable of, will no longer suffice. No one should venture on an exposition of this book without a comprehensive knowledge of all its bearings, and a satisfactory elucidation will assuredly for a long time exceed the powers of any individual student. Such an elucidation involves nothing less than a thorough grasp of its special character within the compass of an eschatological tradition embracing a period of nearly a thousand years. Yet I already begin to fear that Gunkel's canon may soon be so far overstrained as to cause the critical study of the text to fall into complete neglect. Hence it may here be urged that a sound method of verbal criticism will always act as a healthy counterpoise to an arbitrary treatment of mythical sources. I hope to show in the first part of this work how much may be achieved in this field even by textual criticism.

The method based on a study of contemporary history will also have to confine itself within narrower limits. Against this method Gunkel advances the most diverse arguments. He protests especially against the favourite process of interpreting independently isolated passages of Revelation, and points out the absolutely arbitrary character of such a course. A limitation of the contemporary historical method follows, in fact, as a matter of course from the recognition of the claims of traditional history. When we once recognise that at many points the writer is leaning on tradition, we become instinctively more guarded against explanations suggested by contemporary events. But above all Gunkel absolutely rejects those adaptations to current history that date back to times antecedent to the apocalyptic writer as not in harmony with the essential character of Revelation.

But, however encouraging they may be, these deductions require to be somewhat modified. Even when the apocalyptic writer takes over distinctly traditional materials, he often does so not quite purposelessly. He may, in fact, be still thinking of his own and immediately antecedent times. Thus the description of those slain under the altar (Rev. vi. 9 *et seq.*) is after all a mere adaptation of an older tradition. But when borrowing this incident the writer was thinking of the martyrs of his own time, of those that had already suffered, and of those that were to follow. Nor is it altogether beside the question to consider and to ask to what temporal relations he is alluding. For to me Gunkel does not seem to have proved that there are no references in the Johannine Apocalypse to past times. Even the Books of Daniel, chap. vii., and of Enoch, chap. lxxxviii., have also allusions to the period antecedent to that of the assumed writer. Why may we not therefore understand chap. xii. of Revelation to be a retrospective historical introduction to chap. xiii., at least in the mind of the writer who has given it the last touch?

But in any case it must be regretted that Gunkel makes a decided mistake when he attempts to upset the long-standing accepted allusion to current events during the reign of Nero, supporting his contention with much straining of the text, but with little solid argument. Let it be said once for all that the reference to Nero is not to be eliminated from the Revelation of S. John. It is to be feared that Gunkel's reference of the number 666 to the " primeval monster," * whereby he strives to put aside the allusion to Nero,

* תהום קדמניה

will ere long be ranked with those apocalyptic curiosities on which he lavishes so much scorn. But so long as the allusion to Nero justly holds its ground, the interpretation of Revelation in the light of contemporary events will also be justified. Nor will the question be in any way affected by the assurance of Gunkel and of his reviewer Edward Meyer * that this method has here proved a failure.

But here again all exaggeration must be deprecated. A claim to exclusiveness is no recommendation for any new method. Gunkel claims far too much when, for instance, he clings to the fundamental principle that the method based on historical tradition is to be applied wherever the allusion to current events is not quite clear or does not lie on the surface. A cautious inquiry will accept the results based on allusions to contemporary history when such allusions are not strained. But the caution here insisted upon has nothing in common with that hair-splitting reasoning with which Gunkel rejects the Neronic interpretation; it is a caution which will accept all genuine inferences and results of the traditional method, but will admit moot questions wherever both principles are unconvincing, will even allow the possibility of allusions to contemporary events of which we have no knowledge—in a word, it will in many cases apply both methods concurrently.

But in Gunkel's work the student has above all to be on his guard against postulates or assumptions.

* In the Supplement to the *Augsburg Allgemeine Zeitung*, December 13th, 1894.

To attempt, as Gunkel does, to completely reconstruct from our Revelation a now lost old Babylonian myth by patching together a few surviving shreds of some fragmentary contacts, whose connections are no longer clear, is tantamount to flying in the face of all evidence and ignoring the limits of scientific proof. Gunkel's interpretation of Revelation xii. 13 is nothing more than a piece of pure fancy work, which had better have been left undone. Many will be only too ready on this ground to shut their eyes to the real merits of a work which as a whole has certainly opened up new methods of research.

In any case Gunkel has done a real service by following up in a separate treatise the after-effects of the old Babylonian Dragon myth to its last echoes in the New Testament. And even though he may have largely overrated the influence of this myth in the New Testament, he has still considerably sharpened our perception of the mythological element in Revelation.

In some respects I might describe my work as a modest continuation of Gunkel's inquiry. In it proof might be advanced to show that the Antichrist legend is a later anthropomorphic transformation of the Dragon myth, and further that this myth has made itself felt in its traditional form far beyond the time of the New Testament, cropping out again and again now in one now in another feature of its old characteristic aspects. On the other hand, I might in a certain sense justify Gunkel's work. Of the Dragon myth scarcely anything has found its way into the

Apocalypse beyond a few unintelligible fragments. The Apocalypse has, in fact, been to a far greater extent influenced by another eschatological tradition, which is connected with that of the Dragon, and which may still be recognised by the student.

I am also in accord with the traditional method so energetically advocated by Gunkel, and with his equally vigorous contention for the persistence of eschatological tradition. But it did not fall within the scope of my work to embrace the early Babylonian period, with a view to recovering in this field the key to the understanding of Revelation. My aim has rather been to seek my material in the later Christian tradition, with a retrospective view of the New Testament period—that is, so far as such tradition maintains its independence of the New Testament itself. And my belief is that the key thus recovered works better, at least as regards the understanding of Revelation.

At the same time I am quite aware that after all I have not arrived at a thorough understanding of this legendary eschatological imagery. But it may be asked, Can such an understanding ever be arrived at by any process? Gunkel thinks he has found an explanation of the Dragon myth ; but this is precisely what Edward Meyer (*loc. cit.*) demurs to. Here, when all is said and done, everything seems uncertain. Enough will have been done if we can in a measure realise to ourselves the nature of the eschatological imagery prevalent at any given period, say, for instance, in New Testament times, and thus help to unravel this almost inextricable tangle of traditional and contemporary representations, of intelligible and unintelligible elements. But while saying this we do not of course mean to withhold our thanks for any further light that in the course of his investigations Gunkel may still throw on the subject.

For me the main point was to examine the nearest available documents tending to elucidate Revelation, and nearer than the old Babylonian mythology was the early Christian eschatological tradition, which, taken as a whole, is independent of the Johannine document. It is precisely the study of the writings nearest to hand that has been often neglected by Gunkel. The remark applies especially to his comments on chap. xii. of Revelation.

Another matter has to be mentioned in which I am indebted to Gunkel. All praise is due to the restraint which he has imposed upon himself in this work. It was especially in the mythological field, which he undertook to investigate, that lay the greatest temptation to indulge in wild flights into extraneous mythological systems far removed from the subject in hand. Both the Greek and Norse mythologies present numerous parallelisms, and there occur many other traces of the influence of this primeval myth, doubtless one of the earliest evolved by primitive man. Gunkel has happily avoided the danger both of the dilettanteism which here lurked close at hand and of premature judgments on the ascertained facts.

The same can by no means be said of all mythological researches. However stimulating, for instance, may be Dietrich's investigations in the history of religion, however valuable they may be in a domain where he is at home (and here are naturally included his commentaries on the Petrine Apocalypse), still his conclusions on Jewish and early Christian eschatology bear none the less the stamp of the amateur. How superior Gunkel is to this writer appears from the few pages in which he differs from Dietrich in his attempt to elucidate chap. xii. of Revelation. Much serious work has still to be done, many careful inquiries into special points have still to be concluded, before any decided inferences, such as those of Dietrich, can be drawn in detail on the origin of the eschatological representations regarding the destruction of the world, heaven and hell, or even on the fundamental moral concepts involved in the pictures of the last judgment. Nor in my opinion has the time yet arrived for an inquiry into the intricate mythology of the Edda, or for an attempt to discriminate between the Christian and earlier elements of this compilation, as is done by E. H. Meyer in his *Völuspâ*. I mention this work because I have had repeated occasion to refer to it in this treatise. The colossal work of a comparative mythology will have to be done step by step, if it is to give the impression of anything more than a fantastic, amateurish experiment. The temptation to yield to fancy flights is all but irresistible, and in the little that I have brought together from outlying quarters I may have myself perhaps already trespassed too far.

Although the labour still to be done is of a comprehensive character, its sphere of action will be extended only to extraneous works. These investigations do not penetrate into the essence of things, into all that lives and has real force in every religion. For the pith and marrow of all creeds lies in what is special to each, not in what one people or one faith may have borrowed from another ; it lies in the original creations of distinct personalities, not in what one generation may have handed down to another. To understand Revelation we need a fulness of eschatological and mythological knowledge ; to understand the Gospel all this may for the most part be dispensed with. Nevertheless this work has also to be done, and such work remains instructive in many respects. It delivers a lesson of modesty and lowliness, showing how each individual, each generation of men is but a ripple in the stream of the endless life of history ; it teaches what an infinite variety of knowledge, feelings, and sentiments every age unconsciously inherits from previous ages. But it also quickens our vision—and herein lies its fullest value— for all that is original in every living belief ; it shows us indirectly whence flow the living waters of life.

The present work comprises two main divisions. In the first I have endeavoured to give a survey of the extremely difficult relations of the literature bearing on the subject. In the second I have presented a reconstruction of the legend, an exposition of its origin and history. In this second part I quote very fully from the various authorities dealing with

2

the question in hand. This seemed all the more necessary that the literature under consideration is very scattered and of difficult access. The second part also often affords support to the exposition of the mutual relation of the sources to each other—an exposition which, owing to the abundance of materials, had often to be given in a very summary manner.

CHAPTER II.*

A SURVEY of the eschatological parts of the New Testament, and more especially of those referring to the fearful storms and stress of the last days shortly before the general doom, gives a decided impression that we have here nothing more than the fragmentary survivals of a tradition which points at greater associations now shrouded in mystery.

This character of the tradition is most pronounced in chap. xi. of the Revelation of S. John. Specially puzzling is here the sudden appearance of the beast that comes up out of the pit and kills the two witnesses (ver. 7). If we suppose that in the expression "the beast that ascendeth out of the bottomless pit" the hand of the "editor" of Reve-lation has been at work, still there is the reference in ver. 7 to a demoniacal power by which the two witnesses are slain. As this can by no means be separated, as Spitta would have it, from the general context, the fragment remains all the more puzzling. In any case the sudden cessation of the testimony of the witnesses after three years and a half must

* For Notes [1] to [3] of this chapter, see Appendix, p. 263.

still have been brought about by some hostile power. But where are we elsewhere to look for the appearance of the witnesses and of the beast? According to ver. 8, in Jerusalem. Even apart from the words "where also our [their] Lord was crucified," Jerusalem is unmistakably indicated both by the connection with vers. 1 and 2, and by the circumstance that in the earthquake in which the tenth part of the city fell seven thousand men were slain (ver. 13). For the assumption that the scene takes place in Rome there is not a particle of evidence. The assertion that Jerusalem could not be called "the great city" can be shown to be groundless, while the fact that Rome is elsewhere in Revelation also called "the great city" proves nothing for the explanation of this quite exceptional chapter.

But if everything thus points to Jerusalem as the theatre of these events, then comes the question, How are we to explain the appearance in Jerusalem of the beast which is elsewhere in Revelation associated with the Roman empire, with Rome itself, or with Nero returning from the Euphrates? Here a too hasty exposition of a single chapter of Revelation would avail nothing. For after all it is quite possible, nay, even tolerably certain, that we have in this book diverse cycles of thought lying close together. Moreover, who are the two witnesses? Why are they here introduced at all? Why, and against whom, do they forebode the plagues? In what relation do they stand to the beast? Why does the beast of all others slay the witnesses? Who are the dwellers upon the earth who rejoice and make merry and send gifts one to another during the three days and a half that the witnesses lie dead? If we are to suppose that they gathered about Jerusalem, how did they get thither? Is it the Roman legions that are to tread Jerusalem underfoot? But if so, how can these be spoken of as "they that dwell upon the earth"? All these are moot points which will never be solved by discriminating the sources within chap. xi.

Now let us take it as unquestioned that in this chapter the figure of the Antichrist appears in Jerusalem, that he here stands in no relation to Rome and the Roman empire, or to the Gentiles, who, as would seem, tread Jerusalem underfoot. Then a parallel passage will at once be found in the eschatological section of the Second Epistle to the Thessalonians, whose authenticity I accept without however in my researches laying too much weight on this assumption. Here the very mysterious fragmentary manner of the exposition is obviously intentional. The author will not say more than he has said, but refers to his previous *oral* communications, giving the impression of an allusion to some esoteric teaching. In fact Paul speaks of a mystery in the words—"Remember ye not, that, when I was yet with you, I told you these things? And now ye know what withholdeth that he might be revealed in his time. For the mystery of iniquity doth already work: only he who now letteth *will let*, until he be taken out of the way" (chap. ii., vers. 5-7). We read of "the man of sin," a "son of perdition," who is yet to come. This figure also of the Antichrist appears in Jerusalem ; he sitteth in the Temple of God, and proclaims himself God. His advent will be " after the working of Satan " ; he will work " signs and lying wonders," and will beguile them that perish " with all deceivableness of un-righteousness."

Here therefore we have also an Antichrist who has nothing whatever to do with the Roman empire. For the passage is not applicable even to Caligula and his whim to have his statue set up in the Temple of Jerusalem. By such an interpretation we should miss the most essential point—that is to say, the threatened profanation of the Temple by foreign armies. Here we have nothing but signs and wonders and deceits, and it is characteristic of the passage that it contains an altogether unpolitical eschatology—an Antichrist who appears as a false Messiah in Jerusalem and works signs and wonders. And when Paul says that this man of sin will lead astray those destined to perish because " they received not the love of the truth, that they might be saved " (ver. 10), it is quite evident that he is thinking of the Jews, to whom a false Messiah will be sent because they have rejected the true Messiah. But whence does Paul know all this, and who is the one that " letteth," who has to be " taken out of the way " before the coming of the Antichrist ?

I turn to a third allied passage, the section of the Lord's discourse in Matthew xxiv. and Mark xiii. on the Second Coming, and I assume, with many recent expositors, that the distinctly apocalyptic part is a fragment of foreign origin introduced amid genuine utterances of the Lord. It is also evident that compared with that of Mark the text of Matthew is the original. Here we have again the same phenomenon of short mysterious forebodings. The writer speaks of the " abomination of desolation " in the holy place, followed by the flight of the faithful (one scarcely knows from what) ; of a shortening of the days (we know not what days, or whether any definite period of time is meant) ; of the " sign of the Son of man," which still remains a puzzle, although treated lightly by most expositors. In any case the view is steadily gaining ground that the allusion to the siege of Jerusalem and the flight of the Christians to Pella is an explanation introduced as an after-thought into Revelation. Yet one is reluctant to understand the passage except in association with the time of the emperor Caligula. How then is to be explained the flight after the pollution of the Temple ? Was the writer one of the advocates of peace, who wished to dissuade his fellow-countrymen from taking to arms ? But if so, he might have spoken in plainer language. A life-and-death struggle would after all seem probably to have taken place before the setting up of the emperor's statue.

The simplest way out of the difficulty will be to apply 2 Thessalonians to the explanation of Matthew xxiv. Then the profanation will be the Antichrist who takes his seat in the Temple of Jerusalem, and the flight will be that of the faithful from Antichrist and his persecution.

But then the question will again arise, Whence this whole cycle of thought ?　What was the source of this conception of the Antichrist in the Temple of Jerusalem ? Do the last verses of Revelation ii., 2 Thessalonians ii., and Matthew xxiv. all belong to the same legendary matter, and will it be possible again to bring the scattered fragments together ?　Apart from the New Testament, are there any sources still at all available calculated to afford fresh information on this common tradition ?　We can now say that there is, in fact, still extant a superabundance of such material.

When we pass on to the eschatological commentaries of the Fathers on Daniel, Revelation, 2 Thessalonians ii., Matthew xxiv., etc., we everywhere observe the same phenomenon, a multiplicity of details, causing us to ask in amazement, How does it happen that these expositors of the Old and New Testament writings are all alike so full of those wonderful and fantastic representations which occur precisely in this particular domain ?　Even beneath the most arbitrary exegetic fancies and allegorical explanations we may still perceive how this came about.　But in this field of research there is opened up a world of fresh eschatological imagery, for which scarcely any support is sought in the Bible, at least beyond mere suggestions. Yet these very suggestions or assertions everywhere crop out with surprising persistence, so that when the matter is more closely examined we begin to detect order, consistency, and system in what we had regarded as a mere congeries of marvellous fancies.

Doubtless explanations of a chapter in eschatology

are not to be sought in the apostolic Fathers or in the
apologists. But with Irenæus the above-mentioned
statements already begin to be more clearly formulated
and supported by a series of instances. I prefer,
however, to illustrate the point from Hippolytus'
treatise *On the Antichrist*, reserving for the next
section a general survey of the whole material. In
chap. vi. Hippolytus sets forth the following contrasts : " A lion is Christ, and a lion is the Antichrist ;
King is Christ, and king is the Antichrist. . . . In
the circumcision came the Redeemer into the world,
and in like manner will the other come ; the Lord sent
apostles unto all nations, and in the same way will
the other send false apostles ; the Saviour gathered
the scattered sheep, and in like manner will the other
gather the scattered people. The Lord gave a seal to
those that believed in Him, and a seal will the other
likewise give ; in the form of a man appeared the
Saviour, and in the form of a man will the other also
come ; the Lord stood up and exhibited His holy body
as a temple, and the other will also set up the temple
of stone in Jerusalem."

Whence did Hippolytus get all these data concerning the Antichrist ? In any case it cannot be said
that from the figure of Christ the several features in
the figure of the Antichrist were inferred by the law
of contrasts ; it would seem rather that the case was
here and there reversed ; compare, for instance, the
last antithesis, and that other further back, " The Lord
gave a seal to those that believed in Him." In what
follows a biblical passage is quoted only for the first

statement—the Christ, like the Antichrist, was called a lion. Then comes a proof (chap. xv.) that the Antichrist will spring from the tribe of Dan, on the strength of Genesis xlix. 16, 17 and Jeremiah viii. 16. This last notion, so surprisingly widespread amongst the Fathers, seems, however, to have had its origin in those passages of Scripture, though we cannot yet say when it arose. But before any one thought of applying those passages to the Antichrist, the idea must have already prevailed that the Antichrist would spring from the people of Israel.

This idea is also shared by Hippolytus, and thus is obtained another very important factor in the problem. For Hippolytus, the Roman empire is not the kingdom of the Antichrist, which is all the more remarkable that the Johannine Apocalypse distinctly indicates the Roman empire as the last great foe before the end of the world. Nor could Hippolytus be personally at all opposed to such an assumption, considering the judgment he himself pronounces on the Roman empire at the end of chap. xxxiv. He so far agrees with chap. xiii. of Revelation that he certainly understood the allusion in the first part of the chapter to point at the Roman empire ; but then for him the Antichrist is the second beast with the two horns, who will establish his sway after the fall of the Roman empire.

By such an exposition we may gather what violence Hippolytus does to the text of Revelation (see chap. xlix.); nor did his exegesis on this point find much approval in after-times. Yet none the less is the conception itself a commonplace for nearly all the

Fathers, beginning with Irenæus. They hold, not that the Roman empire is the Antichrist, but that the Antichrist will appear after its fall. The Roman empire is the power referred to as "he who now letteth" in 2 Thessalonians ii. 7. In this application the Antichrist saga has made its way into history, and in fact has acquired a historic mission.

Bearing this in view, it becomes extremely remarkable that, despite the after-effect of Revelation, the assumption of the Jewish origin of the Antichrist should acquire such general acceptance as to be so unanimously applied to the solution of the really puzzling passage in 2 Thessalonians. How short-lived, on the other hand, was the notion that the relations in Revelation had reference to Nero, and how infinitely varied and manifold are the interpretations of the passage in question !

Here we are again confronted with the puzzling assumption of a Jewish Antichrist who appears in Jerusalem. Hippolytus, like Irenæus, shows (chap. xliii.) that the two witnesses (Rev. xi.) will be Elias and Enoch. He has of course little difficulty in quoting Scripture for the return of Elias ; but he nowhere tells us how he discovered that Enoch was to be the associate of Elias.

This assumption also that Elias and Enoch are the two witnesses is so prevalent in patristic traditional lore that scarcely any other names are mentioned. How is the firm belief in this tradition to be explained ? In support of his theory, Hippolytus in one place actually quotes as an inspired authority a document absolutely unknown to us (chap. xv.) : " And *another prophet* says : he [the Antichrist] will gather all his power from the rising to the setting of the sun. Those whom he has called and whom he has not called will go with him. He will make white the sea with the sails of his ships, and the plain black with the shields of his hosts. And whoso will war with him shall fall by the sword." This passage he repeats in chap. liv., and in this and the following chapter he brings together specially remarkable statements regarding the Antichrist, statements the evidence for which we vainly seek in the Old or the New Testament. We may assuredly regard as unconvincing the occurrence of the curious combination from Daniel vii. and xi., implying that on his first appearance the Antichrist will overcome the kings of Egypt, of Libya, and Ethiopia, a combination with which again is connected the interpretation of Revelation xvii. In these details, however, Hippolytus is dependent on Irenæus.

It is again still more difficult to understand how Hippolytus knows that the Antichrist's next exploit will be the destruction of Tyre and Berytus (Beyrút). But so much will suffice to show that in his treatise on the Antichrist Hippolytus is dependent on a tradition which no doubt has something in common with many eschatological parts of the Old and New Testaments, but which none the less stands out quite distinctly as an independent concrete tradition. In fact he may well have borrowed the legend from some document already quoted by him as " a prophet."

As a second case in point I may appeal to the
Commentary of Victorinus. On the foreboding of
the famine under the third seal this writer observes :
" But properly speaking the passage has reference to
the times of the Antichrist, when a great famine
will prevail." The flight of the woman in the second
half of Revelation xii. he refers to the flight of the
144,000, who are supposed to have received the faith
through the preaching of Elias, supporting his interpretation with Luke xxi. 21. The water which the
Dragon casts out of his mouth after the woman is
taken to mean that the Antichrist sends out a host
to persecute her, while the earth opening her mouth
signifies the woman's miraculous deliverance from the
host by the Lord.

Although holding fast to the Neronic interpretation,
Victorinus connects it in a remarkable way with
another. Nero will appear under another name as the
Antichrist, and then he continues (chap. xiii.) : " He
will lust after no women, and acknowledge no God
of his fathers. For he will be unable to beguile the
people of the circumcision, unless he appears as the
champion of the law. Nor will he summon the saints
to the worship of idols, but only to accept circumcision,
should he succeed in leading any astray. Lastly, he
will so act that he will be called Christ by them.
The false prophet (Rev. xiii. 11 *et seq.*) will contrive
to have a golden statue set up to him in the Temple
of Jerusalem. The raising of the dead to life is
mentioned among the wonders wrought by this false
prophet."

Revelation xiii. 2 is explained as indicating the captains or leaders of the Antichrist, who are over-taken by the wrath of God in xiv. 20. Here again we see what a wealth of special traditions is revealed by such interpretations. And again we stand before the figure of the Jewish Antichrist, which is here rarely interwoven with the other figure of Nero redivivus.

But to avoid going twice over the same ground, I will break off at this point. Both examples sufficiently bear out the argument as above stated, and it will be enough here to assure the reader that the demonstra-tion might still be carried to a great length. Mean-while I would draw attention to a few considerations. The farther we advance into the centuries, the richer and the more fruitful become the sources. At the same time it is by no means to be supposed that the later documents merely introduce further embellishments into the still extant earlier materials. On the contrary, it is precisely from them that we obtain much supplementary matter needed to fill up the gaps and omissions in the earlier and more frag-mentary documents. How is this to be explained? As seems to me the explanation lies in the fact that in many cases the eschatological revelations have been passed on, not in written records, but in oral tradition, as an esoteric doctrine handled with fear and trembling. Hence it is that not till later times does the tradition come to light in all its abundance. We may learn from Hippolytus (chap. xxix.) what in his time was thought of traditional lore: "This,

beloved, I communicate to thee with fear. . . . For
if the blessed prophets before us, although they knew
it, were unwilling openly to proclaim it in order not
to prepare any perplexity for the souls of men, but
imparted it secretly in parables and enigmas, saying
' whoso readeth let him understand,' how much more
danger do we run if we openly utter what was couched
by them in covert language ! "

With this may be compared *Sibyll.*, X. 290 : " But
not all know this, for not all things are for all." [1] It is
very significant that Sulpicius Severus (*Hist.*, II. 14)
wrote down the Antichrist legend from an oral deliverance of S. Martin of Tours. Hence the secret
teaching concerning the Antichrist was still in the time
of S. Martin passed on from mouth to mouth. An
interesting passage also occurs in Origen on 2 Thessalonians ii. 1 *et seq.* : " Because perhaps amongst the
Jews were certain persons professing to know about
the Last Things either from Scripture or from hidden
sources, therefore he writes this, teaching his disciples
that they may believe no one making such professions " [2]
(*in Matthæum Comm.*, IV. 329).* In Commodian's
Carmen Apologeticum there also occurs the line :
" About which, however, I submit a few hidden things
of which I have read." [3]

In the following chapters I give a survey of the
sources here consulted. Besides the Fathers, the later
and latest Christian Apocalypses come naturally under

* For this passage 1 am indebted to Bonnemann, *Kommentar
zu den Thess.-Briefen.*

consideration. But of course much of this material is still inaccessible, and the Syriac, Coptic, and Slavic manuscripts will yet yield rich fruits. As, however, the tradition of the Antichrist legend is extremely persistent, the still missing documents will change but little in the general character of the tradition.

CHAPTER III.*

THE first group of documents bearing on the subject is connected with that highly interesting Apocalypse which was published in 1890 by Caspari.†

From chap. i. to iv. the treatise has rather the character of a sermon, after which in chap. v. the Apocalypse is related in the usual way in a simple, quiet flow of speech. In the very first chapter a clue

* For Notes [1] to [17] of this chapter, see Appendix, p. 263.

† *Briefe, Abhandlungen*, etc., pp. 208 *et seq.* (*Text*), pp. 429 *et seq.* (*Abhandlung*). The document is contained in the *Codex Barberinus*, XIV. 44, sæc. viii., under the title: "Dicta sancti Effrem de fine mundi et consummatio sæculi et conturbatio gentium"; that is, "The Utterances of S. Ephrem about the End of the World, and the Consummation of the Universe, and the Tribulation of the Nations." It occurs also in a codex of S. Gall, 108, 4°, sæc. viii., under the title: "Incipit sermo sancti Ysidori de fine mundi"; that is, "Here begins the Discourse of S. Isidore on the End of the World."

3

to its dates is afforded in the following sentences :
" And amid all these things are the wars of the Persians
—in those days will two brothers come to the Roman
kingdom, and with one mind they stand forward (?) ;
but because one precedes the other, schism will arise
between them." [1] Caspari has brought proof to show
that these allusions indicate the time of the emperors
Valentinian and Valens, the first of whom was raised
to the purple in 364, and the second soon after chosen
by his brother to share the throne with him. " Schism
will arise between them " is referred by Caspari to the
division of the empire, which took place soon after.
The question might nevertheless be asked, whether
with these words the apocalyptic writer does not
forebode some dissension foreseen by him, but which
has not yet come to pass, whence the future tense " will
arise." This would also agree better with the words
" because one precedes the other." Caspari, however,
is right in supposing the passage was not written before
the close of Valentinian's reign, or about the year 373,
when the war with the Persians broke out again. At
the same time he raises serious doubts against the
inference that the treatise was written about 373. For
in that case we should have to assume that the writer
had projected his own time into the future, after the
manner of the Sibylline utterances. But as this
Sibylline method is not elsewhere to be detected
in the whole treatise, he thinks it more probable
that the writer has quite clumsily interwoven some
extraneous (Sibylline) matter into the text. If so,
we should have nothing but the age of the extant

manuscripts to help us in determining the age of the work.

But all these assumptions of Caspari are groundless. A mere cursory perusal of the document makes it tolerably clear that the author simply reproduces not a contemporary but an early prophecy regarding the Antichrist, merely superadding a short historical and exhortative introduction. This view will be confirmed by the comparative study of the sources appended below.

The author speaks in his own person only in the first chapter, where he partly brings the ensuing revelation into connection with current events, partly introduces it with commonplace exhortations. Thus we see that the first chapter alone is available for determining the period. Nor is it easy to imagine that a writer living centuries later would have accepted such a distinct earlier prophecy had he not seen its fulfilment in his own days. In this Apocalypse on the Antichrist we have accordingly a document composed about the year 373.

Caspari then proceeds to discuss with much acumen the relation of the foregoing Apocalypse to the writings of S. Ephrem.* Unfortunately he has neglected to clear the ground respecting the tradition of the

* For the present I assume the genuine character of the Greek homilies here in question ; nor do I know any reasons against their ascription to S. Ephrem. In any case the whole of this literature is closely associated with the name of Ephrem. Compare, for instance, the Syriac homily on the Antichrist, which will be ·dealt with farther on, and which has also been handed down under the same name.

Ephremite writings under consideration, despite the incredibly careless way that Ephrem has been edited by Assemani. The extant manuscripts have been simply printed off without any attempt at sifting, although from the first a heterogeneous mass of homilies had acquired currency under the name of Ephrem. No doubt some of these formed originally a connected group ; but they were for the most part bundled together in the manuscript collections in the most diverse ways. Thus four distinct documents, *a, b, c, d,* are, for instance, found recurring in such combinations as $a + b$; $a + b + c$; $b + c + d$; $c + d$, and so on ; so that in Assemani the same manuscripts get printed three, four, or five times over—a fact only in the rarest instances noted by the editor.

A case in point is the very first document under consideration, the " Discourse on the Coming of the Lord, and about the End of the World, and on the Coming of the Antichrist," [2] which appears in Vol. I., pp. 222-230 ; and again (all but the first section, that is, pp. 222-225 E of Vol. II.) in Vol. III., pp. 134-143, this, however, being by far the better text. During the first revisions numerous shorter sections disappeared, and the originality of the last recension can be determined only by a comparison with Gerard Vossius' Latin edition of Ephrem (Antwerp, 1619, pp. 172 *et seq.*), which, however, was itself partly based on still more valuable manuscripts, and with a writing of the pseudo-Hippolytus to be considered farther on. Proofs in detail will be given in due course.

An excellent means of restoring the text is, more-

over, presented by the remark made by Professor
W. Meyer that Ephrem's homilies were composed and
even translated in verse, although no doubt verse of
a very peculiar kind, heedless of quantity, stress, or
cadences. Syllables alone are reckoned, an Eastern
process which Ephrem was probably the first to
employ in Syriac. Vossius' Latin edition, where is
still to be seen the transition from one measure to
another, shows that we have here two kinds of versi-
fication. There is first of all the stanza foot of seven
lines, each consisting of fourteen syllables, the cæsura
falling almost invariably in the middle, and every two
verses forming a strophe. Then comes the stanza of
four lines, in which each verse consists of sixteen
syllables, with a cæsura throughout on the eighth,
and wherever possible every fourth syllable coincides
with the close of a word. In quoting Ephrem I have
as far as possible restored this metrical system.

For the Antichrist document I have also been able
to utilise several collections and extracts from manuscripts * kindly placed at my disposal by Professor
Meyer. As the text can be restored with almost
absolute certainty on the above-mentioned principles,
I have not noted the variants occurring in manuscripts, but quote from the recension in Vol. III.,
so far as it is still extant, and for the first part from
W. Meyer's extract and collations. According to
the Latin edition and the pseudo-Hippolytus, the title
runs : " About the End of the World and about the

---

* Vindob. Theol., 165 ; Vatican, 1524, 1815, 2030, 2074.

Antichrist "; [3] and according to the Greek manuscripts :
" Discourse of S. Ephrem on the Antichrist." [4]

Other Ephremite writings bearing on the subject,
comprising four documents differently thrown together
in the different codices, may be tabulated as under :

A. A Discourse about the Cross.[5]
B. A Discourse on the Second Advent of Christ.[6]
C. and D. Questions and Answers concerning the
    Last Judgment.[7]

There are also to be considered the following
writings, here given as they occur in Assemani's
edition :

III., pp. 144-147 : On the Sign of the Cross.[8]
II., pp. 247-258 : Discourse on the Precious and
    Life-giving Cross, and on the Second Coming,
    and about Love and Almsgiving.[9]
II., pp. 192-208 : On the Second Coming of our
    Lord Jesus Christ.[10]
II., pp. 377-393 : Questions and Answers.[11]
II., pp. 209-220 : About the Universal Resurrec-
    tion, and on Repentance and Love.[12]
III., pp. 215 *et seq.* : Questions on Renunciation.[13]
III., pp. 371-375 : About Repentance and the
    Judgment, and on the Second Coming.[14]

In the following scheme I have grouped these
seven writings together just as the pages of the
respective documents correspond, roughly of course,
with each other. Wherever necessary I have more

carefully indicated the openings of the corresponding sections, as well as the conclusion of A, B, C, D, by the subdivisions of the pages in Assemani. By means of the cross-lines the four original documents, from which the seven homilies have been composed, stand out clearly and distinctly.

III.	II.	II.	III.	II.	III.	III.	
	247						
	248 B				371 F		A
	249				372		
144	250 B	192		212 F	373 A		
145	251	193		213	374		B
146	252	194		214	375		
147	253 F	195 (A, B)		215			
	254	166	377	215 F		215	
	255 B	197 B	380 E	217 C		217 B	
	256 BC	198 DE	382 C	218 D		218	C
	257 B	200 B	384 A	219 D		219 A	
	258 A	201 E	385 E	220 F			
		202 A	385 F				
		203	386				
		204	387				
		205 DE	388				
		206	389 E				D
		207	390				
		208	391				
			392 (393)				

Parallelisms with the Apocalypse about the Antichrist are offered especially by our document B, which thus gets printed no less than five times in Assemani.

From a more thorough examination, which for lack
of space cannot here be given in detail, it results that
there are extant two recensions of this document,
which differ not a little from each other, but neither
of which can claim absolute superiority in all respects.
One of these (1) occurs in III., p. 144, and II., p. 192;
the other (2) in II., pp. 250, 212 ; III., p. 373, so that
the last two stand again in the closest connection.
In my quotations the recension is given.

Moreover, chap. ii. of the Apocalypse (comprised
in the exhortative part) shows direct contacts with
Ephrem's " Discourse about Repentance," III., pp.
376-380, and with the twentieth essay on the " Other
Beatitudes," I. 294-299,[15] and still more with the
Latin translation * of the latter treatise (Caspari, pp.
447, 456).   Contacts with the other writings brought
forward by Caspari are unimportant.

On the whole the relations between the Apocalypse
on the Antichrist and the Ephremite writings are
correctly set forth by Caspari.   That the Antichrist
document itself was written by Ephrem is a groundless
assumption of one of the copyists.   But then Caspari
has rightly perceived that the details in Ephrem and
in the Antichrist can neither be derived from nor
explained by each other (see p. 454).

Yet this conclusion itself needs to be more accurately understood.   For Ephrem is by no means
to be taken as the source of all the passages in which
Caspari shows that parallelisms occur.   It seems to
me that a connection with Ephrem has been placed

* " Liber de beatitudine animæ."

beyond doubt only for the exhortative part in chap. ii. And even here it has again to be asked, Whence has Ephrem himself obtained the copious eschatological material which he deals with in his homilies ? Here also the only answer can be that he assuredly did not invent it himself, but borrowed it from one or more of the Apocalypses current in his time. But then immediately follows the important inference that in the Antichrist treatise we have the same apocalyptic material still in the relatively original though already embellished form, on which the writer relies in his homilies; it is even more original in so far that we have here the actual form of the Apocalypse but not of the homily.

There comes next under consideration the homily bearing the name of Hippolytus (Lagarde, p. 92), and entitled : " About the End of the World, and about the Antichrist, and on the Second Coming of our Lord Jesus Christ." [16] This document may be dealt with more briefly. In its first part, with which we are here less concerned, it depends on the genuine work of Hippolytus ; in the second (beginning with chap. xxii.) on Ephrem's homily bearing the same title, which is included in the original recension, III., pp. 134-143. But it is still more intimately related to the homily which is found in the Latin edition, and which is itself closely connected with III., pp. 134-143. The proof of this will be given in the third section by a continuous clause for clause comparison of the texts.

After chap. xxxvi., which again depends on

Hippolytus' genuine work, the pseudo-Hippolytus
utilises those documents in Ephrem's homilies which
I have above indicated by the letters C and D. In
these sections, which deal with the Last Judgment
(compare the title, " And on the Second Coming of
our Lord Jesus Christ "), there also occur many
things which are to be referred to some apocalyptic
tradition still perhaps known to the pseudo-Hippolytus.
But speaking generally the detailed description of
the judgment pronounced on the various classes of
men should apparently be exclusively credited to the
author of the homilies.

To this series belongs also the pseudo-Johannine
Apocalypse, which is comprised in Tischendorf's
Apocalypses Apocryphæ, xviii. *et seq.*, pp. 70 *et seq.* ;
and which varies greatly in the written records. It
professes to give certain revelations made to S. John
on Mount Tabor after the Resurrection, and contains
much the same material as the pseudo-Hippolytus
(chap. xxii. *et seq.*). It takes the form of a dialogue,
and in the second half shows connections with C and
D of Ephrem—that is, the " Questions and Answers."
In fact its interrogatory form may probably be due
to this source—that is, to Ephrem's homilies. Yet in
the opening it adheres more to the form of the
Apocalypse, and no doubt the writer had direct
access to apocalyptic material. Moreover it betrays
direct imitations of the canonical book of Revelation,
as, for instance, in chap. xviii.

With regard to the widely diverging traditions
occurring here and there in some of the manuscripts,

those are to be considered the best in which the text of the pseudo-John approaches nearest to the apocalyptic tradition of our group. Such is especially E Cod. Venet. Marc., Class II., cod. xc., as is best seen in chap. vi. of the Apocalypse. Here in E alone occurs a report on the first appearance of the Antichrist, which corresponds exactly with the tradition contained in our group. After E consideration may next be claimed by B Parisiensis (N. 947, anno 1523), and lastly A Venet. Marc., Class XI., cod. xx. (15th century).

Here may further be mentioned Cyril of Jerusalem, who introduces in his fifteenth catechetical lecture the Antichrist legend in the traditional form occurring in our group. It is noteworthy that Cyril already shows correspondence with Ephrem's " Questions and Answers." I am not quite sure whether a more distinct account of the Last Judgment, possibly the common source drawn upon both by Cyril and Ephrem, may not be assumed as already current in some apocalyptic tradition.

In the same series is comprised the version occurring in the Dioptra of Philip the Solitary, III. 10 *et seq.* (in Migne's *Patrol. Græc.*, CXXVII.), which is likewise closely connected with Ephrem. Nevertheless here also are found some interesting details which cannot be traced directly back to Ephrem.

Lastly, here may be tentatively introduced a fragment to which Professor Bonwetsch has called my attention. It occurs amongst the works of S. Chrysostom (Migne, LXI. 776), under the title, " On the

Second Coming of our Lord Jesus Christ, and about Almsgiving." [17]   Here the fragment opens with the judgment (the sign of the Son of man).   The corresponding Antichrist legend is completely preserved in Slavonic under the name of Palladius.

CHAPTER IV.*

TWO MEDIÆVAL SIBYLLINE DOCUMENTS (BEDE AND USINGER)
—ADSO ON THE ANTICHRIST—PSEUDO-METHODIUS—
S. EPHREM: SYRIAC HOMILY ON THE ANTICHRIST—
REVIEW OF THE GROUP OF EPHREMITE WRITINGS—THE
COMMON SOURCE OF ADSO'S ANTICHRIST AND OF BEDE'S
SIBYL—S. JEROME'S APOCALYPTIC MATERIAL.

I NOW come to a second group of extremely in-teresting documents, whose literary connection, however, presents extraordinary difficulties.

I begin with the latest, a paraphrase or revised text of some earlier Sibyl, which occurs both in Bede (Migne, Vol. XC., p. 1183), and in the *Pantheon* (Book X.) of Godfrey of Viterbo (*ob.* 1190), and which has with some probability been ascribed to Godfrey himself.† A description of nine generations of mankind, in which there are many echoes of the predictions of Lactantius, is followed by the account of a ruler bearing the name of C., after which comes a long series of other rulers, who cannot be more definitely determined, all being indicated merely by their initial

---

* For Notes [1] to [13] of this chapter, see Appendix, p. 264.

† Zezschwitz, 45; Usinger, *Forschungen zur deutschen Geschichte*, X. 629.

letters. The list of the German emperors, however, may
be clearly traced from Charlemagne (K.) to Frederick I.
and Henry VI. Then follow strange, fantastic fables
regarding their successors, and at the end the description of a last ruler, who is spoken of as " king
by name and of steadfast mind." * Then comes the
account of the Antichrist's appearance and of the
end of the world.

Farther on we come upon a similar paraphrase,
which has been published by Usinger (*op. cit.*, pp. 621
et seq.), but which is extant only in a fragmentary
state. It begins somewhat obscurely with a prediction of the period of the three Othos (tenth century), and then carries on the history down to the time
of Henry IV. (1050-1106). † The account of the
reign of Henry merges in that of some Byzantine ruler
with the words : " From him is then to proceed a king
of Byzantium of the Romans and Greeks, having
written on his forehead that he shall uphold the
kingdom of the Christians, overcome the children of
Ishmael, and reduce them and rescue the kingdom of
the Christians from the most vile yoke of the Saracens.
In those days no one under heaven shall be able to
overthrow the kingdom of the Christians. Thereafter
the nation of the Saracens will rise up for seven times,
and they will do all evil things throughout the whole
world, and nearly destroy all Christians. After these

---

* " Rex nomine et animo Constans." At least, so it runs in
the original text of Godfrey of Viterbo (*Monumenta*, 22, 146), not
rex nomine H animo Constans (Gutschmid, 149, Anmerkung 1).

† According to Zezschwitz and Gutschmid (*ib.* 147).

things the kingdom of the Romans will arise and smite them, and thereafter there will be peace and the kingdom of the Christians unto the time of the rule of the Antichrist." [1]

Then follows a brief reference to the Antichrist's rule, to the appearance of Gog and Magog, and the announcement that the last king will found his throne in Jerusalem.

Retracing our steps from these Sibylline writers of the end of the twelfth and eleventh centuries, we come to a work which was written in 954 by the monk Adso * at the request of Queen Gerberga. From Adso it was borrowed by Albuinus, a priest of Cologne, who embodied it in a comprehensive treatise dedicated to Archbishop Herbert. Thus it happened that the work became current under the name of Albuin, and even got printed both amongst Alcuin's and Austin's works (Migne, CI. 1289, and XL. 1130). It forms a collection of eschatological essays, in the last part of which Adso gives a Sibylline treatise on his own authority. To Zezschwitz † is due the credit of having shown that the Sibyl utilised by Adso is the same that lies at the base of the document in Bede. The close agreement begins with the account of the last ruler ; whence it must be inferred that the whole of the previous list of rulers, as in Bede, was not found in the common source, according to which the account of the last ruler ran thus :

* W. Meyer, *Ludus de Antichristo*, Munich, 1882, p. 4.

† *Op. cit.*, p. 42, and in his *Zusammenstellung der Texte*, p. 159.

Bede.	Adso.
And then will arise a king by name and of steadfast mind. The same will be the steadfast king of the Romans and Greeks.[2]	In the time of the said king, whose name will be C., king of the whole Roman empire. . . .[2]

Then follows an account of the glorious appearance of this king, and of the opulence which will prevail in his time ; after which we read :

Bede.	Adso.
And the king himself will have before his eyes the Scripture saying :	He will always have before his eyes the Scripture thus saying :

The king of the Romans [will] claim for himself [acquire] the whole kingdom of the lands [of the Christians]; therefore will he lay waste all the islands and cities [of the heathen], and destroy all the temples of the false gods, and all the pagans will he call to baptism, and the cross of Christ [Jesus] shall be raised over all the temples.[3]

During the reign of this king the Jews are to be converted, and he will vanquish the nations of Gog and Magog with their twelve or twenty-two kingdoms which had once been reduced by Alexander the Great; "[and thereafter the king] will come to Jerusalem, and there laying aside his diadem [and all his royal state], he will resign unto God the Father and His Son Christ Jesus the Christian kingdom."[4] The length of the king's reign is given in Bede as one hundred and twenty-two, in Adso one hundred and twelve, and in manuscripts twelve years. That this last alone is correct, and the others nothing more than fabulous embellishments, is evident from a surprising parallelism in the Greek Apocalypse of Daniel, which will be considered farther on: " And after him another sprung of him will reign twelve years. And he, fore-seeing his death, went to Jerusalem in order to deliver his kingdom unto God." [5]

Who is this king whose description is found in all these sources (compare above Usinger's Sibyl)? By a comparison of the various notices, especially those in Bede (the king by name, etc.) and in the account in the Sibyl of Henry IV.'s time of the victories of the king in question over the Ishmaelites, Gutschmid infers that it was Constans II., so that the common sources would have originated at the beginning of this emperor's reign, a conclusion which is certainly very attractive. At the same time it is to be considered that the reign and personality of Constans II. by no means correspond with the description, which would accord-ingly have to be regarded as purely fantastic; further, that there is no mention of triumphs over the Ishmael-ites in the source of the documents in Adso and Bede; lastly, that the quibble with the name of the king might conceivably point just as well to a Constantius or a Constantine. The account of the king here intro-duced also agrees with the fourth century, the early period of the Christian emperors, quite as well as with the seventh century.

On the other hand, Zezschwitz (p. 43) is fully justified in suggesting that in the concluding part of

4

this apocalyptic tradition events are no longer passing in the Western but in the Eastern empire. At the close the prediction points to its Oriental origin, while the idea of the last Roman emperor going to Jerusalem and there abdicating could have arisen only in times preceding the Crusades. Zezschwitz accordingly extends his investigations to the apocalyptic collection known as the Revelation of the pseudo-Methodius. In the more detailed account of the last emperor's abdication in Jerusalem he shows a direct parallel between the Sibyl of the time of Henry IV. and the pseudo-Methodius (p. 162); he also finds in the description of the appearance of Gog and Magog a parallelism between pseudo-Methodius and Adso.

On the pseudo-Methodius itself no clear idea can be formed pending a trustworthy edition of that work. The available text is found in the *Monumenta Patrum Orthodoxographa*, 2nd ed., Basel, 1569, Vol. I. (Greek 93, Latin 100 pp.). The Greek text, however, is according to Gutschmid (p. 152) a free re-cast dating from the twelfth century. Relatively far more valuable appears to be the *editio princeps*, Cologne, 1475. The editions of the Latin text all derive from that of Augsburg, 1496. Some of the sections of this interesting work, and those the most important for our purpose, have been reproduced by Caspari;* the Greek from the second edition of the *Orthodoxographa*, the Latin from two revised manuscripts.

In Gutschmid's opinion (p. 152) nearly all the materials are lacking in the original Greek text, on

* *Briefe und Abhandlungen*, pp. 463 et seq.

which all attempts have hitherto been made to assign a more accurate date to the document. Such is especially the long section giving a detailed account of some siege of Byzantium. Zezschwitz,* who has taken great pains to determine the date of this document, points to the blockade of Byzantium, which took place in 715 and the following years, and to the three rulers whose names occur in this connection— Philippicus Bardanes, Leo the Isaurian, and Constantine V. (Copronymus). It seems to me that these indications are correct, and I may here point to the interesting parallel passage in the Greek Apocalypse of Daniel (117, 2 *et seq.*).

The ruler here described as the liberator and the restorer of peace is Leo the Isaurian. No doubt he reigns according to the Greek text thirty-six, but according to the Slavonic translation thirty-two years, † like the Leo of the pseudo-Methodius in the revised text. Farther back (117, 55) occurs the passage : " And the great Philip with eighteen tongues and they shall be gathered together in the Seven Hills and prepare for war." [6] Here we have Philippicus Bardanes, while a perfect parallel passage occurs in 117, 61 : " Then shall the ox bellow and the arid hill lament." [7]

There is, however, a discrepancy. The successor to Leo is described in the Apocalypse of Daniel as the last emperor who lays aside his crown in Jerusalem, whereas in the pseudo-Methodius this ruler (Con-

* Pages 64 *et seq.*

† According to a communication kindly made to me by Professor Bonwetsch.

stantine V.) is very unfavourably judged. The passage
in Daniel may, however, possibly be older than the
corresponding passage foisted into pseudo-Methodius;
for the expectation of a good emperor as successor
to Leo could only have arisen before the reign of the
hated Constantine.

We thus obtain a standpoint for fixing the age of
the pseudo-Methodius through the discovery that a
document dating from the eighth century had already
been interpolated into this work. Gutschmid also
thinks that it was certainly composed before the overthrow of the Ommiades, which is again confirmed by
the existence of manuscripts of the Latin translation
as old as the eighth and ninth centuries. Gutschmid
goes even so far as to assert with some confidence that
the work was composed between the years 676-678.

Considering the hopeless confusion of the textual
tradition as embodied in this Methodius, it may seem
somewhat risky to venture any further opinion on
its contents. Nevertheless to me it seems safe to
conclude that the Latin and Greek texts in the *Orthodoxographa* belong to two totally different streams of
tradition, so that wherever these two witnesses agree
they stand on tolerably safe ground. All the pieces
excluded by Gutschmid, on the strength of his better
manuscripts, are also shown by a like collation to
be interpolations now in the Latin, now in the Greek
text.

The pseudo-Methodius is, in fact, a collection of
apocalyptic materials, which, however, is pervaded
by a uniform sentiment. It was obviously composed

under the powerful and vivid impression produced
by the ceaseless and irresistible onslaught of Islám
against the whole civilised world as at that time
constituted. In it may be distinguished about seven
different documents. 1. A survey of the early history
of nations, beginning with Adam. 2. Gideon's victory
over the Ishmaelites, concluding with the ominous
foreboding that these nomads will once again issue from
their settlements in the wilderness and lay the world
in ruins, but that at last the Roman empire will still
come out triumphant. 3. The history of Alexander
the Great ; the erection of the rocky barrier against
Gog and Magog ; the prediction of the irruption of
these nations in the last days (compare Bede and
Adso) ; the marriage of Bisas, first king of Byzantium,
with Khuseth, mother of Alexander,* and of their
daughter Bisantia with Romulus, " who is also called
Armælius." † 4. A comment on the Pauline prediction in 2 Thessalonians, chap. ii., with the indication
that by the kingdom which lasts to the end is to be
understood the Roman empire, despite the ascendency
of the Ishmaelites. 5. On the " reign of terror " of
Islám. 6. On the brilliant victory of a Roman
emperor, who must no doubt be identified with
Constantine IV. when he fixes the date of the work
at 676-678 A.D. : " Then will suddenly arise a king

* On the evolution of these fables, see Zezschwitz, pp. 52 *et seq.*
† " Qui et Armæleus dictus." This gloss, which is not
found in the Greek text, is here introduced because it confirms
the identification of the Jewish Antichrist Armillus, Armilaos,
with Romulus.

of the Greeks or of the Romans, like unto a man
refreshed with wine from sleep." [8]   7. The end :
Gog and Magog and their overthrow by the Roman
emperor ; the birth of the Antichrist ; the emperor's
abdication ; the sway of the Antichrist ; the last
judgment.

Now the relation with the already described sources
stands thus.   Adso and Bede with their common
source coincide only in one point with Methodius (see
below), but are only more remotely connected with
No. 7, while Usinger's Sibyl shows a closer relation
to No. 7, and Adso in the first part of his work with
Nos. 4 and 7.   Adso, however, has here nothing
of the further development of the Methodius saga,
according to which the crown laid aside in Jerusalem
is to be borne heavenwards with the cross.

These remarks enable us to advance a conjecture
regarding the apocalyptic sources which lie far beyond
the Methodius itself.   This work is not, as was still
supposed by Zezschwitz (p. 50), the last link of the
chain bearing on the subject.   Even Gutschmid has
already noticed that Adso, Bede, [and Usinger] lead
us back to an earlier document, which, as he thinks,
dates from the time of Constans II. (642-668).   In the
common source of Adso and Bede the above-mentioned
expansion of the statement regarding the deposition
of the crown is not yet found, though already occurring
in Usinger.

Zezschwitz himself retraces his steps, and conjectures that the historical foundation of the apocalyptic expectations in Methodius is to be sought in

the reign of the emperor Heraclius. During his triumphant entry into Jerusalem, Heraclius is supposed, in accordance with the saga, to have been arrested by an angel at the city gate, and to have laid aside both crown and purple before entering Jerusalem (p. 58). He is also supposed to have summoned to his aid against the Saracens the nations of Gog and Magog, whom Alexander the Great had shut up within the Caspian gates (p. 61). The Heraclius saga would thus be the starting-point of that apocalyptic tradition, with which view Gutschmid agrees. But it may well be asked whether its origin may not be traced still farther back.

We are, in fact, now in the fortunate position of being able to follow up the cycle of legends back to a far more remote time.

A glance at Malvenda's comprehensive work *de Antichristo* (I. 570) might have already brought us, in connection with the Gog and Magog legend, to the paragraph in S. Jerome's epistle to Oceanus (77, 8) to the effect that " the swarms of the Huns burst forth from the remote Mæotis Palus [Sea of Azov] between the gelid Tanais [river Don] and the vast nation of the Massagetæ, where the barriers of Alexander [at Derbend] confine the rude populations to the rocks of Caucasus." * Then Caspari has called attention to the parallelisms between the pseudo-Methodius and the

---

* " Ab ultima Mæotide inter glacialem Tanain et Massage-tarum immanes populos, ubi Caucasi rupibus feras gentes Alexandri claustra cohibent, erupisse Hunnorum examina " (compare Hegesippus, *de Excidio Jer.*, V. 50). The legend that

Discourse of the pseudo-Ephrem (p. 20). Once there occurs an exact parallel in pseudo-Ephrem (chap. iv.) with Methodius in the description of Gog and Magog ; and here also we find (chap. v.) the important passage : " And already the kingdom of the Romans is abolished and *the empire of the Christians is delivered up to God and the Father*, and then comes the consummation, when the kingdom of the Romans shall begin to be consummated and all the principalities and powers brought to an end." [9]

Even allowing that Caspari's doubts regarding the date of the Discourse (about 373) were justified, we are in any case led back beyond the reign of Heraclius. For there is still no trace in the Ephremite Discourse of the irruption of Islám, the foes of the Roman empire being still the Persians. Thus the apocalyptic tradition in question cannot be founded on the Heraclius saga, which could not possibly have sprung up till after the year 629.

But now comes, on the other hand, a welcome confirmation of the correct epilogue in the pseudo-Ephremite Discourse. Professor W. Meyer directs my attention to Th. J. Lamy's *Hymns and Discourses of S. Ephrem the Syrian*,* where we have a sermon preserved in Syriac " about Agog and Magog and the End and the Consummation," † showing the closest

---

Alexander built the Caspian gates against the incursions of the surrounding wild tribes goes even still farther back (Pliny, *Natur. Historia*, VI. 13).

* *Sancti Ephraem Syri Hymni et Sermones*, Vol. III., pp. 187 *et seq.*

† " De Agog et Magog et de fine et consummatione."

connection with the Latin Discourse and with the work of Methodius ; thus :

EPHREM, III. 190.[10]	PSEUDO-EPHREM, I.[10]
Now, like the Nile, which rising floods the land, the regions shall girdle themselves against the Roman empire, and peoples shall war against peoples and kingdom against kingdom, and from one land unto another shall the Romans hurry as if in flight.	In those days shall many rise up against the Roman state, . . . for there shall be commotions amongst the peoples.

But the most striking agreement occurs between Ephrem Syr., chaps. v. *et seq.*, the Discourse of ps.-Ephrem, ch. v., and ps.-Method., VII., chap. v.,* in the account of the savage peoples Gog and Magog, " who dwell beyond those gates which Alexander built." †
Ephrem the Syrian has in common with pseudo-Methodius the enumeration of the twenty-four tribes, while the parallels in the Discourse of Ephrem and in pseudo-Methodius are mere scanty excerpts from the detailed description of these fierce populations. And here are also mentioned Gog and Magog, that is to say, the Huns, whose irruption into the Edessa district

---

* The parallelisms between pseudo-Ephrem and pseudo-Methodius brought together by Caspari (pp. 463 *et seq.*) are explained by their common dependence on Ephrem the Syrian.

† " Qui sunt ultra illas portas quas fecit Alexander."

took place during the time of Ephrem himself, as we learn from an Armenian life of him which states that he wrote against the Huns.*

Here, therefore, we have, as conjectured by Caspari, the common source of the Discourse and of pseudo-Methodius, and probably also the historical event whence arose the Gog and Magog saga in the form with which we are concerned. Then follows in Ephrem the Syrian, beginning with chap. viii., the Antichrist legend proper. Here, however, I have not found any special relations between Ephrem and the Discourse ; and remembering the great persistence of the saga, we have to be very careful in comparing two independent sources. On the other hand, pseudo-Methodius, VII., is manifestly dependent on Ephrem, as may be seen by comparing the account of the wonders wrought by Antichrist and of Enoch and Elias. In the Antichrist saga Ephrem has introduced a .great many archaic elements. The statement (chap. xii.) that Enoch and Elias are awakened by the angels Michael and Gabriel I have met elsewhere only in the Ethiopic Petrine Apocalypse,† in which they are also the assailants of Antichrist. ‡

---

* Lamy, 198, remark 2. With this may be compared the Apocalyptic Commentaries of Andreas, edited by Sylburg (p. 94, 45) : " But some consider Gog and Magog to be hyperborean Scythian peoples, whom we call the most numerous and warlike of all the surrounding territory." [11]

† In pseudo-Johannes, however, chap. ix., the universal awakening of the dead after the murder of the two witnesses is also brought about by Michael and Gabriel.

‡ Cf. also Adso and Bede.

In the account of the destruction of the world by
fire the pseudo-Johannine Apocalypse comes nearest to
Ephrem, while Gog and Magog are destroyed by Michael
the Archangel (chap. xiii.). The same incident occurs
also in the Syriac Apocalypse of Ezra (chap. xiii.),
which has been published by Baethgen from the manuscript Sachau, 131.* This apocalypse will be dealt
with farther on.

Lastly it will be necessary to inquire into the
mutual relations of the various writings which have
been handed down under the name of Ephrem, and
which will have to be repeatedly referred to in the
course of our inquiry. At the very outset doubts
arise with regard especially to the authenticity of
Ephrem's Syriac Discourse itself. In chap. iii. occurs
the passage : "The saints shall lift their voice, and
their clamour shall mount unto heaven, and from the
wilderness shall go forth the people of Hagar, hand-
maiden of Sarah, who made the covenant with
Abraham, husband of Sarah and of Hagar, and they
shall be stirred so that they may come in the name of
the wilderness as the envoy of the son of perdition." [12]

There can be scarcely a doubt that the Arabs are
here meant, and in the following chapters (iii., iv.) a
very vivid description is given of the devastation
which will be caused by this people of the wilderness.
But all the more decidedly is an earlier period indicated
in the description of the Huns, which then follows.
If we omit chap. iii. from the words "and from the
wilderness," and the whole of chap. iv., then chap. v.

* *Zeitschr. für alttestamentliche Wissenschaft.*, VI., pp. 204 *et seq.*

will accurately fit in with the words : "Then will the
divine Justice summon the kings, that is, Gog and
Magog." It is obvious that the twofold description
of an irruption of a savage people as in chaps. iii., v.,
et seq. would be absolutely meaningless.

It may even be more clearly shown that we have
a passage interpolated in the text. In the enumeration
of the twenty-four peoples of Gog and Magog there
is an identical parallelism between Ephrem and the
pseudo-Methodius ; and from a comparison of the two
it is seen that the names Thogarma, Medi, Persæ,
Armeni, "Turcæ" have been interpolated. Then we
get also the number twenty-four which is expressly
given in the Latin version of Methodius ; only the
Khusas are reckoned twice over. But in other respects
the lists in Ephrem the Syrian and in Methodius
(both Greek and Latin texts) fully correspond, which
at first sight might scarcely be supposed possible.*

In other respects there seems to be no objections
to the text as it stands. The vivid description of
the Huns brings us to the lifetime of Ephrem, and

---

* Bearing in mind the above-indicated interpolations, we
find the numbers almost completely corresponding. Thus :
Eph. 1-8 ; Meth. Gr. 1-8 ; Meth. Lat. 1-2, 5-10 (M. Lat.
puts Nos. 18, 17, Mosakh Tubal, in 3 and 4 of the list).
E. 9-13 — M. Gr. 14, 15, 18, 16, 17   M. Lat. 16-20.
E. 14-19 = M. Gr. 9-13 (12 seems = 17 + 18) = M. Lat.
11-13, 4, 3, 15. E. 20-24   M. Lat. 14, 20-24 (in M. Gr.
20 and 21 are missing). In E. I take 20 to be the Nemrukhaei
= M. Lat. Lamarchiani, and a glance at the Syriac text will
show the possibility of this transposition ; 22, however, that
is, Phisolonici, φιλονίκιοι, cannot be fitted in, unless we suppose
it derived from the Syriac ܟܠܒܝܐ̈ 197, 3.

gives credibility to the tradition which assigns this Syriac Discourse to him.

Coming now to Ephrem's authentic Discourse, full support is given to its assumed date about the year 373 by the correct identification of the Huns with the savage people here described. But to the question, Is the Discourse to be also ascribed to Ephrem himself? I think I must give a negative answer. In the Syriac Discourse Ephrem presents a different picture of the destruction of the Roman empire. Thus in chap. viii. : "And there shall arise in the place of this people the kingdom of the Romans, which shall subdue the world unto its confines, and there shall be no one to stand up against it. But when wickedness shall be multiplied on the earth, . . . then shall arise the divine Justice and shall utterly destroy the people, and the man of wickedness [that is, Antichrist] proceeding from perdition shall come upon the earth." [13]

Remembering that the reigning emperor was tainted with the Arian heresy, we cannot be surprised at this judgment of Ephrem. In the Latin Discourse, on the other hand, it is for the first time stated that the Roman empire shall not perish, but voluntarily deliver up its sway; and for this very reason the Discourse cannot be ascribed to Ephrem. But it originated soon after on the base of the details supplied by Ephrem. But then in what relation does the above-described Greek Discourse of Ephrem stand to the Syriac? The fact that it is destitute of any political motives is no reason for doubting its authenticity, because this Discourse deals exclusively with the very last days. It is more important to notice that in the Syriac Ephrem no mention yet occurs of the apparition of the Cross at the universal judgment, a feature to which such prominence is given in the Greek homilies. On the other hand, there is nothing in the Greek Discourse about the part which Michael and Gabriel play in the last days. But on one important and remarkable point the Greek and the Syriac are in accord; in both the servants and messengers of the Antichrist are represented as demons. If we have, in the Greek perhaps, a revision of Ephrem's genuine work, most of the details given by him are doubtless still to be traced back to Ephrem.

Here at last the question of the common source of Adso, II., and of Bede's Sibyl can again be discussed. Should not this Sibyl, with its allusion to the "king by name and of steadfast mind," be after all traced back to some period long antecedent to Constans II.? At least the notion that the last Roman emperor delivers up his crown to God is already found in a document of the fourth century. It by no means dates from the time of Heraclius, and it may be confidently affirmed that the idea of the Roman empire being destroyed before the appearance of the Antichrist must have very soon undergone some such modification after the empire had become Christian. But if we once go beyond the time of Heraclius, then we must assuredly also shift that source back to the fourth century, for the emperor spoken of in it is unanimously described as "king of the Romans and Greeks." Hence there remain but two

alternatives, to look for the "king by name . . .
steadfast" ("Constans") either in the fourth century
or in the time following the reign of Justinian. It
is still, however, possible that in the word "Constans"
we have, not the actual name of the king, but merely
a play of words ; thus here, for instance, the allusion
might perhaps be to Constantius, or even, though less
probably, to Constantine I.

In determining the point we get little help from
the twelve years given as the duration of his reign,
and this term must be regarded as a purely apocalyptic
fancy. The last king is conceived as the counterpart
of Alexander the Great, whose reign lasts twelve
years in the pseudo-Methodius. The influence of the
history of the Macedonian epoch is similarly felt in
the Greek Apocalypse of Daniel,* where is described
yet another partition of the world into four kingdoms,
as taking place after the death of the king, who in
the last times reigns twelve years.

An interesting confirmation of this legend is afforded
by a remark made by Zezschwitz (p. 21). In the
chronicle where Godfrey of Viterbo sings the glories of
Alexander, the Conqueror is introduced as saying :

Reddo tibi restituamque thronum,
Te solo dominante volo tibi regna relinqui.

That is to say : "To thee I deliver up and restore the
throne ; to thee, sole ruler, will I that the kingdom
be resigned." Thus in some particulars are merged
together the Alexander and the Antichrist sagas.

Here may, in conclusion, be examined another special

* Klostermann, 118, 84.

feature from the cycle of traditions under consideration. It occurs in the *Ludus de Antichristo,* a play which was composed about the year 1160, and the author of which has not hitherto been quoted as a special authority because he draws his material mainly from Adso.* Here we read how the Antichrist overcomes the Greek king by war, the French by gifts, and the German by miracles. The source of these fancies has now been discovered by Meyer in the following passage of Adso : " Against the faithful will he rise up in three ways—that is, by terror, by gifts, and by wonders ; to the believers in him will he give gold and silver in abundance ; but those whom he shall fail to corrupt by presents he will overcome by fear, and those whom he shall fail to vanquish by fear he will seek to seduce by signs and wonders " (1294 A).[14] These fancies, however, are still more widespread, as seen in the *Elucidarium* (treated below), where are enumerated four kinds of temptations used by the Antichrist : 1. *divitiæ* (riches) ; 2. *terror* ; 3. *sapientia* (wisdom) ; 4. *signa et prodigia* (signs and wonders). In Eterianus also (see below) occurs the passage : " By threats, blandishments, and all [other] ways will he seduce." [15] But in their essence all these passages may be traced back to S. Jerome.

In his Commentary on Daniel xi. 39, Jerome is already able to tell us that " Antichrist also will lavish many gifts on the beguiled, and will divide the world among his army, and those whom he shall fail

* Cf. W. Meyer, the *Ludus de Antichristo,* pp. 10 *et seq.* and 14 *et seq.*

to quell by terror he will overcome by greed." [16] Scarcely has Jerome extracted this information from the obscure passage in Daniel, which he is even unable to translate, when he falls completely back on apocalyptic tradition, as will be shown farther on.* Here we again clearly see how deep-rooted are even such apparently remote and isolated elements of our apocalyptic tradition. It is noteworthy that we here come for the second time on a parallelism between Jerome and the group of Antichrist documents under consideration. Hence Jerome's apocalyptic tradition, which occurs chiefly in his Commentary on Daniel as well as in his epistle to Algasia (*Quæstio* XI.), belongs also perhaps to the cycle of traditions in question.

In the documents just dealt with we have accordingly a literary series which, beginning with Ephrem, extends through pseudo-Methodius and Adso to the mediæval Sibylline writers and the miracle play composed in the Hohenstaufen epoch. Thus may be seen how the Antichrist legend gets modified when the Roman empire embraces Christianity, and how it preserves traces of such events as the beginning of the migrations of the peoples and the irruption of the Huns. It also tells us about the history of the Byzantine emperors and the destructive effects of the flood of Islâm bursting over the Eastern provinces. Lastly we find it interwoven with the history of the German empire and the Crusades.

---

* Cyprian also goes beyond Jerome in his reference to "Antichrist's threats and corruptions and dens of vice" (*Antichristi minas et corruptelas et lupanaria*) in *de Mortalitate*, 15.

5

CHAPTER V.*

A THIRD group of sources is from later apocalyptic works now to be considered. In the Stichometry of Nicephorus and in the Synopsis of Athanasius there is a Book of Daniel, while a seventh Vision of Daniel is mentioned in a list of apochrypha by Mekhithar of Aïrivank in 1290.† The text of a Greek Apocalypse of Daniel was first published by Tischendorf (*Apocalypses Apocryphæ*, xxx.-xxxiii.), and again in a legible form by Klostermann (*Analecta zur Septuaginta*, Leipzig, 1895, pp. 113 *et seq.*). An Armenian seventh Vision of Daniel has also been published by Gr. Kalemkiar in the Vienna *Zeitschr. für die Kunde des Morgenlandes* (Vol. VI. 109 *et seq.*, 227 *et seq.*).

A comparison of the two documents made by Zahn ‡ before the appearance of Klostermann's text showed that both, although quite different, point back to a common source. Here we shall endeavour to bring out this source still more distinctly.

* For Notes [1] to [5] of this chapter, see Appendix, p. 266.
† Zahn, *Forschungen*, Vol. V., 115, 116.   ‡ *Ibid.*, V. 119.

In the opening, couched in the Sibylline style, the two writings have much in common. Yet these predictions, as they are generally considered, defy all interpretation. But both apocalypses agree in one important detail, a prophecy launched against Rome, the city of the seven hills, which clearly points to the end of the Western empire (compare the Armenian, 237, 9, with the Greek, 116, 28). After referring by name to the reign of Olybrius (472) = Orlogios, that is, if Zahn's conjecture is right,* the texts run :

GREEK.[1]	ARMENIAN.
37. But the sons of perdition standing up will turn their faces to the setting of the sun.	Z. 30. And the king will turn his face towards the west.
38. Woe to thee, O Seven-hilled, from such wrath when thou wert girdled round by a great host, and [when] a youth shall rule over thee wretched.	Then woe to thee, thou Seven-hilled, when thy king is a youth.

Then follows in both a reference to the beginning of the Gothic rule, the dynasty " of another religion, that is Arianus,"† as it reads in Ar. ; or " of the fair race," † as it runs in Gr. But whether we are to understand Ar., 238, 29-32 to refer to the establishment of the exarchate of Ravenna is not quite clear.

* Zahn, *Forschungen*, Vol. V., 118.

† τὸ ξανθὸν γένος.

This particular clause is not found in Gr., hence must be a later insertion.

Then, immediately after the mention of these events, Ar. gives an account of the rule of the Antichrist and of the end, while the Greek Apocalypse also concludes with the details about the Antichrist.

The source of both apocalypses now comes out clearly and distinctly. The essential element is the old apocalypse about the Antichrist, who according to remote tradition was to come when the Roman empire lay in ruins. Nothing was more natural than the revival of this old Antichrist legend (introduced with an allusion to current events) at the time when the Western empire was falling to pieces. In any case, the title of this revelation was doubtless the Apocalypse of Daniel. But it is another question whether the common source itself also bore this name (see above).

Thus the two later legends (Ar. and Gr.) had their origin in the earlier apocalypse. In Ar., 230, 24 *et seq.* the destinies of the Eastern empire are predicted by anticipation. Marcian is mentioned by name (231, 19); the history of Leo I., of Zeno and of the usurper Basiliscus is still clearly related; while Kalemkiar finds events predicted down to the emperor Heraclius—a conjecture, however, which is already questioned by Zahn. If, however, 234 refers to the seven-hilled Babylon,* to the reign of a widow, and to a dragon who is to persecute the foreigners,

---

* The author of Ar. no longer understands it in this sense (231, 16).

then we have here some elements again borrowed from the common source of Ar. and Gr. In Gr. also there is a prediction entirely independent of Ar. It has reference to the history of the Eastern empire, which, as would seem (117, 42), begins with the fall of the Western empire, and lasts till the reign of Constantine V. Thus it becomes quite clear how the interpolation came about. Like the Armenian, the Greek writer has also forgotten the meaning of the " seven-hilled " (119, 88). He accordingly dissociates the sway of the Antichrist from the fall of the Western empire, his relation passing from the Western to the Eastern empire, whereas in Ar. the order is reversed.

In the common source a Sibylline style is evident, and is very pronounced, especially in the opening section of the apocalypses. The very word ἑπτάλοφος (" seven-hilled ") has also become current in Sibylline literature as the distinctive by-name of Rome.

In this connection I may call attention to the article by Kozak on the apocryphal biblical literature amongst the Slavs in the *Yahrbuuch für Protest. Theologie*, 1892, 128 *et seq.* From N. xviii. of Kozak's papers it appears that a *Vision of Daniel* has also been preserved and already printed in the South Slavonic (Serb) and Russian languages, and according to this authority the documents correspond with the Greek Apocalypse of Daniel.* In N. xxxviii. mention

---

* Professor Bonwetsch has kindly favoured me with a trans- lation of some parts of the Slavonic Apocalypse, which seems identical with the Greek.

is made of a *Narration about the Antichrist,* which, as briefly summarised, contains a record of the Byzantine emperor, a prediction of a famine, and the rule of a virgin who receives the Antichrist as a bird, the appearance of John the Theologian and his contention with the Antichrist, the appearance of Elias and his death, the sway of the Antichrist and the end of the world.*

The mention of the rule of a virgin is interesting. With it is to be compared the frequent reference to the rule of a widow in Ar. and in Gr. : " And there being no man available, a polluted woman shall reign in the [city of the] seven hills, and defile the holy altars of God, and standing in the midst of the seven hills shall cry out with a loud voice, saying : Who is God but I, and who shall resist my sway ? And forthwith the seven hills shall be shaken and all life cast into the deep." [2] Then follows (119, 100) the dominion of the Antichrist.

Perhaps some light is thrown by this passage on an obscure part of the Sibylline literature. In Sibyl III. 75 we read : " And then verily the whole world under the hands of a woman—there shall be a ruler and a prevailer in all things—then when a widow shall rule the whole earth—and cast gold and silver into the vast deep—the bronze and eke the iron of mortal men—shall cast into the sea, then truly all the elements—shall be bereft of order when God dwelling on high—shall roll up the heaven." [3]

---

* It may further be mentioned that a fourteenth Vision of Daniel is extant in some Coptic manuscripts (Klostermann, 114).

It is noteworthy that here the appearance of the Antichrist (Belial) comes first.

On the title of the Apocalypse of Daniel it is further to be noted that Lightfoot (quoted by Zahn, 120) draws attention to a miscellaneous codex of the twelfth century in Wright's *Catalogue of Syriac MSS.*, I. 19, which, after the deuterocanonical additions to Daniel, contains a fragment " from the Little Daniel on our Lord (?) and the End of the World." * Here we may perhaps conjecture that we have a part of the Apocalypse, which again lies at the base of the rediscovered source. Zahn is further of opinion that, in accordance with a notice of Ebed Jesu (Assemani, *Bibl. Orient.*, III. 15), Hippolytus had already commented on this apocryphal book of the Little Daniel. Professor Bonwetsch, who was consulted by me on the subject, is inclined to see in the notice of " the Little [Young] Daniel and Susanna " only one and the same work—that is, the apocryphal history of Susanna and Daniel of the Old Testament. I should greatly desire to have this matter cleared up, for it would be very important to find that Hippolytus had already known and commented upon an Apocalypse of Daniel. What has been said higher up regarding Hippolytus is no longer an impossibility. The relations of the Greek Apocalypse of Daniel to the pseudo-Methodius, and especially to the inter-

* Compare what is stated below on a Jewish Book of Daniel of the ninth century. Apocalyptic material also occurs in the *Life of Daniel* contained in *Vitæ Prophetarum* (" Lives of the Prophets ") wrongly attributed to Epiphanius.

polated passage on the siege of Constantinople, has already been discussed (p. 51). Here may further be mentioned the interesting title of a treatise occurring in Fabricius : " The Last Vision of the Great Prophet Daniel," etc.[4]

At the head of a further group of documents I place the apocalyptic writings, which are still extant in the Arabic, the Ethiopic (Geez), and probably also the Syriac languages under the name of *Liber Clementis discipuli S. Petri* (" Book of S. Peter's Disciple Clement "), or also *Petri Apostoli Apocalypsis per Clementem*, etc. (" Apocalypses of the Apostle Peter by Clement," etc.). A review is given by Bratke of the very confused tradition respecting this book.* To Dillmann, however, is due the fullest survey of the Ethiopic translation of this work, which has nowhere yet been printed. But we have to consider the special eschatological sections, which, according to Dillmann, are found in the second and fourth parts, the first being a prediction about Islám, the second another about the rule of the Antichrist. Farther down it will be made evident that both of these now separated sections are essential parts of an original apocalypse, possibly that of S. Peter.

The section most interesting to us contains especially a prophecy on the history of Islám, which Dillmann has interpreted with brilliant success. First comes a reference to twelve rulers of the Ommiades (Muhammad to Abu-Bekr II.), the first four of whom are indicated by their initial letters (Muhammad, Abu-Bekr, Omar,

* *Zeitschr. für Wissenschaft. Theologie*, 1893, I., pp. 454 *et seq.*

Othman). Then the history is continued through six rulers down to Merwan II., after which follows an account of battles fought by the King of the South (Merwan) against the King of the East (the Abassides), and we are told how the King of the East conquers Egypt. The author speaks of four empires: the Eagle representing the Babylonian, the Panther the Greek, the Lion the Roman (of which it is remarked " the king of Rome reigns till my second coming "), and a beast called Arnê (Dragon, Snake), the children of Ed°yô. By this last, which takes the second place, presumably according to its rank, is represented the empire of Islám.

At that time, when the dynasty of the Ommiades was overthrown, the Lion's son rises again and triumphs over Islám, this Lion's son being, according to Dillmann, Constantine Copronymus. Damascus, capital of the Ommiades, is to be destroyed ; but when the Lion's son returns from his expeditions, then the end is near, as was known to Peter. Then comes an unintelligible indication of a period when all this is to happen. Here should probably immediately follow that section about the Antichrist which is now found in the second part of the book. We have here, therefore, an apocalypse, the solution of which is complete in all its details.

To show that in the Arabic Apocalypse of S. Peter we have an almost identical work, the reader may consult Nicoll's *Bibliothecæ Bodleianæ Codices Manuscr. Orient. Catalog.*, Oxford, 1821, II., pp. 149 *et seq.* Unfortunately the contents of chaps. xxxi.-xliv. are not

given. In chap. xlvi. we have already the mention of
the Lion's son, while in chap. xlvii. the four empires
are enumerated as above. The second empire is that
of the Beni'l Abu, the fourth that of the Romans, of
which it is said that "this shall remain till the advent
of Christ." * Chap. xlviii. has a description of the Beni'l
Abu, the beginning of whose rule is determined by the
year 923 from Alexander. A discrepancy is shown in
chaps. lii. and liii., inasmuch as here the Lion's son
is represented as a foe of the Christians, and a promise
given of his overthrow by the archangel Michael. In
chap. lxvii. we are told of "the going forth of the accursed son of Dan, who is Antichrist, and of the descent
of Elias and Enoch, and that these he is to kill and
perform great wonders and many marvels." [5]

In the second and third parts of the Ethiopic Apocalypse of S. Peter were also comprised the fragments
of a "Syriac Apocalypse of Simon Peter," which are
published by Bratke (pp. 468 *et seq.*). A comparison
of the two fragments on the Antichrist here given
at pp. 471 and 481 shows that in the details great
changes naturally occur.

Here therefore we have in all probability an
Ethiopic, an Arabic, and a Syriac recension of the
same work, the apocalyptic elements of which
were composed about the time of the fall of the
Ommiades.

By a lucky chance Dillmann has given us a translation of the following fragment touching the Lion's son
(p. 73 A) : "I will awaken the Lion's son, and he shall

* "Quorum hoc ad Christi adventum mansurum est."

slay utterly all the kings and tread them down, for I
have given him the power thereunto, and therefore is
the appearance of the Lion's son like that of a man who
is awakened from his sleep." This stands in obvious
relation to the passage quoted above (p. 54) from the
book of Methodius (Part VI.). But a close connection
is also manifest between the Ethiopic Petrine Apocalypse and the pseudo-Methodius. It may therefore
be conjectured that the pseudo-Methodius was one of
the sources of the Petrine document, even though in
other respects Gutschmid may be right in identifying
the Byzantine ruler of pseudo-Methodius with Constantine IV.

Starting from this assumption, we shall now
arrive at a solution of the puzzle to which the Syriac
Apocalypse of Ezra published by Baethgen gives rise.*
Obviously the opening of the Apocalypse is a re-cast
of the Petrine Apocalypse. In chap. iii. a Serpent
appears with twelve horns on its head and nine on
its tail. When this is compared with the above given
particulars, it becomes evident that here the allusion
is to the rule of the Ommiades. Certainly the number
nine does not agree with the enumeration in the
Petrine Apocalypse of the second line of rulers sprung
from the House of the Ommiades ; but such a slight
discrepancy is immaterial. An Eagle coming from
the South destroys the last horns of the Serpent—that
is, the sway of the Abassides.

From the East comes a Viper, which stands in

* *Zeitschr. f. alttest. Wissenschaft.*, VI., pp. 200 *et seq.*, from the
MS. Sachau, 131, in the Berlin Royal Library.

association with the land of Egypt, and therefore represents the Fatimite dynasty. We thus see that the two particulars "from the South," "from the East," are taken from the Petrine Apocalypse and wrongly applied. The four kings on the Euphrates river, the Ravens which come from the East, are the Túrki Sultanates, four of which are already mentioned by contemporary historians. Then comes (chap. vii.) the account of the young Lion's victories concluding with the destruction of Damascus, after which follows (chap. viii.) the description of the time of the Antichrist. It is thus made clear that we have here an adaptation of the Petrine Apocalypse dating from somewhere about the time of the first Crusades.

But another interesting observation has still to be made. I hold that the description of the Lion's son in chap. vii. does not derive directly from the Petrine Apocalypse, but from an earlier one dating from the time of Heraclius, which already formed the foundation of the Petrine and of the pseudo-Methodius. Here the account turns entirely on a fight between a Lion and a Bull, of which animal no mention had previously been made. But when we find it stated that he is the King of the Ravens (chap. vii.), it becomes clear even from the image itself that we have here a compilation. The Bull who "stirs up the East" is Chosroes, King of Persia. Chosroes marches with three armies against Heraclius; the Bull also has three horns, with which he tosses. One of his horns wages war with the young Lion (Heraclius); with another army Chosroes laid siege to Constantinople, and in pseudo-Ezra the

Bull plans an evil design against the seven hills and the city of Constantinople.

At that time Heraclius summoned Túrki hordés to his aid, while in 4 Ezra the young Lion strikes an alliance with the Leopard of the North, with whom multitudes advance like winged locusts. Then the young Lion leaps up between the horns of the Bull, both of which he breaks. And then we read at the end : " And the young Lion will march with a mighty host to the Land of Promise, . . . and up to Jerusalem will he ascend with great pomp, and from thence will he depart and march up to his royal city." I can scarcely believe that the whole of this account can originally have referred to any person except Heraclius and his defeat of Chosroes.

In support of this view the following considerations present themselves. In the Ethiopic version we have a little before the passage dealing with the Lion's son a list of emperors brought down to Heraclius.* In pseudo-Methodius also we have the account of the Byzantine emperor making his entry into Jerusalem on his victorious march against Islám. Is this a fancy picture, or, as seems much more probable, an adaptation from some early account dating from the time of Heraclius ? When Heraclius made his entry into Constantinople people thought the end of the world was near. Compare the above-quoted passage of the Petrine Apocalypse : " But when the Lion's son shall have returned from his expeditions,

---

* So also in the Arabic Apocalypse of S. Peter (Lagarde, *Mitteilungen*, IV., pp. 6 *et seq.*).

let Peter know that the time of the end is near." The author of the Armenian Apocalypse of Daniel probably expected the end to come in the time of Heraclius.

Thus we have again secured fresh connecting links. The pseudo-Methodius and the kindred recensions of the Petrine Apocalypse show how the Apocalypse of the Antichrist legend became modified with the rising flood of Islám. The luminous picture of the victorious Lion's son delineated on the obscure background is probably of still earlier date, and has its historic foundation in the events of Heraclius' reign. The Syriac Apocalypse of Ezra is a living witness to show how unintelligible predictions were again and again reproduced in ever fresh combinations.

CHAPTER VI.*

WE now come to a singularly interesting group, in which the chief documents are Commodian's *Carmen Apologeticum* and the Sibylline source of the eschatological details embodied in the Institutes of Lactantius. The connecting element in the writings in question is their common recognition of a twofold appearance of an Antichrist—one as a Roman emperor (the *Nero redivivus*), and another who appears in Jerusalem.

The eschatological part of Commodian begins with ver. 791,† for fixing the date of which we have the trustworthy guidance of Ebert.‡ In the interpretation

---

* For Notes ¹ to ⁷ of this chapter, see Appendix, p. 267.

† In Dombart's edition of the *Corpus Scriptorum Eccles. Lat.*, 15.

‡ In his contributions to the *Abhandlungen der Königlich*

of this work it must be steadily borne in mind that the prophetic fancies of the writer begin with the appearance of the Nero redivivus (Cyrus) in .ver. 823.

The statement in ver. 871 that Nero adopts (*sibi addit*) two Cæsars is not to be explained in the light of contemporary events, but is rather to be interpreted by the passage in ver. 911. In accordance with the early Antichrist legend, this person (the second ruler in Commodian, who nevertheless is the Antichrist proper) on his first appearance overcomes and slays three kings. But these kings had to be found somewhere, and so Commodian has the " happy thought " to make Nero redivivus adopt the two Cæsars, for which the Roman empire itself afforded him a precedent. But it would be more than absurd to ask, Who then were these Cæsars? Hence there remain but two alternatives to help in determining the date of the poem. Following up the clue afforded by the appearance of the Goths, as described in ver. 810, Ebert refers the Apocalypse to the time of Philip the Arab or of Decius, holding, however, that it could scarcely have been written during the severe persecution of Decius. Yet Commodian states (ver. 808) that the beginning of the end was the then raging seventh persecution ; and it is remarkable that in later accounts of these persecutions of the Christians that of Decius is always reckoned as the seventh.* Hence

---

Sächsischen Ges. der Wissenschaften, Vol. V., pp. 387 *et seq.* Rovers' recently attempted elucidation (*Apocalyptische Studien*, pp. 89 *et seq.*) misses the mark.

* Thus Sulpicius Severus, *Historia Sacra*, II. 32 ; Jerome, *de*

it is after all probable enough that Commodian's *Carmen Apologeticum* was really composed during the Decian persecution.

The eschatological matter bearing on the present subject, which we owe to Lactantius, occurs in his *Institutiones Divinæ,* VII., chap. x. *et seq.* He frequently quotes as his authority a Sibyl, VII. 16 (VII. 18 *alia Sibylla*). As in Commodian, here also the Antichrist has a " double," and here also the second Antichrist kills the first, that is, the last ruler of the Roman empire : " There also shall arise another king from Syria, who shall destroy the remnants of that first evil one together with the evil one himself." * It is further noteworthy that, whereas elsewhere according to the universal tradition two witnesses appear against the Antichrist, Elias and Enoch, Lactantius knows of nothing except of an appearance of Elias. In Commodian we have a double tradition ; in vers. 839 and 850 Elias alone is spoken of, but in 853, 856, 858, prophets are mentioned in the plural—evidently an extremely careless fusion of two different traditions.

But, after what has been said, we can scarcely be wrong in conjecturing that the same, or at least very similar, Sibylline sources were accessible to Commodian and Lactantius, between whom in other respects also there is much agreement. Nearest to these assumed common sources comes the passage in

Script. Eccles., chap. lxii. ; Orosius, Book VII. 21 (see Malvenda, *de Antichristo*, II. 132).

* " Alter rex orietur ex Syria qui reliquias illius prioris mali cum ipso simul deleat" (VII. 17).

6

the Sibyl II., pp. 154 *et seq.* Here also we have the appearance of the Antichrist (Beliar) at p. 167, and of Elias alone at p. 187. As in Commodian, the ten (twelve ?) tribes appear in the last days, and the destruction of the world is similarly described (pp. 186 *et seq.*). The description of the new life resembles that occurring in Lactantius. This Sibyl, however, has been retouched, and is far from covering the whole ground embraced by Lactantius and Commodian.

Now this Sibylline source utilised by Commodian must stand in some relation to the treatise of Hippolytus on the Antichrist. Higher up (p. 28) I have drawn attention to the unknown quotation twice made by Hippolytus from an unnamed prophet. A parallelism occurs in the *Carmen Apologeticum*, vers. 891 *et seq.* : " Again shall arise in the slaughter of this Nero—a king from the East with four nations therefrom—and summon to himself very many nations unto the City—who shall bring aid although he be himself most valiant—and fill the sea with ships many a thousand—and whoso shall oppose him shall be slain by the sword—and first he takes the captured Tyre and Sidon." [1]

Although the prophecy is based on Daniel xi. 40, still the parallelism between Hippolytus and Commodian is not explained by the passage from Daniel ; hence there was some common source other than our Book of Daniel. A parallel to this passage occurs also in Hippolytus a little before the place where he for the second time quotes the unnamed prophet in chap. lii. : " But his assault will first be against Tyre and Berytus."² Doubtless a common Sibyl was in any case drawn upon by Commodian and Lactantius, and Hippolytus quotes his authority as prophets. Still both writings cannot have been identical, although they may have stood in the closest relation to each other. It may be assumed that the Sibyl was based on the prophet quoted by Hippolytus; but the reverse can scarcely have been the case. Moreover, the Antichrist legend, as will be shown farther on, is found in a decidedly more original form in Hippolytus than in Lactantius and Commodian. Can Hippolytus after all have at the end already known and commented upon the Little Daniel, and is this very document that quoted as "another prophet"?

In his Dialogue, II. 14, Sulpicius Severus has left us the oral tradition of S. Martin of Tours on the Antichrist and the end. Here also we find the double of the Antichrist. The Antichrist proper here again makes his appearance in Jerusalem, and it is quite distinctly stated that "Nero himself is at last to be destroyed by the Antichrist."³

Lastly, here should be mentioned the short treatise comprised in Lagarde's *Reliquiæ Juris*, etc., 80 *et seq.*, "The First Book of Clement called the Testament of our Lord Jesus Christ."⁴ Here we read, 81, 15: "But there shall arise in the dissolution a king of another nation, lord of many devises, a godless slayer of men, a beguiler . . . hating the faithful, a persecutor." Then (82, 40): "Then shall come the son of perdition, the adversary and boaster and vaunter," etc.⁵

As will be shown later, we have in these apocalypses, where the Antichrist appears in double form, a mingling of two cycles of legends—on the one hand the old and simple Antichrist saga, on the other its political adaptation to Nero redivivus. As above already remarked (p. 29), we have in the Commentary of Victorinus another interesting blending of the currents of thought. Victorinus knows of but one appearance of Antichrist, and for him the demonic figure of Nero is still the Antichrist. Of all commentators on Revelation down to the period of the Reformation he is the only one who was aware that the Neronic saga had any bearing on the Johannine Apocalypse. But for him Nero, the Nero redivivus, has now become the Jewish Antichrist, as will be more fully explained below. The work of Victorinus has accordingly to be included in the group of documents now under consideration.

One branch of the twofold Antichrist tradition, which at last brought about those wonderful combinations, finds its chief witnesses in the still extant Sibylline literature. Here have specially to be considered Books (II.), III., IV., V., VIII. (XII., XIII.), where we have everywhere the fusion of the Neronic with the Antichrist legend.* All the chief points will be dealt with lower down.

Lastly, there remains to be mentioned a fragment of the *Visio Jesaiæ.* In chap. iii. (beginning at about iii. 23) and in chap. iv. we have an interpolated

---

* Cf. Zahn, *Zeitschr. für Kirchliche Wissenschaft und Kirchliches Leben*, 1886, 32-45, 77-87, 337-352.

Antichrist Apocalypse, which is especially interesting, because in it the figure of the Nero redivivus has been foisted into an earlier apocalyptic tradition, which can be clearly recognised. This point also will be established farther on.

In connection with the foregoing may here be appended a reference to the Antichrist Apocalypse interpolated in the already mentioned Book of Clement. In the *Text and Studies* (II. iii., pp. 151 *et seq.*) has recently been published an apocalyptic fragment in Latin, which seems to represent the early source utilised in the Book of Clement. The obviously later detailed description of the destruction of the Church before the coming of the Antichrist (Clement, p. 81, l. 33—p. 82, l. 38) now appears in the light of the Latin parallel as an addendum, so that here we have again a relatively ancient source.

At the end of the Latin fragment the name of the Antichrist is stated to be Dexius,* which James (p. 188) conjectures to be meant for Decius. There is much to support this suggestion, though the weighty objection still remains, that in this (compare Clement), as in all the other apocalypses, no Roman emperor appears to be originally identified with Antichrist. Still the clause might after all be a later gloss, which would then show that our Apocalypse must have already existed in the time of Decius.

In any case it was composed while the persecutions of the Christians were still raging, at least if we may, as seems highly probable, refer to it the passage in

* " *Dexius erit nomen Antichristi.*"

Clement, p. 81, l. 15 *et seq.* : " But there shall arise in the dissolution a king of another nation . . . hating the faithful, a persecutor ; and he shall rule over barbarous nations and shed much blood, . . . and there shall be in all cities and in all places rapacity and incursions of robbers and bloodshed." [6]

This description would apply in a special manner to Decius.

To show that we have here an earlier source, we may conclude with the subjoined striking parallelisms with some eschatological parts of 4 Ezra :

And a sound and a voice and seething of the sea.	Ezra, chap. v. 7. The sea of Sodom . . . shall give out a voice by night.
And on the earth shall be monsters, a generation of dragons of men (?) and likewise of serpents.	Chap. v. 8. And the beasts of the field shall stray beyond their ground, and women . . . shall bring forth monsters.
And presently a woman shall wed [and] bring forth children uttering perfect words.[7]	Chap. vi. 21. And babes of a year shall speak with their voices, and the pregnant shall bring forth immature babes of three and four months.[7]

CHAPTER VII.

QUITE a special inquiry, such as would be impossible till we had reached this point, is called for by the recently discovered Apocalypse of Zephaniah. A series of fragments from this source are found in the Upper and Lower Sahidic dialects of Coptic, representing two recensions of a single work, as appears from a comparison of the fragments where they run parallel. These have all been collated and translated by Stern,* though we are concerned only with the fifth and sixth. †

It is no easy matter to fix the time of this Apocalypse. To be sure it is already quoted by Clement of Alexandria ; ‡ but the passage cited by him, which strongly recalls the *Ascensio Jesaiæ*, does not occur amongst our fragments.§ Even were it recovered,

---

.* *Zeitschrift für ägyptische Sprache*, 1886, pp. 115 *et seq.*

† *Ib.*, pp. 122 *et seq.*

‡ Cf. the passage in Fabricius, *Cod. Pseud. Vet. Test.*, I. 1140.

§ Cf. the close analogy with the *Ascensio* at the end of the fourth fragment, p. 122.

it might be assumed with some confidence on *à priori*
grounds that the document quoted by Clement has
survived to our time only in a greatly modified
form. Such is the inference to be drawn from all the
observations hitherto made, and even from a mere
comparison of both recensions of the Apocalypse itself.

Stern (p. 135) from their language and contents
refers the fragments to the fourth century, which
would give us a certain standpoint for estimating the
period of the document lying at the base of both
recensions. Further determinations of the date can
be obtained only from the beginning of the fifth
fragment, although here the two recensions show
great discrepancies. The details regarding the struggle
between the Persian and Assyrian kings with their
fabulous imagery are found only in the Upper, not
in the Lower Sahidic recension. But both have one
characteristic feature in common. Immediately before
the appearance of the Antichrist they each, although
even here with great differences, describe the dominion
of a ruler, who restores peace and favours Christianity,
and is hostile to the heathen. The key to this passage
is afforded by the foregoing inquiry into the history
of the Antichrist saga. Here we find, although still
only half understood and overladen with fantastic
accessories, the characteristic element that was added
to the saga during the epoch of the first Christian
emperors (see above, p. 62).* Hence the original

---

* According to the Zephanian Apocalypse the Antichrist is
to come in the fourth year of the peaceful emperor, while
elsewhere twelve years are given as the duration of his reign.

draft of the Zephanian Apocalypse, as it now stands, would also date at the earliest from the second half of the fourth century, so that both recensions should perhaps be referred to a somewhat later time than that assigned to them by Stern.

Immediately before the description of the peaceful king the following passage occurs in the Upper Sahidic version :

"And when they shall behold a king rising up in the North, then shall they call him the King of Assyria and the King of Unrighteousness. On Egypt shall he bring his many wars and disorders."

This extract vividly recalls Lactantius, VII. 16. In both places a special forerunner of the Antichrist is spoken of ; in both this forerunner is called a king from the North, although in Lactantius the second king comes from Syria.

In the Lower Sahidic recension alone (although it cannot be positively asserted that it was not originally found also in the Upper Sahidic) there occurs at p. 124 the following highly remarkable description of the advent of Christ:

"The Christ, when He cometh, shall come in the form of a dove, with a crown of doves about Him, hovering on the clouds of heaven, with the sign of the Cross before Him, whom * all the world shall behold like unto the sun shining from the

---

* *Whom* in reference to Christ, although it may be asked whether the relative might not refer to the sign of the Cross. Farther on I will give the parallel passages from Ephrem embodying a similar conception.

regions of the rising to the regions of the setting thereof."

We are warned by this fantastic image also not to go too far back in search of the source of our document. Material representations of these apocalyptic fancies may be found even in later times. From a poem by Paulinus of Nola describing such a conception, F. Wickoff has reconstructed the mosaics of the apsis in the Church of S. Felix at Nola.* Here we see the Cross appearing in the sky encircled by a crown of doves, emblematic of Christ with the twelve Apostles. A similar picture is seen in the apsis of the Church of S. Clement in Rome.†

With the other writings already discussed the Zephanian Apocalypse shows the most manifold literary relations, as in the account of the wonders worked by the Antichrist with pseudo-Methodius, and the description of the Last Days of the Antichrist (p. 128), and in many other places with the Ephremite group. In the account of the glorious times preceding the Antichrist rule Zephaniah agrees with pseudo-Johannes, with Adso, and the other writings bearing on the subject.

But it is above all noteworthy that the description of the Antichrist (p. 125) stands in the closest literary connection with a series of Jewish apocalypses to be dealt with farther on. Surprising parallels are shown especially by the Apocalypse of Elias found in the

---

* _Römische Quartalschrift_, 1889.

† De Rossi, _Mus. Christ._, Plates VII., VIII. For these particulars I am indebted to my colleague Dr. Achelis.

Bet-ha-Midrash. It would seem that in this document, before all others, the many earlier records worked into it should be investigated. Moreover, the Zephanian Apocalypse comprises many other original and archaic elements which shall be discussed in their proper place. Meanwhile the assumption in any case does not lack support that, behind this Coptic Apocalypse of Zephaniah, there stands a much earlier work, which is probably of Jewish origin. In fact the Zephanian work is found, like the Vision of Daniel, the Ascension (Vision) of Jesse and others, in a series of canonical lists amongst the Old Testament Apocrypha.

It would be a laborious task to give even an approximate survey of the patristic literature which touches on this subject. Here I must confine myself to the most important, while referring the reader to Malvenda's careful and valuable collations in his work on the Antichrist.*

In this connection the foremost place amongst the commentaries on the Johannine Apocalypse is taken by that of Victorinus, which has already been referred to in the Introduction. Thanks especially to its exuberant and archaic exegesis, this work is of the very highest interest. The later Latin commentaries depend all alike on the spiritualistic interpretations of Ticonius. Hence amongst them are only occasionally found some stray realistic features derived from the Antichrist

* *De Antichristo*, pp. 2 *et seq.* I may here remark that in my quotations from the Fathers I have in many places been aided by Malvenda's indications.

tradition. Valuable also is the Commentary of Andreas, as well as that of his follower, Aretha. In Andreas is comprised a quantity of very important materials, which come at many points in contact with the tradition emanating from Ephrem. Compare, for instance, the identification of Gog and Magog with the Huns. In the later Commentary of Beatus there is a special section showing how the Antichrist is to be recognised.*

Nor can the commentaries on Daniel be overlooked, and especially the interpretations of chaps. vii., xi., and xii., where the commentaries of Jerome and of Theodoretus are of the first importance. Much valuable material is found also in the commentaries on 2 Thessalonians, chap. ii., such as those of the so-called Ambrosiaster, Pelagius, Chrysostom, Theodoretus, and Theophylactus ; those on Matthew, chap. xxiv., and the corresponding passage of Mark (Hilarius, Ambrosius, Chrysostom, the author of the unfinished work on Matthew in Chrysostom, Euthymius) ; on John v. 43 (Chrysostom, Theophylactus, Euthymius) ; lastly on Genesis xlix. and Deuteronomy xxxii. (Ambrosius, Eucherius).

We have further some more lengthy treatises, such especially as Irenæus, *Adversus Hæreses*, V., chaps. xxviii. *et seq.*, where the details in many places come in contact with Hippolytus, *de Antichristo* ; Jerome, epistle *ad Algasiam* (121), Quæstio XI.; Prosper Aquitanicus (?), *de Promissionibus et Prædictionibus*, IV., p. 4, l. 16 ; Theodoretus, *Hæret. Fabulæ*, Book V. (see section 23 on the Antichrist); S. John of Damascus,

* "Qualiter cognoscatur Antichristus," pp. 443 *et seq.*

Ἔκθεσις τῆς ὀρθοδ. πίστεως, iv. 27. The reader should also consult the *Quæstiones ad Antiochum ducem,* included amongst the works of Athanasius (Migne, XXVIII.).

But specially important are also some mediæval sources, conspicuous amongst which are the Predictions of S. Hildegard (cf. *Scivias,* Book III. ; Migne, CXCVI.), and less so the *Revelationes Stæ Birgittæ.* Then should above all be mentioned the *Elucidarium* of Honorius of Autun (Migne, CLXXII.), in which, as in Adso and apparently subordinate to him, the tradition of the Antichrist is included. On Honorius of Autun and his important position in the history of literature, see E. H. Meyer's *Völuspá,* pp. 41 *et seq.* Lastly I may mention the details in Hugo Eterianus, *Liber de Regressu Animarum ab Inferis,* chaps. xxiv. *et seq.* (Migne, CCII., p. 168). I would, however, here state emphatically that for the present I make no attempt to give a complete indication of the authorities on the history of the Antichrist legend in the mediæval period.* Such an inquiry would greatly exceed my limits.

But even without extending our researches farther in this direction, the above-mentioned sources cover a very considerable period of time. In the third and fourth chapters the documents coming in some instances down to the eleventh and twelfth centuries led us on the other hand back to the works of Ephrem. In the fifth and

---

* Much information will still be found in Zezschwitz, especially at pp. 26 *et seq.* of his Observations on the German poem of the *Endchrist.*

sixth chapters is especially seen the development of
the apocalyptic outlook during the Byzantine empire,
while the seventh carried us far beyond Ephrem to the
times of Commodian, Lactantius, Victorinus, Hippolytus, and Irenæus. A survey of patristic litdrature
reveals the immense extent of the influence exercised
by the Antichrist tradition on the early Christian
writers.   During the first thousand years of the
history of Christendom the eschatological expectations
of the faithful may be said to have been determined,
not by the Revelation of S. John, but by our apocalyptic tradition.

Hitherto our sources have been carried back no
farther than the second century. The eschatological
material occurring in the Apostolic Fathers and
apologists is too slight for consideration.   But a vista
has already been opened up of a Jewish tradition
reaching farther back than that of the early Fathers
of the Church ; attention has also already been called
to some coincidences of our tradition with the Fourth
Book of Ezra. This observation, should it be confirmed, brings us at once back to the time of the
New Testament and the antecedent period.

CHAPTER VIII.*

HERE has in the first place to be considered the Sibylline literature, and especially Sibyl III. 46-91. On the strength of a series of parallel passages with Book VIII., Alexandre refers it to a time prior to this book, and considers that the work in question has been put together from every possible part of the Sibylline literature. He gives no reason for this assumption, while a simple comparison of both Messianic descriptions in III., pp. 46 *et seq.*, and VIII., pp. 169 *et seq.*, suffices to clearly show that the priority lies with our document. So far from being more recent, this writing is to be regarded as one of the earliest of Sibylline literature. When the Sibyl begins, " But when Rome shall hold sway over

* For Notes [1] to [8] of this chapter, see Appendix, p. 268.

Egypt,"[1] and then proceeds to speak of three rulers of Rome (p. 51), and later of a widow who reigns over the world, it is obvious that the times of Antony and Cleopatra are here clearly indicated.*

In its second part the Sibyl contains a short account of the Antichrist and the destruction of the world. Here he is called Beliar, and a difficulty is certainly presented by the statement that this Beliar is to come " from the Sebastenoi " †—that is, the descendants of the Sebasti. It might seem as if such an expression could not have arisen till after the reign of Augustus, or Sebastus as he was called by the Greeks. But since everything else in the document in question points so clearly to the period prior to Augustus, it may here be simply inferred that the title *Sebastus* was from the first plainly understood by the Eastern peoples as referring to the Roman emperors, and that the Sebasti might consequently have already been spoken of before the time of Augustus.

It therefore appears that the Sibyl expects the Antichrist to spring from the dynasty of the Roman Cæsars. Hence we have here already a political application of the Antichrist legend, for Beliar, as will be seen farther on, had originally nothing to do with a Roman emperor. It is also evident that this identification of the Antichrist with a Roman ruler was by no means made during or after the reign of Nero, but at a much earlier period.

---

* Cf. Friedlieb, *Prolegomena.*

† ἐκ Σεβαστηνῶν ; from Σεβαστός, revered, venerable—hence answering to the Latin *Augustus.*

Bearing this in mind, we also begin to understand the puzzling statement in Suetonius (chap. xl.) that to Nero during his lifetime was already foretold the dominion of the East, and even specially that of the kingdom of Judah. Here we have a Sibylline prophecy that Nero is to be the Antichrist, and that he will consequently, like the Antichrist himself, be regarded as king of the Jews.* In this Sibyl, III. 45 *et seq.*, there are no Christian elements. On the contrary, its Jewish origin may be confidently inferred from the vers. 69 *et seq.*; so that from·this aspect of the case our deduction is established.

This political interpretation of the Beliar Apocalypse points at some earlier source, in which such an interpretation had not yet been made.

A description of Beliar, such as might here be postulated, is presented in Sibyl II. 167 *et seq.*, although no doubt in a very summary manner. That a literary connection exists between the two passages at 154 and 213 is shown by a comparison of the two descriptions of the destruction of the world by fire in III. 80-92 and II. 196-213. The original conception of the Beliar saga is found, as we see, in Sibyl II., though even here no longer in its pristine state. For the document, as must be admitted, has already undergone a Christian transformation.† But that here also a Jewish Sibyl forms the background must also be frankly admitted. Thoroughly Jewish, for instance, is especially the expectation of the return

---

* Cf. Zahn, *Zeitschr. für Kirch. Wiss. u. Kirch. Leben*, VII. **337**.
† Cf. vers. 168, 170, 178-182.

7

of the ten (twelve) lost tribes (170 *et seq.*). The
obscure vers. 174 *et seq.* find their explanation only
in the later Jewish tradition. On the assumption of a
Christian origin, the account of *one* precursor of the
Thesbite Elias (187 *et seq.*) also presents something
unusual ; while the " triple signs " * will also probably
find their explanation in the Jewish traditions.

We may go farther. Friedlieb † has shown with
much probability that Sibyls I. 1-323 and II. 6-33
constitute originally a Jewish prediction, in which the
Sibyl foretells the history of the ten generations of
man from the beginning to the end. In the Sibyl
the end seems to be missing; but I now hold that
this is really found in a slightly modified form in
II. 154-213. For in the fourth Sibyl after the
account of the universal doom (47) we read : " But
verily all these things shall be accomplished in the
tenth generation; but now will I tell who shall be
from the first generation." [2] In fact the fourth is
merely an echo of an earlier sibyl, in which was
described the fate of the ten generations of man down
to the judgment. This is clearly shown in what
follows, where a strained attempt is made to harmonise
the assumption of ten generations (vers. 50, 55) with
four universal empires.

Equally clear is Sibyl VIII. 199 : " But when the
tenth generation [shall descend] into the house of
Hades " ; [3] after which comes the account of the

* τρίσσα σήματα.

† *Oracula Sibyllina*, XX. Here it is rightly seen that the
Christian interpolations begin with I. 324 and II. 34.

rule of a woman, as is also described in Sibyl III. 77 in the last days. That here the consummation is expected after the tenth generation cannot mislead us as to the final result, which may also be described as taking place after the tenth generation in the source drawn upon by Sibyls I. and II. An eleventh generation of men is even spoken of by Sibyl IV. 20.

Here we may also briefly refer to those passages in which mention is made of the rule of a woman at the end of the world. In Sibyl III. 77 we read: "Then when a widow shall rule over the whole world";[4] and in VIII. 20: "Thereafter great [shall be] the power of a woman; surely shall God Himself increase many evils when she shall be crowned with royal honour."[5]

Have we here merely an allusion to Cleopatra? Or rather the exposition of an earlier mysterious prediction touching the sway of a mighty woman in the last days? The line in Sibyl V. 18, "And an unvanquished woman falling on the waves,"[6] gives a picture of Cleopatra distorted to a superhuman demonic form.

From this the expectation of a woman's rule would appear to have also found its way into the Greek Apocalypse of Daniel.

Here I would venture with some hesitation to offer a suggestion. If the Antichrist, as will be shown farther on, is to be regarded as the embodiment in human form of the old figure of the Dragon, may we not have in this woman "falling on the waves" a surviving reminiscence of the same marine monster originally conceived as of the female sex? The passage, however, may also recall the woman of Babylon "that sitteth upon many waters."

From this a fresh ray of light falls on the Sibyl imbedded in Bede. For here also we have in the opening part a survey of the generations of men. I cannot, however, explain how the ten have shrunk to nine generations in Bede. But if the decidedly later central part be removed, that account will then be immediately followed by a prediction of the Antichrist and of the last things. Thus are completed the links in a chain of written tradition, which embraces a period of about a thousand years.*

In conclusion it may be mentioned that in the Christian re-cast of Sibyl II. the description of hell shows a close relationship with the earlier Petrine Apocalypse. And in this form, as will be more fully explained farther on, the Sibylline document makes its influence felt down even to the Edda poems.

Of Jewish literature there are here also to be considered some sections of 4 Ezra and of the Book of Baruch. Amongst these are especially to be mentioned the accounts of the signs of the last times in

---

* Perhaps Ezra also (xiv. 11) read, according to the Ethiopic version : " For in ten parts is the world divided " (*decem enim partibus dispositus est mundus*). With the literature here under consideration may also be compared some isolated passages of the Sibyl. Such is the description of the end of the world in IV. 172 *et seq.* (V. 288 *et seq.*) ; V. 376 *et seq.* ; VII. 118 ; VIII. 15 ; VIII. 203 *et seq.* ; but above all the acrostic (VIII. 217 *et seq.* and VIII. 337 *et seq.*) already known to Lactantius ; lastly, all passages referring to the Nero redivivus, as above pointed out.

4 Ezra, which are loosely connected with the first three chief visions.* Here in the opening of V. 1 *et seq.* the reference is quite clear to the fall of the Roman empire. It will be shown below that the prediction " he shall reign whom they expect not " † also alludes to the Antichrist. Attention will moreover be drawn to many points of contact occurring elsewhere in the accounts of the signs of the end. ‡

For reasons which will be fully explained farther on, special attention will have to be paid to the Testament of Dan, comprised amongst the Testaments of the Twelve Patriarchs. Unfortunately the passage bearing on our subject has reached us in a very corrupt form. Mention has already been made of the *Ascensio Jesaiæ* (see above, p. 87). I think I shall be able to show that the passage here interpolated (chaps. iii. and iv.) is of Jewish origin. Further details follow below.

Coming to the later Jewish apocalyptic writings, I must here confine myself to briefly pointing out that their evolution was completed in direct association with the Antichrist legend. Leaving the exploration of this field to specialists, I will confine myself to a

* Cf. V. 1 *et seq.* ; VI. 20 *et seq.*

† " Regnabit quem non sperant."

‡ I would also call attention to Ezra v. 4 = Sibyl VIII. 203 ; Ezra xi. 21 = Sibyl II. 155. Cf. further 4 Ezra xiii. and Baruch, chaps. xxxvi.-xl., chap. xxvii. (48, 34), chap. lxx. ; besides the above-mentioned parallelisms between 4 Ezra and the Book of Clement. Moreover, Sibyl II. 155, etc., goes probably back to Hesiod ; cf. Dietrich, *Nekyia,* p. 184 (Anmerkung 2), Sibyl II. 165 *et seq.*, and the Egyptian Gospel in Clement of Alexandria (Strom. iii., p. 445). But I cannot follow Dietrich in his further comments on Sibyl II.

few indications which can make no claim to exhaust
the subject.

Higher up attention has already been called to the
expectation of the return of the ten tribes of Israel,
a notion by which Commodian amongst others was
influenced. It belongs to the very earliest elements
of the apocalyptic tradition with which we are here
concerned, and is already found in Ezra xiii. 34 *et seq.*
Here it is stated that under God's miraculous aid the
ten tribes wander away beyond the Euphrates to a far-
distant land, whence they are some day to return. The
same myth occurs again in Commodian's *Carmen Apologeticum*, where God leads against the second Antichrist
a people of whom we read (942) : " But enclosed are
the Jews [in the land] beyond the Persian stream,
where God willed they should bide to the end." [7]
Then follows immediately a detailed description of the
glorious wonderland where the Israelites dwell.

So also in the Othoth ha-Mashiakh (for which see
below) a glowing description is given of the homeward
march of the ten tribes of Israel from the river Gozan
out of the land of Khalakh and Khabor, this being
the tenth and last sign of the end—that is, after the
appearance of the Messiah. That the ten tribes dwell
beyond a great river is likewise in accordance with
an ancient legend, from which were later developed
in the Rabbinic traditions monstrous fables about the
river Sabbation.*

* See Eisenmenger, II. 533 *et seq.* On the Book of the Danite
Eldad mentioned here (1238), cf. Malvenda, II. 206. The foundation of these fables is already found in Josephus, *B. J.*, VII. 24.

In Sibyl II. 170-176 we have also an account of the return of the ten tribes and of their victories ; and the passage, though very short, is important. It would appear from the extremely obscure text as if the triumph of the ten tribes is not to be final, but that they are again to be overcome by the Gentiles.

Thus, however, the legend of the ten tribes assumes a close resemblance to that of Gog and Magog. From this it also becomes evident that a fusion of both took place in the hands of mediæval Christian writers. We read, for instance, in Godfrey of Viterbo (XI.) that " Alexander shut in Gog and Magog for ever. The eleven tribes of the Hebrews he compassed round in the mountains for ever." [8]

With this is to be mentioned another and later tradition—that is, the assumption of two distinct Messiahs, one overcome and slain in battle, the other triumphant. The notion of a suffering and dying Messiah would seem to have been suggested by disputations with the Christians, by reference, for instance, to such telling passages of Scripture as those of Zechariah xii. 10 *et seq.* Justin, however (*Dialogus cum Tryphone*), knows nothing yet of these speculations, and considering his great familiarity with the Jewish theological treatises, this argument based on his silence is not without weight. A standpoint for approximately determining the date of this conception is afforded by the fact that a very distinct application of Zechariah xii. 10 to the Messiah ben Joseph is already found in the Jerusalem Talmud.*

* See Wünsche, *Leiden des Messias,* 110 *et seq.*

But then comes the question, What gave rise to the conception of a Messiah ben Joseph or ben Ephraim? It may presumably have been suggested by the already existing legend of the return of the ten tribes of Israel. The Messiah ben Joseph is the leader of the ten tribes on their return, and in fact he is so described in the later work of Mikwêh Israel.[*]

But it may still be doubted whether all this suffices to sufficiently account for the origin of the two Messiahs.

Here I would merely raise the question whether the notions both of the two witnesses, widespread in the Christian Apocalyptics, and of the two Messiahs, may not both rest upon a common source, which, however, is still to be sought farther back than Jewish tradition. As Victorinus in his Commentary calls the two prophets (Apoc. 11) the eagle wings of the woman, so we read in Yalkut Khadash: "His [Israel's] two wings shall be the two Messiahs, the Messiah ben Joseph and the Messiah ben David."[†]

But, to return to the further development of the cycle of legends, that Messiah of the ten tribes had to suffer and perish, and the commentators appear to have assumed that Gog and Magog were the power by which he was to be overthrown. [‡] Thus stands the tradition in the *Haggaditic* or Homiletic Exposition of

[*] Fol. 47, 48 (Wünsche, 115 *et seq.*).

[†] Fol. 132 (Wünsche, 114).

[‡] On the influence of the Alexander saga on this point, see Wünsche, 117.

the Messiah * and in the *Pesikta Sutarta,* † and a translation also occurs in Schöttgen's *Messias Judæo-rum.* ‡ Other evidence of the same tradition may be seen in Wünsche, 117.

At this stage of its development the legend begins to be again influenced by this Jewish apocalyptic tradition through the tradition of the Antichrist.

The figure that now stands out in the foreground of the new apocalyptic picture is that of Armillus, which is the Hebrew form of Romulus. This name is itself significant, for the political application of the Anti-christ legend, which disappeared in the Christian tradition, was preserved in the Jewish. The Romans —kingdom of Edom, children of Esau, dominion of Sammael—remained the fierce hereditary foes of the Jews, more especially after the Roman empire had become Christian. Hence the Antichrist power, the Antichrist himself, is Armillus (Romulus).

As already remarked, a trace of this Jewish apocalyptic conception is already found in the Latin, though not in the Greek, text of Methodius, where it is expressly stated that Romulus is Armæleus. §

The following are the writings with which we are here concerned : (1) The Mysteries of Simon ben

---

* Jellinek, Bet ha-Midrash, III. 141 *et seq.* Jellinek pro-nounces this work to be one of the earliest (III., XXVIII.). The Pirke (Sayings) of the Messiah, III. 68-78, seems dependent on it.

† Fol. 58, 1 (twelfth century, Schürer, I. 103).

‡ German translation, Leipzig, 1748, pp. 163 *et seq.*

§ " Romulus, qui et Armæleus."

Yokhai,* which Graetz has dealt with in his *History
of the Jews* (V. 191 *et seq.*). It gives a clear account
of the period of Merwan II., and was evidently composed at the time of the overthrow of the Ommiades
rulers. (2) A closely related eschatological tractate on
the Antichrist and the two Messiahs included in the
Midrash va-Yosha on Exodus xiv. 30 ; xv. 1-8.†
(3) The Othoth ha-Mashiakh, ‡ of which there is a
translation in Eisenmenger, II. 703 *et seq.* (4) The
Book of Zorobabel, § which covers the period from the
destruction of the Temple to the end, some 990 (970)
years, hence cannot have been written later than the
eleventh century. The three last-mentioned books,
which seem to have had a common history, were
published collectively in the year 1524 ‖ in Constantinople, but judging from the specimens given by
Eisenmenger (II. 708 *et seq.*) in a recension showing
considerable variants.

In the Mysteries of Simon and in the Signs of the
Messiah, the eschatological predictions properly so
called begin with the prophecy of a nine months'
renewed dominion of the " wicked " Roman (Byzantine)
empire. In this characteristic statement we see the

---

* Jellinek, III. 78 *et seq.* ; the chief passages translated by
Wünsche, 120.

† Jellinek, I. 35 *et seq.* This work was known to Yalkut, and
was consequently composed before the thirteenth century.

‡ Jellinek, II. 58 *et seq.*, from the Amsterdam edition,
אבקת רוכל.

§ Jellinek, II. 54 *et seq.*

‖ Eisenmenger, II. 708 ; Jellinek mentions (II., XXXIII.) an
edition dated Constantinople, 1519.

connection between the Christian legend and these
Jewish apocalypses.   Here also, since the time of
the book of Methodius, a dominant trait is the
expectation that in the end the Byzantine empire
will prevail over Islam and conquer Palestine.   Then
in both apocalypses appears the Messiah ben Joseph,
who overthrows the Roman empire * and rebuilds the
Temple, after which comes Armillus.

In all the documents except the Midrash va-Yosha
we find the puzzling statement that Armillus is to
be begotten by Satan of a stone, and in the Signs
of the Messiah † he is expressly called the Antichrist.
Then follows in all except the Book of Zorobabel
a description of this Antichrist, who is represented
as a frightful monster.   Then comes everywhere an
account of the flight of Israel to the wilderness, and
the death of the Messiah ben Joseph in the battle
with Armillus ; only in the Midrash va-Yosha this
Messiah is slain in Jerusalem.   Both in the Signs of the
Messiah and in Zorobabel, Armillus is already distinctly
described as a false Messiah.   But in the other sources
also he is prominently mentioned in connection with
the Romano-Byzantine empire, which, in fact, is
alluded to by his very name.   Here again is clearly
seen the influence of the Christian legend.

Then comes the Messiah, the son of David, called

* In the Midrash va-Yosha, which seems to represent a
somewhat earlier tradition, we have the reference to the Roman
empire replaced by an account of the destruction of Gog and
Magog.

† Jellinek, II. 60.

also the Menakhem ben Ammiel, while the Messiah
ben Joseph takes also the name of Nehemia ben Uziel.
Now the son of David slays Armillus with the breath
of his mouth ; in the Signs of the Messiah, however,
Armillus is killed by God Himself.   It is characteristic
of these sources that the description of the end does
not abruptly break off with this event, as it does in
the Christian tradition.   For there still follows the
description of the revival of the New Jerusalem, and
also the resurrection of the dead, and in the Signs
of the Messiah the return of the ten tribes.   In the
Mysteries of Simon we have even the description of
a kingdom lasting for two millenniums, after which
comes the last judgment.   It is noteworthy that in this
Jewish tradition there is much more in common with
the Johannine Apocalypse than is found in the Christian tradition.   We have especially in the Book of
Zorobabel some striking points of contact, for instance,
with Revelation, chap. xvii.   So also the description
in the last part of the Mysteries of Simon : "And
fire falls from heaven and consumes Jerusalem, and
sweeps from the midst of her all strangers and
uncircumcised and unclean."* Direct parallelisms
with John are also found in the interesting Apocalypse
of Elias.†

It should be mentioned that here this figure of Elias
comes on the scene, although quite in the background,
together with that of the Messiah ben David.   With
this may be compared what has been stated above

---

* Wünsche, 121.   † Jellinek, III. 65.

(p. 82) about Lactantius and Commodian ; and also Sibyl II. 187.

In the development of the Jewish legend a special place is taken by an apocalypse which has been preserved in the Persian language, and for the text and translation of which we are indebted to Zotenberg.* The very title, History of Daniel, is significant, and recalls the evidences brought forward higher up in support of the early existence of an Apocalypse of Daniel.

The treatise in question begins with a description of the Muhammadan caliphs, Muhammad himself being easily recognised in the opening (407). In the ruler with his three sons we may also confidently recognise Harún ar-Rashíd,† after whom mention is made of two other rulers. Hence the Apocalypse must date from the first half of the ninth century.

Then follow the eschatological predictions, beginning with an account of the victory of a Roman ruler over Islám, and of his reign lasting for nine months (see above, p. 106). Then we are told another, whose name is not given, is to come, who will proclaim himself as the Messiah, and whose personal appearance is described in the usual way. With him will come Gog and Magog, while Israel takes refuge in the wilderness. Then we read : " Thereupon a man shall appear in that distant place, and every Israelite shall leave his seat, and they shall all be gathered." That

* Merx, *Archiv,* I. 386 *et seq.*

† 411, 12 ; I have to‚ thank my colleague Dr. Rahlfs for this communication.

man shall be of the children of Ephraim, and they will all of them flock to that wicked one, who says, " I am the Messiah, your king, your possession."

The Israelites will ask signs of him, which he cannot perform ; and especially is he unable to raise the 'dead again. Then he persecutes the Israelites, and Israel flees to the desert. Then are the Israelites made partakers in the grace of God, who opens the floodgates of heaven ; a month will be as a week, a week as a day, a day as an hour. Then shall Michael and Gabriel appear to the Israelites in the wilderness, and they shall slay the false Messiah.

Thereupon comes the Messiah ben David and kills the wicked one (that is, the above-mentioned ruler) with the breath of his mouth; " and the banner of the Messiah, son of David, shall appear." The same shall kill the whole host of Gog and Magog, after which comes Elias. Then shall the new era be announced with four blasts of the trumpet. The dead arise ; the Israelites are gathered from all quarters of the world (on the wings of Simurg ?) ; a pillar of fire appears in the Temple, the glory of God is made manifest, and all mountains disappear. Then follows for thirteen hundred years the time of rejoicing and of domination, and then the everlasting great doom.

Obviously the Apocalypse is a genuine collection of manifold traditions, and betrays the influence of the Christian legend in far greater measure than the other sources. From this influence, which may even be closely followed in the style of composition itself, it also becomes probable that here the Messiah ben Joseph has been transformed to the Antichrist. The statement, however, on this point is not quite clear. Presumably Abar ben-el may have also had a similar tradition in mind, when in his work, the *Mashmia Yeshua*, he utters the enigmatical sentence : "The Messiah, son of Joseph, whom we expect to come in the beginning of the deliverance, is the Antichrist, whose coming they, the Christians, predict." * Or in these few surviving fragments have we not rather a primeval tradition about some false Messiah destined to appear amongst the Jews? But no final judgment can yet be pronounced on this point. In any case we have in the remarkable document under consideration a great mass of archaic traditions. In its whole composition it also shows the closest connection with the Mysteries of Simon. Let me add that we are here told how at first the Jews do not believe in the Messiah ben David, who thereupon hides himself, until at last he appears to them as the Son of man in the clouds of heaven.†

But on the whole the conclusion may be hazarded that the Jewish cycle of legends taken collectively, with the figure of Armillus and of both Messiahs, was developed in this connection in the seventh and eighth centuries under the influence of the Antichrist saga.

The survey of this Jewish literature has revealed numerous interminglings of the Jewish and Christian

* Eisenmenger, II. 747.

† With this may be compared the end of the Midrash va-Yosha.

traditions of our apocalyptic material.   In the light
of the evidence brought together in chap. vii., the
conjecture becomes a certainty that the expectation
of an Antichrist had its origin on Jewish ground.
Thus the tradition might have been traced back to a
period prior to that of the New Testament writings,
while full confirmation is given to the view advanced
in the Introduction that the apocalyptic documents
there described imply the existence of an earlier
tradition.   Thus, while the Antichrist legend was
adopted by the Christians from the Jews, the fully
developed Christian tradition reacted in its turn on
the Jewish eschatology during the sixth, seventh,
and eighth centuries.

But this eschatological tradition of the Antichrist
has also made its influence felt beyond the pale of
the Christian and Jewish worlds.   Here I shall bring
together a few notices on the subject, without making
any pretence to completeness.

In a full and careful inquiry into the *Völuspâ* of
the elder Edda (Berlin, 1889), E. H. Meyer has
endeavoured to follow step by step the influence of
Christian tradition on the poem which covers the
whole ground from the creation to the last judgment.
Still more definitely has he advanced the view that
the author of this poem depends essentially on the
theological works of Honorius of Autun, and especially
on the *Elucidarium*.   But if the *Völuspâ* depends on
the one hand on Honorius, it is influenced on the
other by the Antichrist legend, and in fact works up
the same material.   Still, despite its comprehensive

and learned treatment, the question seems to me not yet cleared up. For Meyer's assumption the strongest argument seems to be the fact that the last great battle between the good and evil powers of the world, that is to say the end, begins with the passage : *

> Brothers will one another slay, and
> Murderers one of another become ;
> Kindred their kinsfolk will kill ;
> Heavy times are in the world. . . .

As will be seen farther on, this has become an almost stereotyped introduction to the tradition of the Antichrist. The description also recalls the punishments in Hades,† while the opening strongly reminds one of the Sibylline literature as known to us. Hence a general connection of the Edda with the Christian literature and with the Antichrist legend admits of no denial.

But in the details much remains uncertain. The difficulties we had to contend with in the elucidation of these poems may be seen, for instance, in strophe 47 (in Meyer, 46). Here the usual translation is, "The world all burns at the blast of the horn"; whereas Meyer (190) here reads, "The Healer shines on that old renowned cross." If Meyer is right, which, however, is doubtful, owing to the express mention that follows of Heimdall's horn, then we have here

---

* A. Holtzmann, *die ältere Edda übersetzt und erklärt*, Leipzig, 1875, p. 23.

† Page 23, ver. 43.

again a characteristic feature of the Antichrist tradition.

Altogether Meyer seems to me to have gone much too far in his attempt to establish direct Christian influences in the Eddas. He greatly underrates the primeval mythological stuff contained in these lays. Take, for instance, what is told in *Völuspá* (3) of the giant Ymir and of Chaos, and in *Vaf-drúonismál* (21) of the creation of the universe. It is a great mistake to derive these primitive myths from a passage in Honorius, where all analogy completely breaks down. According to Honorius the body of (the first) man is formed from the several elements of the earth. From this Meyer argues that the creation myth of the Edda has been evolved by a kind of reverse process ! Equally strained and wide of the mark seems Meyer's attempt to derive from Revelation the magnificent description of the five battles of the gods, with which the end of the world is introduced (*Völuspá*, strophes 50 *et seq.*). With what an effort the required number five is here obtained by the expedient of tacking on Hades and Death to the three hostile powers, the Beast, the Dragon, and the False Prophet ! * Nor does Meyer seem to me to establish with his vague parallelisms the identity of Súrtr (strophe 51) with the Antichrist (p. 206). To my mind primeval myths stand in the background of the descriptions of the battles between the gods, as well as in the account of the two monsters, the Midgard Serpent and Fenris the Wolf.

* θηρίον, δρακών, ψευδοπροφήτης.

But if the influence of the Antichrist saga on the earlier Edda can be spoken of only as slight, it is otherwise with the *Muspilli*, an old Bavarian poem, dating from the ninth century. In this half-heathen, half-Christian work, the local colouring employed in the description of the destruction of the world is taken bodily from our tradition. This statement needs no further proof, as the parallel passages bearing on the point will be given farther on.*

Clear traces of the Antichrist legend are also found in the literature of the Parsees extant in the Pehlevi language. Here attention is claimed especially by the Bahman Yast Apocalypse, of which a translation is contained in the *Sacred Books of the East*, Vol. V., 191 *et seq.* As far as I can make out, the Bahman Yast is based on an apocalypse which was composed at the time of the overthrow of the Iránian (Persian) monarchy by the Muhammadan Arabs in the seventh century. In II. 14 *et seq.* Zaratustra (Zoroaster) sees a tree with seven branches, which alludes in the usual way to seven dynasties. The sixth is that of Chosroes (the Sassanides), and in the seventh is described the irruption into happy Irán of the demons with upraised spear and streaming hair. This irruption of Islám was witnessed by the author of the original Apocalypse, who after that event expects the end of the world. It is this consummation that is described under the direct influence of the Antichrist

* For this reference to the *Muspilli* I have to thank my young friend W. Lueken.

legend, as will appear from the large number of parallel passages quoted farther on.*

This Apocalypse appears to have undergone a revision in the time of the Crusades (see especially III. 3 *et seq.*), when an intricate eschatological system with several Messiahs was also foisted into the text.†

Last of all the Antichrist legend found its way to the Arab world. In Tabari's Chronicle ‡ we have an interesting excursus on the Antichrist. He is to be a king of the Jews, who rules the whole world, whose figure overtops the welkin, and whose name will be Dejjâl. He will appear at the end of time, when Gog and Magog break through the walls built up against them by Alexander the Great. § On his march he will be accompanied by monsters, snakes, scorpions, dragons; he will reduce the greater part of mankind, and no one will be able to resist him in war. He will march from east to west, to the north and to the south, and his sway will last forty days. But the

* Cf. II. 30 *et seq.*, the signs of the end ; II. 54, the rule of the Wicked Spirit ; III. 13, the birth of the Messiah, with the sign of the star announcing the event ; III. 24, the two messengers, Nêriôsang and Srôsh ; III. 26 *et seq.* (cf. 30), the advent of the Messiah (Pêshyôtanû), and the overthrow of the Antichrist with his whole host.

† On the Persian eschatology, see also Spiegel, *Avesta*, Leipzig, 1852, pp. 32 *et seq.*

‡ Translated by Zotenberg, Paris, 1867. See chap. xxiii., p. 67. For this reference I am indebted to Professor W. Meyer.

§ This cycle of sagas, for the diffusion of which see Zezschwitz, p. 170, is also given in detail in Tabari, cxii., p. 518.

faithful will flee before him ; and then Jesus, together with the Mahdi (the Guided) Muhammad ben Abdallah, will overthrow the Antichrist.*

This relation with its reminiscences both of Jewish and Christian traditions, the Bahman Yast Apocalypse, and the Jewish eschatologies above collated, all serve to illustrate in a striking manner the religious syncretism (combination, communion) that prevailed during the sixth, seventh, and eighth centuries between Christians, Jews, Muhammadans, and Parsees.

* Dietrich, *Abraxas*, 125 (Anmerkung 1), mentions an old Muhammadan tradition that Jesus is to vanquish the Antichrist (Dajjat) before the walls of Lydda.

PART II.

HISTORY OF THE ANTICHRIST LEGEND.

CHAPTER IX.*

SIGNS AND FOREWARNINGS—THE FALL OF THE ROMAN EMPIRE
BEFORE THE END—ORIGIN OF THE ANTICHRIST.

ATTENTION has already been called (p. 86) to
the striking analogy between 4 Ezra and
the Apocalypse which forms the basis of the
Book of Clement in the account of the premonitory
signs of the end; and it was further seen how
individual traits reappear in Sibyl II. and in Ephr. Gr.
Such parallelisms show of themselves that we have
here a widely ramifying current of tradition. Our
limited space prevents the reproduction of all the
excerpts bearing on the point. But the various
descriptions of tremendous convulsions in the realm
of nature, all cast in the same groove of thought, may
be compared, as they are recorded in 4 Ezra v. 1
et seq. and vi. 21 *et seq.*, and again in pseudo-Hippolytus, chaps. viii., xcvi. 26, and in Lactantius,
VII. 16.

But in the Antichrist legend a specially characteristic feature recurs again and again. It turns on the
account of the ever-increasing hatred which will be

---

* For Notes [1] to [9] of this chapter, see Appendix, p. 269.

stirred up in the world even between kith and kin,
and which goes back to Micah vii. 6 : " A man's
enemies are the men of his own house." Thus in
4 Ezra v. 9 : " And all friends shall overcome one
another utterly " ;[1] and vi. 24 : " And it shall happen
in that time [that] friends shall overthrow friends as
foes."[2] In pseudo-Hippolytus the section describing
the signs of the last days begins with a detailed account
of this strife between kindred, with which compare
the opening of pseudo-Ephrem, chap. i.

So intimately associated is this trait with the
Antichrist tradition that even in quite remote authorities it affords the very first indication of the influence
of the legend. Thus, as already seen, we read in the
Völuspâ how " brothers will one another slay," etc.
So in the Bahman Yast the unmistakable influence of
our saga begins with the description (II. 30) : " All
men will become deceivers, great friends will become
of different parties, the affection of the father will
depart from the son, and that of the brother from
his brother, . . . and the mother will be parted and
estranged from the daughter." The uprising of nation
against nation, as in Matthew xxiv. 7, is also frequently
described in the opening of the apocalypses,* and
lamentations are poured out especially on the discord,
the unrighteousness, and misrule prevailing in the
world. Here may be mentioned 4 Ezra ; the
Apocalypse of Baruch, chap. xlix. 32 *et seq.*, and
chap. lxx. (cf. xxv. 3) ; Lactantius, VII. 15, all of

* Cf. 4 Ezra v. 5 ; Lactantius, VII. 15 ; pseudo-Ephrem
chap. i. ; Book of Clement, etc.

which stand in perceptible literary connection with each other.*

In many apocalypses the general descriptions of the forewarnings are replaced by more definite pictures of current events. But the mention of one distinct premonitory sign constantly recurs in nearly all the sources. The end is at hand when the Roman empire perishes.

In 2 Thessalonians ii. 6, 7 we read : "And now ye know what withholdeth that he might be revealed in his time. For the mystery of iniquity doth already work : only he who now letteth *will let*, until he be taken out of the way." With this compare 4 Ezra v. 3 : "And of disorderly condition shall that region be which thou now beholdest dominant, and they shall see it desolate ; but if the Most High shall grant thee to live and thou behold [those things which] after the third [hath passed away ?] in disorder. . . ."³ Here the allusion is to the fourth (Roman) empire which succeeds the third (Greek), and after the fall of which the end comes.

Irenæus (V. 26), drawing on Daniel ii. and Revelation xvii., is able to tell us that in the last days the Roman empire will be partitioned into ten kingdoms, after which the Antichrist will appear in the character of a foreign ruler. Hippolytus (chaps. xxv. and liv.) †

* Cf. also the detailed descriptions in the *Ascensio Jesaiæ*, III. 23 *et seq.*, in Bk. K., in pseudo-Hippolytus, and elsewhere.

† Cf. with this Jerome on Daniel vii. 8 : "Ergo dicamus quod omnes scriptores ecclesiastici tradiderunt" ("Therefore let us relate what all the Church writers have delivered ").

borrows from Irenæus, and neither of these writers has derived his knowledge of the future from a mere investigation of Daniel and Revelation.

Special consideration is next claimed by Tertullian (*Apologetics*, 32) : " There is also a greater need for us to pray for the emperors as also for the whole state of the empire, and for Roman affairs *since we know that by the provision* [*prosperity ?*] *of the Roman empire the* mighty power impending on the whole world and threatening the very close of the century with frightful calamities *shall be delayed* ; and as we are loth to suffer these things, while we pray for their postponement we favour the stability of Rome." And again, *ad Scapulam* (2) : " The Christian is hostile to no one, least of all to the emperor, to whom . . . he wishes well, with the whole Roman empire, so long as the world shall last, for *so long* it shall last," [4] that is, so long as Rome endures.

In VII. 15 (634, 18) Lactantius writes : "The Sibyls, however, openly speak of Rome being destined to perish. Hystaspes also, who was a very ancient king of the Medes, . . . predicted long before that the empire and name of Rome should be effaced from the globe." And in 16 (635, 1) : " But how this shall come to pass I will explain. . . . In the first place, the empire shall be parcelled out, and the supreme authority being dissipated and broken up shall be lessened, . . . until ten kings exist all together ; . . . these . . . shall squander everything and impair and consume." VII. 25 (664, 18) : " The very fact proclaims the fall and destruction to be near, except that so long as Rome is safe it seems that nothing of this need be feared. But when indeed that head of the world shall fall and the assault begin that the Sibyls speak of coming to pass, who can doubt that the end has already come ? . . . That is the city that has hitherto upheld all things, and we should pray and beseech the God of heaven, if indeed His decrees and mandates can be postponed, that that detested tyrant may not come sooner than we think." [5]

So in pseudo-Ephrem, 1 : "And when the kingdom of the Romans shall begin to be consumed by the sword then the advent of the Evil One is at hand." 5 : " And already is the kingdom of the Romans swept away, *and the empire of the Christians is delivered unto God and the Father*, and when the kingdom of the Romans shall begin to be consumed then shall come the consummation." [6]

And Cyril, xv. 11: " The man magician . . . seizing for himself the power of the kingdom of the Romans, . . . and this predicted Antichrist cometh when are fulfilled the seasons of the kingdom of the Romans." [7]

In the works of Ephrem (I. 192) we find under the name of Jacob of Edessa an exposition of the prophecy in Genesis xlix. 16 on Dan, where the words " that biteth the horse heels so that his rider shall fall backward " are referred to the Antichrist : " That that empire belongeth to those that are called Latins, the Spirit hath already . . . declared and taught through Hippolytus in that book in which he interprets the Revelation of John the Theologian." [8]

This widespread accordance acquires extraordinary

significance from the following consideration. In the
Johannine Apocalypse the Roman empire is plainly
enough indicated as the last anti-Christian power, and
it might be supposed that those vivid pictures of fierce
hatred and sublime imagery would for ever have
branded imperial Rome as the anti-Christian power
that rises up against God. The legend of Nero
redivivus survived long enough in association with the
prophecies of Revelation ; the whole of the Sibylline
literature is overshadowed by this weird demoniac
personality ; even Victorinus was still familiar with
the relations of the Johannine Apocalypse to Nero.

How then, it may once more be asked (see above, p. 26),
was it possible that such a conception as an Antichrist
hostile to Rome could have arisen in the very teeth of
Revelation and in direct opposition to its teachings ?
Surely the Roman empire gave the Christians reason
enough to regard it as the last anti-Christian power,
and in one of its rulers to see the Antichrist himself,
the devil incarnate. How did it come about that the
very opposite notion acquired such unlimited preva-
lence ? For now the Roman empire so far from being
the Antichrist stands in the way of his coming, while
he is declared to be a non-Roman ruler. How was
it possible that, even where the Neronic saga still
survived, as with Lactantius, Commodian, and S. Martin
of Tours, Nero redivivus came to be looked upon as
the last Roman emperor, precursor of the Antichrist ?
Hippolytus fully understands that in the first half of
Revelation xiii. the allusion is to the Roman empire.
Yet for him (chap. xlix.) the second beast " coming

out of the earth " is the Antichrist rule which is to
come after the Roman empire. Hence he has to refer
the two horns of the beast to the false prophet who,
according to the Apocalypse itself, was to accompany
the Antichrist. Then the description of the second
beast as minister of the first he explains in such a way
as to represent the second beast as ruling the world
" according to the law of Augustus " * (the first).
Whence originates this persistent and violent distor-
tion of the clear sense of Revelation ?

It might be pointed out that 2 Thessalonians ii.
reacted on the eschatology of the Fathers of the
Church. Still it is *à priori* improbable that this short
Pauline allusion could have had a more potent influence than the whole of Revelation, which at least
in the first age (Irenæus, Hippolytus, Tertullian,
Victorinus) enjoyed unquestioned authority. But then
fresh problems present themselves. Whence did Paul
himself, or whoever was the author of 2 Thessalonians, derive this notion ?   And how does it
happen that the extremely enigmatical allusions of
this epistle were expounded with such confidence,
definiteness, and unanimity by the whole body of
patristic writers ? Austin alone seems to hesitate,
remarking (*City of God*, XX. 19) that " some think
this was said of the Roman empire." [9] Chrysostom
also mentions another interpretation. But with this
general unanimity compare the wild gropings of
modern expositors, some of whom suppose that in
the passage of Thessalonians Paul expresses himself

* κατὰ τὸν Αὐγούστου νόμον.

in this mysterious manner in order to avoid openly
speaking of the fall of the Roman empire.*

Nor are we helped much by a reference to the
influence of Daniel vii., on the strength of which the
last beast with the ten horns is supposed to represent the Roman empire. But in that case one scarcely
sees how the idea could have arisen of explaining
the small (eleventh) horn as some foreign non-Roman
ruler. Even from Revelation xvii. such an inference
could not be arrived at independently. Here no
doubt the Neronic Antichrist marches with the ten
kings against Rome ; but here also he is too clearly
identified with the Roman emperor himself. In fact
the endless embarrassment of the Fathers in expounding the passage in question plainly shows that the
writers did not draw their apocalyptic ideas from, but
rather read them into, this chapter of Revelation.

There is but one solution of the problem. Before
the composition of this work a fully developed Antichrist legend was already current, no doubt derived
partly from, but also partly independent of, Daniel.
This legend was still destitute of any political meaning,
such as the application of the coming of the Antichrist to the Roman empire, to Nero redivivus, or to
any other Roman ruler. On the contrary, the Roman
empire is regarded in the tradition as the power which
so long as it holds together wards off the frightful
time of the last days. It is, moreover, highly
probable that this conception of the Roman empire

---

* Cf. Jerome, *Epist. ad Algasiam* ; Austin, Chrysostom, and
others.

must have arisen some considerable time before the destruction of Jerusalem.

The sources of this tradition are deeply rooted in the past. It had already influenced Paul; and that we have here no genuine Christian eschatology is evident from its contacts with 4 Ezra. It will be shown farther on that chaps. li. and following of this book are to be taken as direct sources of the Antichrist saga. Both Paul and 4 Ezra clearly exhibited the enigmatic and purely suggestive treatment of the esoteric tradition which we had assumed for all this eschatological legendary matter. Gunkel (224) conjectures that in the " he who now letteth " of Paul is contained an earlier mythological tradition. That by these words Paul himself understood the Roman empire from the parallel passages handed down to his time I have no doubt. But what may have been originally understood by the expression is comparatively speaking irrelevant so far as regards the exegesis of the New Testament.

The Book of Revelation itself was unable to give another direction to this tradition. In the second century the earlier figure of the Antichrist might seem to have been once for all banished by the ghost-like image of the Nero redivivus, as current, for instance, in the Sibylline literature. But that the lingering influence of the Johannine Apocalypse and of the Neronic legend should have so rapidly died out was also essentially due to the fact that the old hallowed tradition in its turn soon obliterated the later political application of the Antichrist legend. Henceforth the

9

figure of the Nero redivivus still persists at most as
a secondary form in apocalyptic imagery, or else, as
in ·Victorinus, it becomes identified with the earlier
embodiment of the Antichrist originating in pre-
Roman times.

It was precisely in this form, in which it was not
directed against Rome, that the Antichrist legend
exercised a most powerful political influence.   For
what could have been of more far-reaching conse-
quence than the idea, everywhere current in the early
Christian communities, that after all the Roman
empire did not represent the Antichrist rule—that, on
the contrary, the time of the Antichrist would be far
more dreadful and calamitous?   The Roman empire
and the Cæsars were prayed for, because they were
looked upon as the last bulwark against the coming
sway of the Antichrist, as is evident from the above-
quoted passages from Tertullian and Lactantius.

We have also seen how the legend took another
turn with the conversion of the empire to Christianity.
Henceforth it became impossible any longer to imagine
that the holy Roman empire could perish at all.
Accordingly the last Cæsar is not vanquished, but
voluntarily delivers up his crown to God.   Probably
we have this new application of the saga already in
pseudo-Ephrem, chap. v. : " And the empire of the
Christians is delivered up to God and the Father." *
This would harmonise with the assumption that such

* With this, inspired by 1 Corinthians xv. 24, compare the
above-quoted passages in Adso and pseudo-Methodius and in
Bede's and Usinger's Sibyls ; also the parallelisms in Wetstein

a notion had already been developed in the first half of the fourth century.

Thus the legend went wandering about, ever assuming new aspects under the shifting conditions of the times. When Rome fell at last and was followed by the rule of the Northern Barbarians, hopes were turned towards the new Rome (Constantinople) and the Byzantine emperors.* Then arose a holy Roman empire of German nationality, and the legend again wandered westwards, as we find it in Adso. But with the epoch of the Crusades thoughts were once more turned eagerly towards Jerusalem, and the notion again became possible that a last Roman emperor might after all deliver up his crown to God in the holy city. Thus was the saga quickened to new life, becoming in the renewed freshness of all its details the source of the twelfth-century miracle play of "the Antichrist."

With the Reformation it assumes a new aspect, for the necessity now arises of opposing the dangerous tendency of the Protestants to identify the power of the Antichrist with modern Rome and the Papacy. The Roman Catholic interpreters, some of them men of vast erudition, accordingly fell back on the early unpolitical tradition of the Antichrist, gathering traces of it from all quarters in huge tomes full of colossal industry. Here it will suffice to mention

(*N. Test.*, II. 167, 24) from Abarbanel and Elieser's *Pirke* ("Sayings") (Zezschwitz, p. 167).

* Cf. Apocalypse of Daniel (above, pp. 67 *et seq.*), and pseudo-Methodius.

such writings as the Commentaries of Ribeira and Alcassar, the works of Cardinal Bellarmine and of Malvenda, from all of which there is still much to learn.   Thus were laid the foundations of a scientific inquiry into these apocalyptic and mythological traditions, which in the course of ages have assumed so many marvellous phases.   Their persistency as well as the progress of their evolution can be measured only by the duration of recorded time.

CHAPTER X.*

HERE we shall touch only on the more important
points, without attempting to exhaust the
subject. Fuller details will be given in subsequent
chapters.

We already learn from Paul that the Man of Sin
shall be seated in the Temple of God : " Even him,
whose coming is after the working of Satan with all
power and signs and lying wonders, and with all
deceivableness of unrighteousness in them that perish ;
because they received not the love of the truth, that
they might be saved. And for this cause God shall
send them strong delusion, that they should believe
a lie : that they all might be damned who believed
not the truth, but had pleasure in unrighteousness "
(2 Thess. ii. 9-12). That Paul is here thinking of the
unbelieving Jews, who have rejected the true Messiah,
and have therefore received the false one from God,
there can scarcely be any doubt. A direct parallel is
presented by John v. 43 : " I am come in My Father's

* For Notes [1] to [50] of this chapter, see Appendix, p. 270.

name, and ye receive Me not : if another shall come in his own name, him ye will receive." I do not know who else can here be understood except the Antichrist. For a perfectly distinct person is spoken of, and the allusion can surely not be to Bar-Cochab. We thus come nearer to a solution of the enigma, how the beast, coming out of the bottomless pit, appears in Jerusalem (Rev. xi.). In the course of our inquiry clear proof will also be given that the abomination of desolation spoken of by Daniel the prophet, standing in the holy place (Matt. xxiv. 15), is the Antichrist. We are ever and everywhere confronted with this spectacle of an Antichrist, who appears in Jerusalem, a godless power, who in the last days rises up amid the holy people, a false Messiah equipped with signs and wonders.

We now also understand how Hippolytus came to know (chap. vi.) that " in the circumcision the Saviour came into the world, and he [Antichrist] in like manner shall come."[1] It also becomes clear how the idea occurred to Victorinus of speaking of Nero in such language as this : " Him therefore God having raised up shall send as a king worthy to the worthy [of such], and as a Christ such as the Jews deserved. . . . And since he shall bring another name, he shall likewise institute another life, so that him the Jews may receive as Christ, [for] saith Daniel (xi. 37), ' Neither shall he regard the God of his fathers, nor the desire of women,' he who hereto-fore had been most foul, for no one shall be able to seduce the people of circumcision unless [he be himself] a defender of the law." [2] So universal is the unanimity on this point that it will suffice to adduce one more witness, Jerome on Daniel xi. 21 : " But our [expositors] interpret both better and more correctly that at the end of the world these things shall be done by the Antichrist, who is to rise up from a small nation—that is, the nation of the Jews." [3]

In Lactantius alone occurs the variant (VII. 17, 638, 14) : " Another king shall rise up out of Syria " ; [4] but even by Lactantius this alien king is described as the pseudo-Messiah. So also Commodian (vers. 891 *et seq.*) : "Again there shall arise . . . a king out of the East." [5] But at 933 he also is spoken of as a false Messiah : " For us Nero, for the Jews He [Christ], is made the Antichrist." [6] Moreover, this ruler, after slaying Nero, marches on Judæa, which is obviously assumed to be the seat of his power. Thus, in the Jewish source common to Lactantius and Commodian, the false Messiah is again transformed to a hostile ruler, but in such a way as to leave the original figure clearly perceptible.

Still more clearly and distinctly is now seen the whole aspect of that apocalypic tradition : an Antichrist is expected, but not from the Roman empire, which, on the contrary, is the power that still bars the way to the appearance of the Antichrist. Hence the godless power, a false Messiah who claims divine worship, arises in Jerusalem in the midst of Israel itself.

But is it conceivable that in this form the prediction can have at all originated on Jewish ground ? How did the notion arise ? Have we not here an apocalyptic dream of nascent Christianity inspired by hatred of the Jews? In any case this must be a very early prediction which was current in the first centuries of the new era, and which had already assumed a definite form for Paul—a prediction which, being at first un-political, dates neither from the time of Caligula nor of Nero.

The name, however, of the Antichrist (1 John ii. 18 ; 2 John 7) is not older than the New Testament. By Paul he is spoken of quite in a general way as the "man of sin," "the son of perdition" (2 Thess. ii. 3). Yet even Paul seems already to know of some distinct name, as seen from the following passages :

2 Corinthians vi. 15 : "And what concord hath Christ with Belial ? " This association of Christ with Belial (Beliar) is significative.

Testam. Patriarcharum, Dan 5 : "And unto you shall ascend from the tribe of Judah and of Levi the salvation of the Lord, and he shall make war against Beliar."[7]

Sibyl II. 37 : "And Beliar shall come and work many signs for men."[8]

Sibyl III. 63 : "But hereafter shall Beliar come from the Sebastenes."[9] Compare also III. 73.

Ascensio Jesaiæ, IV. 2 : "Beliar a great angel, king of this world, shall descend . . . in the form of man."[10] This name Belial occurs also in the Dioptra ; and in the Book of Zorobabel Belial is the father of Antichrist ; with which compare the Commentary of Andreas, 92, 2.

Paul was thus acquainted with a distinct name of

the Antichrist—Belial or Beliar, being somewhat
equivalent to the expression "man of sin." It is
noteworthy this very name has a wide currency in
Jewish literature. The above-quoted Sibylline passages
are certainly taken, one (II.) directly the other indirectly, from Jewish writings ; and the extract from
the Testament of Dan seems to me to be derived
from the fundamental Jewish element in that book.
The *Ascensio Jesaiæ* (III. and IV.) is also probably
based on a short Jewish apocalypse, while in a late
Jewish document the name of Belial has survived
with reference to the Antichrist. The original meaning
of this word will be dealt with farther on.

The following descriptions of the Antichrist may
also be quoted for the sake of their literary associations :

Irenæus, V. 25 : " He . . . shall come . . . as an
apostate and wicked one and murderer, as a robber." [11]

Pseudo-Ephrem, 5 : " Then shall appear that most
wicked and detestable dragon, he whom Moses named
in Deuteronomy, saying, ' Dan is a lion's whelp ; he
shall leap from Bashan.' For he croucheth that he
may seize and destroy and slay. . . . But a lion's
whelp not as the lion of the tribe of Dan, but roaring
with rage that he may devour." [12] With this compare
Hippolytus, *de Antichristo,* chap. xiv. ; and the descriptions in pseudo-Methodius and Adso (1292 B).

Ephr. Gr., II. 225 *et seq.* : [13]

For since the thief—and the persecutor and cruel one
Shall first come—in his own times
Wishing to steal and—to slay and destroy.

Pseudo-Johannine Apocalypse, 6 : " Then shall

appear the denier and he who is born of darkness, who is called the Antichrist." [14]

Greek Apocalypse of Daniel, 104 : " And the thrice accursed demon shall prevail." [15]

Noteworthy are also the following :

4 Ezra v. 6 : " And he shall reign whom the dwellers on earth expect not." [16]

Irenæus, V. 30, 2 : " He who shall come of a sudden claiming the dominion for himself." [17]

Armenian Apocalypse of Daniel, 239, 1 : " After the coming of him whom they desired not nor hoped for."

By a collation of these parallelisms we may perhaps restore a passage in the *Ascensio Jesaiæ*, V. 13: " And many of the faithful and of the saints, when they beheld Him whom they expected (not) [the Lord Jesus Christ suspended, when I Jesse saw Him who was suspended and ascended (?), and the believers also in Him, of those but few shall remain in those days, His ministers] fleeing from desert to desert, awaiting the coming of Him (the Lord)." [18] The mention of the crucifixion of Christ in the middle of a description of the Antichrist times is quite meaningless.   But if the clause in square brackets be struck out, there remains the puzzling " whom they expected," which in the light of the parallel passages should perhaps read " whom they expected not." Then the sense will be completed by simply supplying the words " the Lord " at the end of the sentence.

These preliminaries bring us to the specially important subject of THE DEVIL AND THE ANTICHRIST. On the mutual relations of these two personalities the greatest discordance prevails in traditional lore. Yet it is of the greatest interest to investigate these discrepancies and conflicting fancies. For this very chaos of clashing views enables us to get behind the beginnings of our eschatological tradition, and thus follow them up to their essential original form.

The Fathers of the Church, whose writings have acquired great influence in this exegesis, speak very plainly and distinctly. Foremost amongst them is Jerome on Daniel vii. 8: "Nor let us think that he [Antichrist] . . . is the devil or a demon, but *one of men* in whom Satan is wholly to dwell bodily." [19] Quite in a similar sense runs Chrysostom's exposition of 2 Thessalonians ii., in Homily 2: "But who is this one? Think you, Satan? By no means, but some man possessed of all his energy." [20] So also Irenæus, V. 25, 1: "Receiving all the virtue of the devil, . . . summing up within himself the apostasy of the devil." In any case it is clear enough that this, and this alone, is the New Testament view of the Antichrist. The influence of Jerome may be distinctly traced in the Western Church, and that of Chrysostom in the Eastern Church.* Henceforth the assumption that the Antichrist is the devil himself practically dies out of ecclesiastical tradition.

Yet the very interpretations of Jerome and Chry-

* For Jerome, cf. Haymo of Halberstadt on 2 Thessalonians ii.; for Chrysostom, John of Damascus, Ἔκθεσις τῆς ὀρθοδόξου πίστεως, Verona, 1531, p. 135; also the Commentaries of Œcumenius and Theophylactus on the passage of 2 Thessalonians in question.

sostom presuppose an earlier tradition, in which Satan
was identified with Antichrist, or at least was brought
into a much closer relation with him than is assumed
in the notion of a man possessed of satanic energy.

To begin with the earliest evidence, in Hippolytus
the relations are already far from clear. Here
(chap. vi.) we read : " In the form of man appeared
the Saviour, and he also [the Antichrist] shall come in
the form of man." [21] From this quite another representation might be inferred. Farther on, where we
are told of the birth of the Antichrist in the tribe of
Dan, it is added (chap. xiv.): " ' Dan shall be a
serpent.' . . . But who is the serpent except the
deceiver from the beginning, he who in Genesis is
called the beguiler of Eve and the crusher of Adam ? " [22]
In what follows the Antichrist would seem to be
called " the devil's son." Although the identification
is not complete, still for Hippolytus the Antichrist is
in any case Satan incarnate.

But in Firmicus Maternus the identification is
clenched with the words : " The devil is Antichrist
himself." * Equally clear is the passage of pseudo-
Hippolytus, xxii. 105, 21 : " Because the Saviour of
the world, wishing to save mankind, was born of the
immaculate Virgin Mary, and in the form of flesh
trod underfoot the enemy by the special virtue of His
own divinity, in the same way the devil also shall
come of a polluted woman on the earth, but be born
by deception of a virgin, for our God dwelt with us in
the flesh. . . . But the devil, even if he take flesh

* *Liber de Erroribus,* chap. xxii.

he does so by simulation." [23]   The passage points back
to the source of pseudo-Hippolytus, and to Ephr.
Gr., III. 134 C :

" Let us learn, my friends—in what form shall come on
earth—the shameless serpent—Since the Redeemer—wishing to save all mankind—was born of a Virgin—and in
human form—crushed the enemy—with the holy power—
of His godhead." 137 E : "This then the enemy having
learnt—that again shall the Lord come from heaven—in the
glory of His divinity—thus bethought him—to assume the
form—of His coming—and [thus] beguile all men. . . . So
in very truth shall he be born—of a defiled woman—his
instrument—[though] he shall not [really] be incarnate." [24]

Although here everything is based on the notion
that Satan, simulating the birth of the Lord, appears
personally in the Antichrist, still at the close the
point of this notion is blunted, the Antichrist after all
appearing only as the " organ " or instrument of Satan.
It is strange that the pseudo-Hippolytus, who depends
on Ephrem, here shows quite a strained sequence
of thought.   Are we to suppose that Ephrem was
accessible to him in some other recension?   Moreover,
as will be seen farther on, the Antichrist is elsewhere
also in the homily of the Greek Ephrem [25] absolutely
described as a demoniac superhuman figure.   But so
far as the Ephremite Greek text runs, the relation
between Satan and Antichrist is after all here conceived
in a different way from Jerome and Chrysostom.
This is at once seen from the parallel passage (already
alluded to in Hippolytus) between the appearance of

Satan on earth in the Antichrist and the miraculous birth of Christ. So also Ambrosiaster on 2 Thessalonians ii. 3 : " As the Son of God in His human birth manifested His divine nature, so also shall Satan appear in human form." A like comparison, though in a somewhat weakened manner, is drawn by Theodoretus commenting on 2 Thessalonians ii. 3 : " For the persecutor of men simulates the incarnation of our God and Saviour ; and as He by assuming our human nature accomplished our salvation, so that one also by making choice of a man capable of receiving the fulness of his power shall tempt men." [26] In this last conception Theodoretus certainly approximates to the idea of Jerome and Chrysostom, but still he obviously goes beyond them.

Another parallel occurs in the work passing under the name of Prosper Aquitanicus, *On the Promises and Predictions of God*, IV. 8, where the Antichrist appears in a man, "just as, on the other hand, the holy angel in the Book of Tobias assumed the form and resemblance . . . of Azarias." [27] But somewhat different again seems the relation in Lactantius : " begotten of an evil spirit " ; [28] and in S. Martin of Tours : " conceived of an evil spirit." [29]

We thus see how the tradition wavers between the concept of the Antichrist as of a man controlled by the devil and that of his identification with Satan. But it is manifest that the notion of him as of a superhuman spectral and demoniacal apparition is widespread and primeval ; possibly this is the earlier, and consequently comes again and again to the surface.

Side by side with these ideas we find still a characteristic intermediate form in later writers, who firmly hold that the Antichrist was to come into the world in the natural way from human parents, but that Satan must at least have co-operated in his conception.

How are we to explain these discrepancies in the notion of the Antichrist? In my opinion only by a reference to the origin of the Antichrist legend itself. Whence comes the idea of such a personality at all, that is, of a hostile pseudo-Messiah, who rises up in the midst of the people of God themselves, as represented in Paul, Matthew xxiv., Revelation xi., and here obviously on the ground of Jewish traditions? Gunkel (pp. 221 *et seq.*) is fully justified in holding that the expectation of an Antichrist in no way originated in any distinct political situation, and that all explanations have failed that are based on current events, whether those of Caligula's or of Nero's reign. Such times of political excitement give rise to no new eschatological yearnings, whose growth and being are a much slower process, in fact one to be measured by centuries. Long-standing expectations may indeed be interpreted by contemporary history, but no fresh imagery takes its rise in this way. Gunkel holds that we are to regard the Antichrist tradition as a Jewish dogma, which had its origin in such visions as those of Daniel vii. and the like, by imparting a spiritual meaning to a tradition which had at first a political character.

But to me it still seems that it is a far cry from Daniel vii. to 2 Thessalonians. How did the description of a foreign dominion revolting against God give rise to thé idea of a godless power rising up against God in the midst of the people of God themselves? Moreover, the notion of the Antichrist seated in the Temple of Jerusalem is so concrete and vivid, that it becomes difficult to imagine it inspired by Daniel's foreboding of the dreadful desolation of the holy place. With the knowledge that Daniel's prophecy itself was not uttered for a definite purpose, but rested on an earlier tradition, Gunkel held in his hands the clue to a correct solution of the problem. My belief is that we have here merely an exposition, and that behind this Antichrist saga there lies an earlier myth. As convincingly shown by Gunkel himself,* we find in the Old and here and there in the New Testament literature very numerous traces of a primeval Creation myth, which was later transformed to an expectation of the last things. As may still be seen in Revelation, there existed in the popular Jewish belief the foreboding of another revolt of the old marine monster with whom God had warred at the creation, but who in the last days was again to rise and contend in heaven-storming battle with God. The expectation is not of any hostile ruler and of the oppression of Israel by him and his army, but of a struggle of Satan directly with God, of a conflict of the Dragon with the Almighty throned in heaven. To me the Antichrist legend seems a simple incarnation of that old Dragon myth, which has in the first instance nothing to do with particular political powers and occurrences. For the Dragon is substituted the man armed with

* *Schöpfung und Chaos,* passim.

miraculous power who makes himself God's equal— a man who in the eyes of the Jews could be no other than the false Messiah.

But the Antichrist legend is after all unable quite to conceal its origin in a far wilder and more fantastic world of thought and sentiments, from which it has received an indelible impression. During its further development there continually arises behind the Antichrist the still wilder figure of the God-hating demon, of Satan, ever seeking to thrust Him aside. The history of the saga bears on its face the impress of our assumption regarding its origin, as will be more clearly seen in the following remarks.

To begin with, the Antichrist is even still frequently represented as a dragon and a demon. Especially is this the case in Ephr. Gr., whose homily opens with the announcement that he is about to speak " on the most shameless and terrible dragon who is to bring disorder into the whole world." [30] Here the term " dragon " often recurs, and as in Ephr. Syr. the messengers and ministers of the Dragon are demons. So the pseudo-Ephrem : " Then shall appear that most wicked and detested dragon " ; * while in the Greek Apocalypse of Daniel (116, 35) we have the characteristic expression : " The serpent that sleepeth shall awaken." [31] At 119, 105, the Antichrist is " the thrice accursed demon " ; and in Cyril (xv. 15) " the fearful

---

* " Tunc apparebit ille nequissimus et abominabilis draco " (cf. chap. viii.). In chap. vii. also the Antichrist is the " nequissimus serpens," with which compare the " signum serpentinum " of chap. viii.

beast, the great dragon, unconquerable by men " ; [32]
while Philip the Solitary " compares him to the subtle
and deceitful dragon," [33] as in Genesis xlix. 17.

Without further quotations, and especially omitting
those passages in which the figure of the Dragon
might somehow have arisen under the influence of
Revelation xii., I turn to some highly interesting
and suggestive details.

In the opening of Ephr. Gr. we have the following
description of the Antichrist, which nowhere recurs in
later writings :

> A great conflict, Brethren—in those times
> Amongst all men—but especially amongst the faithful,
> When there shall be—signs and wonders
> [Wrought] by the Dragon—in great abundance (?)
> When he shall again—manifest himself as God
> In fearful phantasms—flying in the air
> And [show] all the demons—in the form of angels
> Flying in terror—before the tyrant,
> For he crieth out loudly—changing his forms also—
> To strike infinite dread—into all men.[34]

A detailed description drawn directly from this
source occurs in pseudo-Hippolytus, xxix. 111, 10 :
" For his demons he shall represent as angels of light,
and hosts of bodiless [spirits] he shall lead forth, of
whom there is no number, and before the face of all he
exhibits him received into heaven with trumpets and
shouts and great cries hailing him with unutterable
hymns, and shining like a light that shareth in
darkness, and now flying aloft unto heaven, and now
coming down on the earth in great glory, and again

marshalling the demons as angels to do the will of him with much fear and trembling." [35]

A reflection of this image occurs in Philip the Solitary : " Flying aloft as an angel, nay as a demon, and fashioning terrors and wonders unto deception." [36]

Perhaps light is thrown by these passages on a puzzling sentence in the old Apocalypse of Baruch, where it is stated (chap. xxvii.) that in the eighth time of the Messianic end there shall come " a multitude of phantasms and a gathering of demons (?)." Here we may have a parallel to those later and fuller descriptions.

But is all this strange and absolutely unique imagery really nothing more than fantastic accounts of the marvellous works of the Antichrist ? We are warned to be guarded in our conclusions by the very circumstance that we have here evidently cropping out that Dragon myth which lies behind the Antichrist legend. And in point of fact it is highly probable that this marvellous spectacle of the Antichrist encircled by his angels and flying in the air had originally a far more serious meaning.

Here we are carried further by the consideration that the Antichrist saga is beyond question connected with another cycle of legends, which has become interwoven with the person of Simon Magus of Samaria.* In the following remarks it will be shown that the further

---

* Cf. *The Acts of the Apostles*, ed. Lipsius and Bonnet, I., 1891 ; *Actus Petri cum Simone*, chaps. xxxi., xxxii. ; *Martyrium Petri et Pauli*, *ib.*, 118 *et seq.*, chaps. liii.-lvi. ; *Acta Petri et Pauli*, 178 *et seq.* ; *Passio Petri et Pauli*, 223 *et seq.* ; *Arnobius*

development of the history of Simon Magus in the apocryphal legendary matter of apostolic times has been carried out under the influence of the Antichrist legend.

When the Simon Magus legend is viewed from this standpoint, we are at once struck by a parallelism in this connection.   In the fabulous relation dating back to the second century and perhaps earlier, the magician's end is brought about in the following way. After promising to fly heavenwards before the assembled multitude, and thus prove himself God, he is borne aloft by the aid of demons ; but on the prayer of Peter he tumbles down, and so perishes miserably.   A special original version occurs in Arnobius, II. 12 : " For they [the Romans] had seen the flight of Simon Magus and his fiery chariots dissipated by the breath of Peter and vanish at the name of Christ ; they had seen . . . the truster in false gods betrayed by them in their terror and precipitated by his own weight."   But either way the legend of the flight to heaven already acquires a deeper meaning, and in the case of Simon it becomes an essay to prove his divinity—an ascension ! We are also told that on beholding him soar upwards the people begin to hail him as a god.   The narrative is thus seen to be a direct revolt against God.*

adv. Gentes, II. 12 ; Cyril, *Catechetical Lecture*, VI. 15 ; Sulpicius Severus, *Sacr. Hist.*, II. 28 ; Theodoretus, *Hæretic. Fabularum*, I. 1 ; Austin, *de Hæresibus*, I. ; *Constit. Apost.*, VI. 9.

* Cf. also *Actus Petri cum Simone*, chap. iv., where Simon performs his flight in Rome ; and *Martyrium Petri et Pauli*, II., where amongst his wonders it is related that he has been able to appear flying in the air.

It now becomes highly significant to note that in the *Scivias* of S. Hildegard the same end is related of the Antichrist. Here we read : " For when he shall have fulfilled all the pleasure of the devil, the beguiler, because in the just judgment of God he shall not by any means be permitted any longer to have so much potency for his wickedness and cruelty, he shall gather all his host and say unto the believers in him that he intendeth to go aloft—and lo ! as if stricken by a thunderbolt suddenly coming [down] he strikes his head with such force that he is both cast down from that mountain and delivereth his soul unto death." [37]

The supposition must be at once excluded that S. Hildegard invented these fancies herself ; evidently she must have been acquainted with some surviving primeval traditions, whence she drew her predictions. Nor is this description of the fate of the Antichrist borrowed from the Simon Magus legend. We need but ask ourselves whether this idea of the attempted, or here only planned, ascension adapts itself better to the Antichrist or to Simon Magus. We infer rather that in S. Hildegard's Visions is preserved a variant of the Antichrist legend, which is itself presupposed by the Simon Magus saga.

The Antichrist perishes in the attempt to fly aloft and thus prove himself God, and by God is hurled down.* How is it possible here to overlook the deeper

---

* Cf. for instance, *Constit.*, VI. 9, 165, 11 : Λέγων εἰς οὐρανοὺς ἀνιέναι κἀκεῖθεν αὐτοῖς τὰ ἀγαθὰ ἐπιχορηγεῖν (" Saying that he goes unto heaven and thence sends them [all] good things "). This

sense of the saga and its connection in this point with the earlier Dragon myth ? The notion that the Dragon storms the heavens and in the assault on the throne of God is cast down is found quite clearly expressed in the New Testament, and Revelation xii. is assuredly based on the same myth. In chap. xiii., ver. 6, also we have an echo of the legend in the words " to blaspheme His name, and His tabernacle, and them that dwell in heaven "; so also, " I saw Satan like unto the lightning falling from heaven."

In that variant of the Antichrist legend and in that of Simon Magus we have reminiscences of the primeval myth, which even Ephrem seems to have known, only with him the ascension of Antichrist becomes a miraculous spectacle.

In Ephrem (see above, p. 146) it is further related that in his flight the Dragon changes his form, with which may be compared the *Martyrdom of SS. Peter and Paul*, chap. xiv. : " But he [Simon] began suddenly to change his forms, so as instantly to become a child, and after a little an old man, and again a youth ; . . . and he raged, having the devil a helper." [38]

Then we read of the Antichrist in Philip's Dioptra : " But also altogether like Proteus by changes of forms and colours [he makes himself] one from another, . . . flying on high like an angel, nay, like a

announcement is of frequent occurrence, as in *Mart. Petri et Pauli*, where Simon says to Nero : Πέμψω τοὺς ἀγγέλους μου πρός σε καὶ ποιήσω σε ἐλθεῖν πρός με (" I will send my angels to thee and cause thee to come unto me ").

demon, and fashioning portents and wonders unto deception." [39]   So also in the Apocalypse of Ezra (p. 29) we have concerning the Antichrist : " And he becomes a child and an old man, and no one believeth in him that he is my beloved son." [40]   Similarly in the Apocalypse of Zephaniah (123) in the sight of the onlookers he transforms himself, growing at one time young at another aged.   Here is clearly seen how both cycles of legends come in contact.

In early Christian (New Testament) times the Antichrist saga had already acquired a political tendency with reference to Nero.   When the figure of this ruler, returning with the Parthians after the lapse of a generation, had gradually been distorted to a demoniac and spectral being, the elements of the primeval Dragon myth also found their way into this picture of Nero returning from the lower regions. Cases in point are presented in superabundance by the Sibyls.   Thus V. 214 :

Weep thou also, O Corinth, for the dire undoing of thee ;
For when with their twisted threads the three sister Fates,
Having ensnared him fleeing by the Isthmian oracle,
Shall raise him on high, then let all look to it.[41]

In VIII. 88 the figure of the Dragon stands out clearly :

The fiery-eyed Dragon when he cometh on the waves
With full belly, and shall oppress the children of thee,
Famine also pending and fratricidal strife,
Then is nigh the end of the world and the last day.[42]

And again, VIII. 154 :

From the Asian land [he shall come] mounted on the Trojan
    chariot,
With the python's (?) fury; but when the isthmus he shall
    cross,
Changing from sea to sea in eager search of all,
Then shall he encounter the great beast of black blood.[43]

And V. 28 :

And whoso hath fifty horns (?) received, lord shall he be,
A dire serpent begetting heavy war.

32 :

And the height 'tween two seas shall he sever and with gore
    befoul,
And unseen shall be the pernicious one ; [but] again shall
    he return,
Holding himself equal to God, and shall contend that He
    is not.[44]

Here is lastly to be mentioned yet another reference
in Ephr. Syr., 7,* where the Antichrist comes from a
place which is translated by Lamy " perdition," but
which probably means from the lower world, that is,
the Hebrew *Abaddon.*† Although in Revelation this
is a *personal* name, it is translated in the Old Testament by the Syriac term in question.

Andreas, who in his Commentary points to many
coincidences with Ephrem, remarks on Revelation
xi. 7 : " The Antichrist coming out of the dark and

* וܩ,ܥ   † אבדון

deep recesses of the ground, to which the devil had been condemned." [45] Here might again be compared the Abaddon of Revelation ix. 11, and the expression " son of perdition " in 2 Thessalonians ii. 3.

Note on Belial.

As above remarked, Paul was already acquainted with this name as that of the Antichrist (2 Cor. ii. 3), and the Greek expression " man of sin " (properly " man of lawlessness ") is probably a translation of the Hebrew *Beli-'al.** We thus come upon firm Jewish traditional ground. Who then is Belial? The best explanation occurs in *Ascensio Jesaiæ*, IV. 2 : " . . . And after the consummation the angel Berial shall descend, the great king of this world, over which he ruleth since it existeth, and he shall descend from his firmament [in the form of man, king of wickedness, matricide . . . he is king of this world]. . . . This angel Berial [in the form of this estate] shall come, and with him shall come all the powers of this world, and they shall hearken unto him in all things as he shall will." [46]

It may be, and indeed is probable enough, that the reference to Nero (see the clauses in square brackets) is not here made for the first time. Still we clearly see that originally Belial had naught to do with Nero, but is an evil angel, who is called the ruler of this world, who has his abode in cloudland, and to whom

* בְּלִיַּעַל

are subject other angels, the " powers of this world."
Of this Belial it is announced that he is to set up his
dominion at the end of the world.

In equally plain language Belial is also described as
the ruler of the last time in Sibyl III. 63 *et seq.*,
where he is brought into relation with Nero : " And
from the Sebastenes shall come Beliar." Although
this reference is lacking in Sibyl II. 167, Belial is also
in the Testament of the Twelve Patriarchs an evil
spirit, apparently the devil or Satan himself, and here
also we read of the " spirits of Beliar." [47]   Likewise in
the Testament of Daniel, Belial is spoken of as the
foe of the last days ; as in chap. v., where it is said
of the Messiah that " He shall make war against
Beliar, and the vengeance of victory shall He grant
for our translation [to heaven]." [48]   Some of the
following passages also have perhaps been modified in
a Christian sense.   Thus, while Codex R reads " in
the *kingdom* of Jerusalem," all the others have " in the
new Jerusalem."

Some light may now be shed on a passage in the
Ascensio Jesaiæ, VII. 9 : " And we ascend into the
firmament, I and he, and there I beheld Sammael and
his powers, and a great battle was there and Satanic
speeches, and one was wrangling with another ; . . . and
I asked the angel : What is this strife ?   And he said
to me : So is it since this world existeth until now, and
this contest [abideth] until He shall come whom thou
art to behold, and He shall destroy it [the world]." [49]
It is not clear in what relation Sammael stands to
Belial, and possibly Sammael was not originally in the

text at all.* But in any case here also we read of an evil spirit whose domain is the sky (" firmament "), and who in the last days is to be vanquished.

How is the figure of Belial himself to be explained ? Whatever view be taken, it is a figure which from its name and tradition must have originated on Jewish ground, and in it we have seemingly to recognise a first phase of the Antichrist legend. The Dragon who revolts against God is here metamorphosed to a wicked angel who becomes the ruler of the æthereal regions and prince of this world. Thus is accomplished the first step in the migrations of the Babylonian mythology.

As seen, Paul is already familiar with the figure of Belial as the opponent of the Messiah in the last days. But what can Christ and Belial have in common ? But with Paul Belial has already ceased to be an angel or a demon, and becomes " the man of lawlessness."

This determination is of unusual importance. Even allowing that the notion of the Antichrist seated in

---

* The Latin text (Dillmann, 77) varies greatly ; but the Ethiopic version is confirmed by the Latin fragment, p. 85. Still there remains the possibility that the original reading has been preserved by the Latin text I., as compared with the two other documents. This text knows absolutely nothing of Sammael, while in the recension represented by the Ethiopic and Latin II. Sammael and Belial are brought into artistic relation one with the other. Thus p. 84 (III. 13) : "Fuit enim Beliac bilem habens in Esaiam propter quod in se ostenderit Samael " (" For Beliac was enraged against Isaiah for that he held up Samael against him ").

the Temple originated with Christianity in opposition
to the Jews, nevertheless it has its roots in Judaism,
that is, in the distinctly Jewish expectation of the
revolt of the aërial spirit, Belial, and this again in
the Babylonian Dragon myth.

The Antichrist in the Character of a Monster.

In this connection it may further be mentioned that
a description of the Antichrist as of a human monster
is found widely diffused. Such a variant of the
Antichrist occurs in the Apocalypse of Ezra, where
we read (Tischendorf, *Apocalypses Apocryphæ*, xxix.):
"The form of the face of him as of a field; his
right eye as the morning star, and the other one
that quaileth not; his mouth one cubit; his teeth
of one span; his fingers like unto sickles, the
imprint of his feet two spans, and on his brow the
inscription Antichrist." [50]

So also in some manuscripts of the pseudo-
Johannine Apocalypse, chap. vii.

Moreover, we have in the Armenian Apocalypse of
Daniel (239, 11) a different description couched in
similar language, as also in the Book of Clement,
with which compare the part extant in Latin. Then
the same fanciful description reappears in the accounts
of Armillus occurring in the late Jewish apocalypses.
So also in the Apocalypse of Elias, where, however,
no reference yet occurs to Armillus, though, strange
to say, appeal is made to a Vision of Daniel. In the
Midrash va-Yosha (Wünsche, 119) we read: "He

shall be bald-headed, with a small and a large eye ; his right arm shall be a span long, but his left two and a half ells ; on his brow shall be a scab, his right ear stopped, but the other open." Similar accounts may be seen in the Mysteries of Simon ben Yokhai, in the Book of Zorobabel, in the Signs of the Messiah, and in the Persian History of Daniel.*

It is very noteworthy that a description clothed with this distinctly Jewish tradition occurs also in the Apocalypse of Zephaniah, p. 125. Such a coincidence points at the original Jewish character of the work. With this compare also the extravagant description of the personal appearance of Judas Iscariot in the fragment of Papias.† About its source there can no longer be any doubt.

* Cf. also *Quæstiones ad Antiochum*, 109 (Migne, XXVIII.) : Καί σημεῖον τι ἐν τῇ χειρὶ τῇ μιᾷ καὶ ἐν τῷ ὀφθαλμῷ τῷ ἑνὶ κέκτηται ("And he hath received a certain sign in one hand and in one eye ").

† *Patres Apost.*, I. 94. Cf. also the comparison drawn in pseudo-Methodius, p. 99, between Antichrist and Judas.

CHAPTER XI.*

FROM a collation of Daniel xi. 43 with vii. 8 there arises the notion that at the outset of his career Antichrist will vanquish the kings of Egypt, Libya, and Ethiopia—that is to say, three of the ten last kings of the Roman empire. This Rabbinical interpretation seems to be utilised in the Antichrist legend, and the tradition is already known to Irenæus (V. 26, 1) and to Hippolytus (li. 27, 7).† These writers apply it even to the interpretation of Revelation, striving in direct opposition to the text to connect the seven heads and the ten horns of the beast in such a way as to assume that both images represent the Roman kings of the last days, of whom Antichrist kills three and subdues the remaining seven.

---

* For Notes [1] to [52] of this chapter, see Appendix, p. 276.

† Cf. also Jerome on Daniel xi. 43, and many other expositors of Revelation and of Daniel, all writing under the influence of Jerome.

In Ephr. Gr. we find the same fancy interwoven with the Antichrist saga, III. 138 D :

> And forthwith is set up—his kingdom,
> And in his wrath shall he smite—three great kings.[1]

This trait belongs so essentially to the substance of the legend, that Commodian, in accordance with contemporary historical precedents, associates two Cæsars with his Nero, precursor of the Antichrist, the object being to enable the Antichrist to triumph over three kings (911 *et seq.*) :

> And to oppose him shall three Cæsars go forth ;
> Whom having slain he gives as food to the birds.[2]

Hence nothing could be more absurd than to attempt to explain this passage of Commodian by reference to historical events. Here we have, in fact, nothing but an eschatological picture.

A further parallel is presented by Sibyl V. 222 :

> And first having by a mighty stroke from the roots
> Three heads severed, he will give them to be scattered
>   amongst others,
> So that they may eat the royal polluted flesh of their
>   fathers !

The persistency with which this eschatological fancy was propagated, despite the silence of Revelation on the subject, again shows that the following age was influenced not by this work, but by our eschatological tradition.

For the notion derived from Daniel xi. 41 of an alliance between Antichrist, Moab, and Ammon, see

Hippolytus (li. 27, 1), Greek Ephrem (III. 138 C), and pseudo-Ephrem (chap. vii.).

It is, however, possible that this element, suggested by an exposition of Daniel, may not have found its way into the tradition till later times. As already seen, the Antichrist Apocalypse holds on the whole a position independent of Daniel. But of course this does not exclude the idea that in some respects it may have been developed under the influence of that work. Considering its manifold points of contact with Daniel in certain details, fresh significance is added to the remarks above made (p. 71) in reference to the early existence of an apocryphal Apocalypse of Daniel—the Little Daniel, the History of Daniel, the Last Visions of Daniel.

After triumphing over those three kings, the Antichrist is to take his seat in the Temple of Jerusalem.

This characteristic belief, already mentioned in 2 Thessalonians ii. 3, prevailed to an extraordinary extent, and is very frequently referred to by Irenæus, as in V. 30, 4 : " But when this Antichrist shall have wasted everything in this world, . . . he shall seat himself in the Temple "; and in V. 25, 1 : " And [shall] indeed depose the idols, that he may persuade [the people] that he is himself God, setting himself up as the one idol." [3] So also Hippolytus, lii. 27, 12 (liii. 27, 19) : " He shall begin to be exalted in his heart, and rise up against God, holding sway over the whole world." [4]   The Sibyl XII. (x.) : " Making himself God's equal, he shall argue that He is not." [5]

Pseudo-Ephrem : "And entering that [Temple] he shall seat himself as God, and command all nations to worship him."[6] And the pseudo-Johannine Apocalypse, 6, Cod. E : "And him he represents as God, and shall set up the place of him on the place of Calvary (?)."[7]

It is remarkable that the incident occurs neither in the Greek Ephrem nor in pseudo-Hippolytus, while but a very slight allusion is made to it in Philip the Solitary.

On the other hand, it is still mentioned by Hilarius commenting on Matthew xv. ; by the Syriac Ephrem, 8; by pseudo-Methodius, 99 ; John of Damascus.; Jerome (on Daniel vii. 25 ; xi. 30, etc.) ; by Adso and Bede's Sibyl.

A special variant, also dating somewhat far back, occurs in the *Ascensio Jesaiœ*, IV. 6 : "And he shall say, I am God, the excellent and greatest, and before me was no one." IV. 11 : "And his image shall be set up before his face in all the cities."[8]

In Victorinus on Revelation xiii. 15 : "He shall also cause a golden statue to be set up to the Antichrist in the Temple of Jerusalem, that a fleeing [fallen ?] angel may enter and thence emit voices and oracles."[9]

In the Ethiopic Apocalypse of Peter: "And his statue shall stand in the churches and before all in Jerusalem, the holy city of the great king."

Can these variants in the tradition date perhaps from the time of Caligula, seeing that a tendency has also been shown to explain 2 Thessalonians ii.

11

and Revelation xiii. by the events of the same period ?

But if the Antichrist is to be seated in the Temple of Jerusalem, then the Temple must exist, and must consequently be re-erected after the destruction of Jerusalem. Hence this incident in the tradition is also of very early occurrence, although of course forming no part of its original substance. Thus Hippolytus, c. 6, 5, 11 : " The Saviour raised up and manifested His holy body as a temple ; in the same way he also [the Antichrist] shall raise up the temple of stone in Jerusalem." [10]

Greek Ephrem, III. 138 C :

Whence also as preferring—the place and the temple
To all those he displays—his exercise (?) of foreknowledge.[11]

Cyril, xv. 15 : " In order the more to deceive them [the Jews] he builds for himself the Temple in great haste, giving out that he is of the race of David." [12]

The Greek Apocalypse of Daniel : " And the Jews he shall exalt, and dwell in the Temple that had been razed to the ground." [13]

Andreas, xlv. 42 : " And be seated in the Temple . . . to be erected by him as expected by the Jews contending with God." [14]

Adso, 1293 C : " The ruined Temple also, which Solomon [had] raised to God, he shall [re]-build and restore to its [former] state." [15]

Haymo on 2 Thessalonians ii. 4 : " And they shall rebuild the Temple that the Romans had destroyed, and he shall seat himself therein." [16]

Elucidarium : " Antichrist shall rebuild the old Jerusalem, in which he shall order himself to be worshipped as God." [17]

Lastly, in Lactantius, VII. 16, 639, 7, or rather in his Jewish source, we have a most remarkable variant : " Then shall he strive to raise the Temple of God, and the righteous people shall he oppress." [18] Commodian, from whom something similar might be expected, has no reference at all to this incident.

But the last-quoted passage gives rise to some reflections. Is not the notion of a ruler hostile to and contending with God, a ruler arising amid the Jews, having the centre of his sway in Jerusalem, and seating himself in the Temple of Jerusalem,—is not such a notion essentially Christian, and not of Jewish origin in times prior to the New Testament epoch, so that here Lactantius may have somehow preserved the old type of the legend ? And this, even if it were a question of a false Messiah, such as the figure of " the man of lawlessness " already partly grasped by Paul ! For surely this utterly reckless revolt against God and the seat in the Temple scarcely harmonise with the idea of a false Messiah.

Is there any means at all of explaining this remarkable element in the Antichrist legend ? It depends not a little on one consideration. If we wish to get on the right track, the first thing to be done is to get rid of all interpretations based on current events. In this we adhere to the above-enunciated principle, that, during the excitement caused by momentous contemporary occurrences, the apocalyptic writer, speaking generally, does not invent new, but applies old imagery. From the disorders of Caligula's reign it is impossible· to elucidate Revelation xiii., 2 Thessalonians ii., or Matthew xxiv. From Caligula's well-known doings how could the idea have arisen of the Antichrist seating himself in the Temple of Jerusalem, even had this incident survived only in the above-quoted variants in the *Ascensio Jesaiæ*, in Victorinus, and the Ethiopic Apocalypse of Peter ? As matters stand it must, on the contrary, be inferred that the variant, as in 2 Thessalonians ii., was perhaps revived in the exciting time of Caligula, being based on an earlier representation. The belief, however, was at that time current that the old prediction of Beliar enthroned in the Temple of Jerusalem would be fulfilled by Caligula's threat to set up his statue in the Temple.

Where, then, are we to look for a solution ? The question must in any case be asked, whether this notion may not, after all, be somehow conceived as a belief prevailing amongst the later Jews. For it already occurs with great distinctness in the most divers places in the New Testament, and we know that such eschatological notions are of very slow growth.

Involuntarily our eyes are turned searchingly in the direction of the Dragon myth, in the hope of here finding light. It has already been seen that "the man of lawlessness" is nothing more than an incarnation of the old foe of God, the demoniacal Dragon. Now this Dragon storms the welkin, the heavenly abode of God. A distinct echo of this old representation occurs in Revelation xiii. 6 : " And he openeth his mouth in blasphemy against God, to blaspheme His name and His tabernacle, and them that dwell in heaven " (the angelic hosts). So also the Dragon storms (blasphemes) the abode of God in heaven, the Antichrist ejects God from His sanctuary on earth, seats himself in the Temple of Jerusalem.

Such may perhaps be the solution of this highly enigmatic fancy. If so, we can at least understand how such an idea could have arisen and spread amongst the Jews. It may not have spread far, but, as was only natural, dawning Christianity eagerly seized on and further developed it. Paul especially adopted the notion, and a place was even given in the inspired writings to a short Jewish apocalypse which dealt with the Antichrist times, the frightful desolation of the Temple. For it becomes clearer and clearer that Matthew xxiv. 15-31 represents such an apocalypse of the Antichrist. So also the author of Revelation, chap. xi., makes the beast coming out of the bottomless pit quite naturally appear in Jerusalem, although amongst the later Jews this incident was completely forgotten. By them the Antichrist after the first century was brought into direct relation with the Roman Cæsars and the Roman empire. But the Antichrist legend is older than the special hate harboured by the Jews against the Roman destroyer of their Jerusalem.

And thus this representation with its dualistic feature borrowed from the Dragon myth remains an

exotic growth on the soil of Judaism. The idea of
a demoniac power hostile to God and ejecting Him
from His Temple very soon became degraded to the
simple expectation of a false Messiah.

For Paul the Antichrist is this false Messiah, who
works by the power of Satan with signs and wonders,
and who, above all, is sent by God to the Jews because
they refuse belief in the true Messiah.   Attention has
already been called to an interesting parallel in
John v. 43 : " I am come in My Father's name, and
ye receive Me not : if another shall come in his own
name, him ye will receive." The other, who shall
come in his own name, is the Antichrist.   So is the
passage expounded by nearly all the Fathers, from
whom in this field of inquiry there is much to learn.*

Thus in our authorities the Antichrist is everywhere
described as a false Messiah appearing amongst the
Jews.   Hippolytus, chap. vi., already draws the comparison between the true and the false Messiah : " The
Saviour has gathered the scattered   sheep,   and   he

---

* Cf. Malvenda, *de Antichr.*, I. 599 ; Commentaries on John
v. 43, by Chrysostom, Cyril of Alexandria, Euthymius, Bede ;
Irenæus, V. 25, 3 ; Cyril's *Catechetical Lectures*, XII. 2 ; Aretas
on Revelation xi. 7 ; Ambrosius *on Psalm* xliii. 19 ; Prosper,
Dimidium Temp., 9 ; Rufinus, *Expositio Symboli*, 34 ; Jerome, *ad
Algasiam, in Abdiam*, V. 18 ; Adso, 1296 A ; Hugo Eterianus,
chap. xxiii.   Both of the last quoted collate a series of the
Fathers on the characters of the Antichrist ; cf. the Commentaries of Ambrosiaster, Theodoretus, Theophylactus, Œcumenius ; Jerome, *ad Algasiam*, 11 ; Theodoretus, *Hæret. Fabul.*,
V. 23 ; John of Damascus, *Altercatio Synagogæ et Ecclesiæ*,
chap. xiv., etc.

[Antichrist] also shall likewise gather the scattered people." [19] And Hippolytus, liii. 27, 30 : " For he shall summon all the people to himself from all the land of dispersion, making them as his own children, proclaiming that he will restore the land and reconstitute the kingdom." [20]

Characteristic details are even already found in Irenæus, who applies the contrast between the unrighteous judge and the widow (Mark xviii.) to the Antichrist (V. 25, 3) : " To whom the widow unmindful of God, that is, the earthly Jerusalem, appeals for vengeance on her adversary." [21] So also Victorinus in his Commentary (on chap. xiii.), although he associates the Antichrist with Nero : " Him therefore shall God having raised up send as a worthy king to the worthy [of him], and a Christ such as the Jews deserved." [22] In Commodian we read (927 *et seq.*) :

But thence marches the Conqueror into the land of Judah ;
. . . Many signs does he work that they may believe,
Because unto their seduction has the wicked one been sent.
. . . For us Nero has become the Antichrist, he for the Jews.[23]

Throughout the whole cycle of literature associated with the name of Ephrem the same thought prevails. Ephr. Syr. : " But in him shall the Jews exult, and girdle themselves to come unto him ; but he shall blaspheme, saying, I am the Father and the Son," etc.[24] Ephr. Gr., III. 238 A :

Honouring unto excess—the race of the Jews.
For they shall await—his coming.

238 C :

But more doth the people—the murderous people of the Jews
Honour and rejoice—in the kingdom of him.[25]

After this passage pseudo-Hippolytus (xxiv. 107,
12) gives a somewhat lengthy exposition.

Cyril, xv. 10 : " And through the name of Christ
he deceiveth the Jews expecting the Anointed." [26]

Pseudo-Ephrem : "Then shall the Jews give [him]
thanks that he hath restored the use of the former
testament."[27]

Pseudo-Johannine Apocalypse, 6, Cod. E. : " And
there shall be gathered the ignorant and unlettered,
saying one to another, Do we indeed find him
just ? " [28]

Greek Apocalypse of Daniel : " And he shall work
wonders and incredible things, and shall exalt the
Jews." [29]

Hence respecting the diffusion of the tradition
Jerome is able truthfully to say (on Daniel xi. 23) :
" But our [expositors] interpret both better and more
correctly, that at the end of the world these things
shall be done by the Antichrist, who is to spring of a
' small people,' that is, from the Jewish nation." [30]

Compare further the Ethiopic Apocalypse of Peter :
" In those days shall a king come, evil-minded and
evil-doer ; on that day shall Zabulon rise up and
Naphthali stretch his neck on high and Capernaum
exult, . . . because they shall take that man for
Christ."

Adso, 1296 A : " Then shall [all the Jews] flock unto

him, and thinking they receive Christ they shall
receive the devil." [31]

Hence the Antichrist will get circumcised, as in
Hippolytus, chap. v.: "In the circumcision came the
Saviour into the world, and he [Antichrist] will come
in like manner." [32]

Hence also Victorinus says of the Nero redivivus
(on Revelation xiii.) : "And because he shall bring
another name, so shall he also institute another life,
that so the Jews may accept him as Christ, for saith
Daniel that he shall not regard the desire of women,
although he was before most corrupt, nor regard any
god of [his] fathers, for the upholder alone of the law
shall be able to beguile the people of the circumcision." [33]

The same strange and mistaken translation of the
passage in Daniel (xi. 37) occurs in pseudo-Ephrem, 7:
"Then shall be fulfilled that utterance of the prophet
Daniel, 'And the God of his fathers shall he know
not, nor shall he know the desire of women.'" [34]   But
Lactantius also must have had under his eyes the
same relation as Victorinus, although with him the
old connection can no longer be recognised.   Thus
VII. 16 635, 15: "New counsels in his breast
shall he harbour, that . . . at last by change of name
and removal of the seat of empire there may ensue
disorder and perturbation amongst mankind." [35]

With these may further be compared the following
passages :

Adso, 1293 C : "And he shall circumcise himself, and
lie that he is the Son of God Almighty "; and else-

where (1296 A): " Coming to Jerusalem he shall be circumcised, saying to the Jews, I am the Christ promised unto you, who have come for your weal that I may gather and defend you that are scattered." [36]

Haymo, on 2 Thessalonians ii.: " And when he shall come to Jerusalem he will circumcise himself, saying to the Jews, I am the Christ promised to you." [37]

Elsewhere the rite of circumcision is enforced, as in Victorinus : " Nor is he lastly to call back the saints to the worship of idols, but to observe the circumcision ; and should he be able to seduce any, them he will in the end compel to call him Christ." [38]

A noteworthy parallel drawn from the Simon Magus legend occurs in the *Martyrdom of SS. Peter and Paul* : " Nero asked, Was Simon then circumcised ? Peter answered, [Surely], for otherwise he could not have beguiled the souls, except by explaining that he was a Jew, and showing that he taught the law of God." [39]

This notion of the Antichrist appearing as the false Messiah is further developed in the series of Ephremite writings. Ephr. Gr., II. 137 :

> In the form of him—shall come the all-polluted
> As a false wily thief—to beguile all beings,
> Humble and gentle—hating the speech of the unjust,
> Overturning the idols—honouring piety,
> A good lover of the poor—exceeding fair,
> Altogether well disposed—pleasant towards all.[40]

An exact parallel occurs in pseudo-Hippolytus, xxiii. 106, 18 ; while in pseudo-Ephrem, chap. vi., we read of "that impious corrupter more of souls than of bodies, that subtle dragon [who] in his youth seems to move about under the form of justice before he assumes empire." [41]

Pseudo-Johannine Apocalypse, 6, Cod. E : " And he begins by judging with mildness and much charity and consideration for sinners, and as he says makes allowance for sin." [42]

Cyril, xv. 10 : " At first indeed he simulates discretion and humanity, as a wise and shrewd person [might exercise] clemency." [43]

John of Damascus : " And at the beginning of his reign he simulates benevolence." [44]

With all this is associated the notion that the Antichrist was expected to come from the tribe of Dan. This is an indication that the apocalyptic tradition in question originated under the influence of the Jewish hagadic (homiletic) interpretation. For the belief itself arose out of the Rabbinical exposition of such passages as Deuteronomy xxxiii. 22, Genesis xlix. 17, and Jeremiah viii. 16, and is everywhere in patristic literature supported by reference to these passages.*

* Cf. Malvenda, I. 140 ; Caspari, 217, Anmerkung 22. This idea is already found in Irenæus, V. 30, 2 (on Jeremiah viii. 16); Hippolytus, chaps. xiv., xv., and after him pseudo-Hippolytus, chaps. xviii., xix. ; Ambrosius, *de Benedict. Patriarcharum*, 7 (on Psalm xl.) ; Eucherius, *on Genesis*, III., p. 188 ; Austin, *in Josuam, Quæstio* XXII. ; Jacob of Edessa (in Ephrem, I. 192 *et seq.*) ; pseudo-Ephrem, chap. vi. ; Theodoretus, *on Genesis, Quæst.* CX. ;

This notion is probably of long standing. At least we have in Irenæus, V. 30, 2 : " And for this reason this tribe [Dan] is not numbered in Revelation amongst those that are saved." [45] It seems to me that this interpretation, especially as it is now a mere link in the chain of a much wider connection, is the only one possessing a certain degree of probability. If so, the idea must have already been known to the author of Revelation, chap. vii.

With this is connected the more definite assumption of later authorities that the Antichrist would come from Babylon, where the tribe of Dan was supposed to dwell. Here we seem to feel the later influence of Jerome, who writes (on Daniel xi. 37) : " But our [expositors] interpret in the above sense everything concerning the Antichrist, who is to be born of the Jewish people and to come from Babylon." [46]

The above-suggested connection is seen most distinctly in Andreas' comment on Revelation xvi. 12 : " It is probable also that the Antichrist shall come from the eastern parts of the land of Persia, where is the tribe of Dan of the Hebrew race." [47]

We may now trace farther afield this idea of the Antichrist coming from the East, although not yet in connection with the notion of his origin in the tribe of Dan.

Prosper Aquitanicus, *Dimid. Temp.*, 9 ; Gregory, *Moralia*, XXXI. 24 ; pseudo-Methodius ; Anastasius Sinaita, in *Hexæmeron*, Lib. X., 1018 B ; Adso, 1292 B ; Bede's Sibyl ; Hugo Eterianus ; Primasius and Ambros. Ansbertus, Commentaries (on Revelation xi. 7).

Lactantius, VII. 17 : " Another king shall arise in the East." [48]

Still more weighty is the passage in Commodian, 932 : " A man [coming] from the Persian land proclaims himself immortal." [49]

On the other hand, we have in pseudo-Methodius a different tradition : " He is begotten in Choraza [Chorasmia ?], because amongst them hath the Lord tarried, and in Bethsaida (?), because there he was nourished." [50] Both Adso (1293 B) and the *Elucidarium* betray the influence of this tradition in so far as to hold that the Antichrist grows up in the said regions. The origin of the fancy is now clear.

It is significant, however, that the notion of the Antichrist springing from the tribe of Dan is unknown to Ephrem and the sources directly dependent on him. To me this seems another proof of the great antiquity of the views regarding the Antichrist which are here in question.

Nevertheless the opinion that the Antichrist is to come from Dan occurs also in the Testament of the Twelve Patriarchs (Dan, chap. vi.), a document probably of Jewish origin. Unfortunately the text is here so corrupt that no definite conclusions can be arrived at. Beliar, however, is described as the Antichrist in the prediction (chap. v.) which is made touching the children of Dan : " And unto you shall the salvation of the Lord arise from the tribe of Judah and of Levi ; and he shall make war against Beliar." [51]

Now this Beliar seems to stand in a definite relation to the children of Dan : " For I knew in [from] the

Book of Enoch the Just that your ruler is Satan, and that all the spirits of fornication and of arrogance shall be subservient to Levi, in order to lie in wait (?) for the children of Levi, to make them sin before the Lord." [52]   As it stands the passage is meaningless, for what sense can there be in their being subservient or obedient to Levi, in order to lie in wait for his children ? In Codex R, however, " Levi " is missing ; and if it be struck out, then " shall be obedient " remains without its object.   But the error would seem to lie in this last expression, for which a Latin manuscript version has " sese applicabit "—that is, all the evil spirits " will plot," etc.   But possibly we should read ὑποδύσονται— that is, all the evil spirits shall strive to ensnare the children of Levi.   Thus we arrive at the suggested idea of the sons of Dan in league with Beliar and his angels against Levi.   In what follows, however, this idea again disappears, for here emphasis is laid above all on the sinfulness of the children of Levi and of Judah. It is urgently to be desired that the whole apparatus of the text of this work be made available for study.

Meanwhile the important fact remains that in this very Testament of Dan, where we had conjectured such an incident, allusion is made to a league between Satan and the children of Dan.   Here, however, there is yet no question of the Antichrist's birth in the tribe of Dan.   In the Testament of Dan Beliar is not yet even a human being, but is conceived as an evil demon— the demon, however, who in the last days is to revolt against God.

CHAPTER XII.*

IN our authorities prominence is given above all to
signs and wonders in heaven. But respecting
these, as well as all other manifestations, it is everywhere insisted upon that the works wrought by the
Antichrist are only lying and magical portents. Thus
Sibyl III. 64 :

And the mountain-tops he shall make stand still, and the ocean
And the great flaming sun and the bright moon.[1]

Ascensio Jesaiæ, IV. 5 : " And at his word the sun
shall rise at night, and the moon also he shall cause
to appear at the sixth hour " (after dawn).[2]

Here it again becomes clear that 4 Ezra v. 1 *et seq.*
is influenced by the Antichrist legend. Thus v. 4 :
" And suddenly shall the sun shine again at night, and
the moon during the day." [3] With this is also connected Revelation, chap. xiii. 13, as will be seen later.
To the same distinctly Jewish cycle of traditions
is also to be referred Lactantius, VII. 17, 639, 4 :

---

* For Notes [1] to [35] of this chapter, see Appendix, p. 281.

" He shall bid fire fall from heaven, and the sun stand still on its course "[4] (an echo of Revelation).

Apocalypse of Zephaniah, 124 : " To the sun he shall say, Fall, and he falleth. He shall say, Light, and he lighteth. To the moon he shall say, Be as blood, and so shall it be. From the sky he shall make it vanish."

Ephr. Syr., 9 : " Then shall he begin to show lying signs in heaven and on earth, in the sea and on the dry land ; rain shall he call upon, and it shall come down."[5]

Pseudo-Methodius, 93 B : " The sun shall he turn to darkness, and the moon to blood."[6]

Ethiopic Apocalypse of Peter : " The sun shall he cause to rise in the West, and the moon towards Ælam."

Pseudo-Hippolytus, xxvi. 108, 28 : " The day he shall make dark, and the night day ; the sun he shall turn aside whither he willeth, and before the spectators shall he show all the elements of the earth and of the sea absolutely obedient to the power of his display."[7]

Moreover, special prominence is given to his miraculous cures ; but here again all his wonders are emphatically declared to be mere shams.

Thus Sibyl III. 66 *et seq.* :

And the dead he shall raise, and many wonders work
For man ; but for him fruitless they shall be
And deceptive, and surely many mortals he shall beguile.[8]

Pseudo-Hippolytus, xxiii. 106, 14 : " And after all these things he shall signs perform, . . . but not real, but in deceit, that he may beguile those impious as himself." 24 : " The leprous cleansing, the palsied lifting up, driving out demons, raising the dead." [9]

Apocalypse of Zephaniah, 125 : " The halt he shall cause to walk, the deaf to hear, the dumb to speak, the blind to see ; the leprous he shall cleanse, the sick shall he heal, and the spirits drive from the possessed."

Ephr. Syr. : " He shall cry out to the leprous, and they shall be made clean ; to the blind, and they shall see the light : he shall call the deaf, and they shall hear ; the dumb, and they shall speak." [10]

Pseudo-Methodius, 99 : " The blind shall see, the halt shall walk, the demons shall be healed, . . . and in his false signs and fanciful portents." [11]

Andreas, lvi. 27 : " By whom [that is, the devil] he shall seem to raise the dead, to perform signs for those of distorted mental vision." [12]

The Armenian Apocalypse of Daniel, 239, 15 : " Of stones making bread, causing the blind to see, the maimed to walk."

Elucidarium : " For he shall work such stupendous marvels, as to bid fire come down from heaven . . . and the dead arise." [13]

But in this stereotyped description, presumably based on Matthew xi. 2 *et seq.*, and consequently of later introduction, it is often expressly remarked that the Antichrist fails to quicken the dead. Thus in Apocalypse of Zephaniah, 125 : " He shall do the things that Christ shall do, all but the awakening of the dead. Therein shall ye know that he is the son of lawlessness, that he hath no power over the soul."

Eph. Syr., 9 : " For indeed many signs shall he do that our Lord hath done in the world ; but the departed he shall not raise because he hath no power over spirits." [14]

Diemer, *Deutsche Gedichte* (" German Poems ") of the eleventh and twelfth centuries, 280 :

> But from the signs that he shall make
> No good shall anybody take,
> Nor shall he any dead awake. [15]

Quæstiones ad Antiochum Ducem, 109 : " Some say that after working all the other wonders the Antichrist could not raise a dead man." [16]

The tradition runs somewhat differently in Cyril, xv. 14 : " For the father of deceit shall simulate the works of deceit, that the multitude may think it sees the dead raised that is not raised." [17]

Adso, 1293 D : " The dead forsooth [are] to be resuscitated in the sight of men, . . . [but they are lies and beside the truth] " ; [18] with which compare Haymo on 2 Thessalonians ii.

Elucidarium : " He shall raise the dead, not verily, but the devil shall enter some [dead man's] body . . . and speak in him, that he may seem alive." [19]

In the late Jewish History of Daniel it is also stated emphatically that the Antichrist succeeds in working all the wonders demanded of him, but fails to quicken the dead. In Eph. Syr., chap. xi., say Elias and Enoch to the Antichrist : " If thou art God, call on the departed, and they shall arise ; for it is written in the books of the prophets and also by the apostles, that, when He shall appear, Christ shall raise the dead from their graves." [20]

But here again quite a special tradition is preserved in Greek Ephrem, III. 138 E :

Magnifying his miracles—performing his portents,
Deceiver and not in truth—manifesting these things.
In such fashion—the tyrant removeth
The mountains, and simulates (?)—falsely and not truly
While the multitude stands by—many nations and peoples
Applauding him—for his illusions. [21]

There follows a lengthy account of how the Antichrist removes mountains by fraud and only in appearance. Then we read (139 C) :

Again this same dragon—stretches out his hands
And gathers the multitude—of reptiles and birds;
And likewise he moves over—the surface of the deep,
And as on dry ground—he walks thereon.
But he simulates all these things. [22]

A perfect parallel to the first half of these details occurs in pseudo-Hippolytus, xxvi. 108, 19 *et seq.* With them may also be compared the pseudo-Johannine Apocalypse, chap. vii., Cod. E : " The mountains and hills he shall move aside, and shall beckon with his polluted hands : Come hither to me all [of you]; and by illusions and deception they assemble in the same place." [23]

A noteworthy parallel is found in the Apocalypse of Zephaniah, 125 : " He shall walk on the sea and on the rivers as on dry ground."

It is noteworthy that very similar traits are found in the Simon Magus legend and its fabulous descriptions. In the *Acts of Peter with Simon,* xxviii. *et seq.,* we have, for instance, a long account of how Simon Magus is able so reanimate a dead body, but only in appearance, and the charm vanishes as soon as he withdraws from the corpse, which is then really resuscitated by Peter. In the various sources the whole contest between Peter and Simon culminates in this incident of Simon's failure and of Peter's success in raising the dead. In the *Recognitiones,* III. 47, Simon's wonders are thus related : " I have flown through the air ; mingling with the fire, I have been made one body with it ; I have caused statues to be moved ; I have reanimated the extinct ; I have made stones to bread ; I have flown from mountain to mountain ; I have crossed over upheld by angels' hands ; I have alighted on the ground." [24]

Similarly the Homily ii. 32 : " Statues he causes to walk, and rolling in the fire is not burnt ; at times also he flies, and of stones makes loaves ; he becomes a snake, is changed to a goat ; puts on two faces." 33 : " Working wonders to astonish and deceive, not healing works unto conversion and salvation." [25]

To such parallels the patristic writers were often attracted. In his Commentary, chap. xxxvii. 58, 39 *et seq.,* Andreas points out how in the presence of Peter Simon had almost raised a dead body, and infers that in like manner the precursor of the Antichrist (Revelation xiii. 11 *et seq.*) will also perform his signs and wonders. He also alludes, in connection with Revelation xiii. 3, to a wonderful resuscitation to be effected by Antichrist, and again (lvi. 13) Andreas calls attention to the precedent of Simon Magus.

So Eterianus, *de Regressu Animarum* (" On Apparitions "), 23 : " For by his magic art and illusions he will beguile men, as is supposed to have been done by Simon Magus, who seemed to do what he did not." [26]

From Revelation xiii. 3 it was later inferred that in order to place himself completely on a level with Christ, the Antichrist will suffer death, and then raise himself from the dead. I find the earliest allusion in Primasius, and then in Gregory, *Epistle*, xiii. 1.*

Here Adso again calls attention to the parallel with Simon Magus : " By his magic art and deception he will deceive men, as Simon Magus deceived the man who, thinking to kill him, kills a ram instead." [27] Here we see how both legends are merged in one, so that it becomes difficult to say to which belongs the priority.

There is even a much earlier and interesting passage, which preserves the original representation from which the two cycles of legends became intermingled.

In Homily ii. 17 Peter says : " Thus truly, as the true prophet hath told us, the false gospel must first come through the fraud of some one [that is, Simon], and then, after the destruction of the holy place, the true evangel is to be secretly sent, . . . and thereafter towards the end again must the Antichrist first come,

* From Primasius it is borrowed by Bede, pseudo-Ambrosius, Ansbertus, Haymo ; and it is also known to S. Hildegard cf. Malvenda, II. 125 *et seq.*).

and then the very Christ our Saviour shall appear, and after that, the eternal light having risen, all the deeds of darkness shall vanish." *

It will here be worth while to sum up the results so far established. In the collective Christian tradition the Antichrist rule is not the Roman empire, which on the contrary is conceived as the "letter," the obstacle that stands in the way, and this despite Revelation and the early history of Christianity. The Antichrist is the false Messiah appearing in the midst of the Jews in Jerusalem, working signs and wonders through the power of Satan, and seating himself in the Temple of God. As ruler of the Jews he is joyfully greeted by them. He is no peaceful monarch, no political personality, but a purely eschatological figure in every sense of the word.

Thus is the concept already presented to us in the New Testament. According to Paul the "man of lawlessness" is the false Messiah, who is sent to the Jews to punish them for having rejected the true Messiah. So also John v. 43, while the clause interpolated in Matthew xxiv. is drawn from the same

---

* Cf. *Rec.*, II. 60. Here Simon's wonders are compared with those which the evil one will have power to work in the last days. Simon performs merely useless miracles, whereas at the end of the world cures and such-like (resuscitations are not mentioned) will be effected by the powers of evil. Thus here also we have the Antichrist tradition standing in the background of the Simon Magus legend. In this connection it may further be mentioned that what we are told of Simon's miraculous birth (*Rec.*, II. 14) finds an echo in the Antichrist saga.

apocalyptic tradition. The writer who imagined chap. xi. of Revelation could have had no difficulty in making the beast coming out of the bottomless pit appear in Jerusalem.

When we more diligently examine the Revelation of S. John, where traces may to some extent still be met of the same eschatological tradition, attention is above all claimed by chap. xiii. 11 *et seq*. The idea of "the beast coming up out of the ground" is based originally on that of the Antichrist. He represents no hostile, foreign political power, but comes "like a lamb," and in the mind of the apocalyptic writer he is the false prophet not greatly to be distinguished from the false Messiah. He speaks "as a dragon"—here again another survival— an evidence that the figure of the Antichrist grew out of the Dragon myth. He works signs and wonders, which show a certain resemblance with those of the Antichrist as brought together just before. The specially characteristic trait of the "mark in their right hand, or in their foreheads," and the buying and selling in virtue of that mark, will find their explanation farther on in the Antichrist legend.

This second beast comes out of the ground and appears in the land of Palestine,* whereas the first beast, the Roman empire or one of its Cæsars, naturally rises out of the sea, comes over the sea.

* This explanation, I think, suits better than that proposed by Gunkel, who traces both beasts in chap. viii. back to the old myth of two primeval monsters dominating the sea and the dry land.

The apocalyptic writer, for whom the universal sway of Rome has become the manifestation of the Antichrist, and who expected the Antichrist in the Nero redivivus, could make nothing better of the old unpolitical and purely eschatological figure of the Antichrist than degrade him to the position of a servant of the first beast. But in the process the writer has naturally ascribed to the earlier figure all those characters in virtue of which the second beast is brought into association with the first.*

We now also clearly see how Hippolytus, despite his extremely confused exposition, was able to hold that the second beast is the Antichrist, who appears after the fall of the first—that is, of the Roman empire. He was acquainted with the old legend, and in the second half of chap. xiii. still distinctly recognised the original figure of the Antichrist.

Here we are in the presence of a decisive introspective view of the essence and growth of the whole myth in which we are interested. The Antichrist legend was evolved out of the old Dragon myth about the time of the New Testament writings. This legend thus again acquires political significance with reference to the Roman empire and the Nero redivivus. For reckless criticism alone will venture to deny that the picture of the Nero redivivus stands in the foreground of Revelation, chaps. xiii. and xvii. This picture is, in fact, so inextricably interwoven with the

* Such are Rev. xiii. 12 ; 14 ; last clause of 15 (the first clause is drawn from the old saga) ; last clause of 17 ; 18.

whole representation that it seems to me impossible to disentangle it from all the details.

Especially in Jewish circles has this political application of the Antichrist legend retained all its freshness. It dominates the Sibylline literature precisely in those parts which are directly due to Jewish influence. Thanks to the postponement of Nero's return for over a generation, the simple expectation of his reappearance with the Parthians became transformed to the fantastic belief in a Nero redivivus. Thus it came about that the elements of the old Dragon myth became incorporated in the Neronic saga, so marvellous is the tendency of such currents of legendary matter to merge in a common stream. In this form we already meet the Neronic saga in Revelation xiii. and xvii., but still more distinctly in the Sybilline documents. Here Nero has become a python, a wrath-breathing dragon, a weird ghost-like demoniac being wafted through the air by the Fates. Nay, to me it seems not quite impossible that, as Gunkel holds, the enigmatic expression in Revelation xvii. 8 originally referred to the old Serpent, who, already once overthrown in his struggle with God, shall in the last days again revolt against God and His heavenly kingdom. Here we read of " the beast that was, and is not, and yet is "—that is, will again " ascend out of the bottomless pit, and go into perdition." Thus the writer would seem to have applied to Nero this dark passage, which presumably was scarcely any longer intelligible to himself. In the later Greek Apocalypse of Daniel

we are even told that the slumbering Serpent shall
again awake.

Amongst the Jews this turning of the saga against
the Roman empire was preserved, completely effacing
its original form. The hatred cherished against Edom
under the sway of Sammael survived till the seventh
and eighth centuries, when the old Antichrist legend
again came to the surface. But even so their un-
dying hatred of Christian, as before of Pagan, Rome
is betrayed in the very name of Armillus (Romulus)
associated with the revived legend. Armillus, however, is no Roman Cæsar, but a ruler destined to
come after the domination of the godly empire
(Byzantium).

Amongst the early Christians, thanks no doubt
partly to their detestation of the Jews, the feeling
of hostility against Rome, as expressed in Revelation,
very soon disappeared, as is already to be seen in
Tertullian. The Antichrist comes from the midst
of the Jews, and is above all a satanic pseudo-
Messianic figure—such is the universal belief. Nevertheless this old conception displays such tenacity
and persistence that a doubling of the Antichrist
figure is the result, at least in a few writers amongst
whom the application of the legend to the Roman
empire survives under the influence of the Jewish
Sybilline literature. In this connection Lactantius,
Commodian, and S. Martin of Tours come under
consideration. By all three the immediate precursor
of the Antichrist (who appears with the fall of the
Roman empire) is more or less distinctly identified

with the Nero redivivus, whereas the second appearance, that is, the Antichrist proper, by whom Nero is overcome and killed, bears the familiar characters of the true Antichrist. And although he is not here represented as coming from the Jews, his power is nevertheless set up in Jerusalem, he is welcomed by the Jews as the Messiah, he works signs and wonders, and so on. Here we have a strange spectacle, the saga in course of time assuming a double and even a threefold aspect. But these separate aspects of the same figure become once more merged in one. The very remark above made in connection with Lactantius, Commodian, and S. Martin of Tours confirms in a striking manner the explanation of the two beasts given in our comments on Revelation xiii. Here, as there, we have a blending of the two streams of tradition ; only the old figure of the Antichrist, which in Revelation is made subordinate to its own shadow, to its political interpretation, is by those writers made predominant.

Thus we also understand how the old and most distinct reference in Revelation to the Nero redivivus so soon disappears from the tradition of the patristic writers. Victorinus, with whom alone it holds its ground, has, however, left us a surprising jumble of the Jewish pseudo-Messiah and Nero redivivus, in which the latter actually appears as the Jewish Messiah. But Revelation is mainly interpreted in the light of the earlier eschatological traditions. And on the whole the further evolution of these traditions during the ensuing centuries has taken place under the influence, not of the Johannine Apocalypse, but of those earlier reminiscences.

A close study of the effect of Revelation on the Fathers, as seen in their expositions, almost produces the impression that these writers possessed no living eschatological imagery, and that such imagery lay dormant till reawakened in mediæval times.

Thus the saga with which we are here occupied may be likened to the figure of Proteus ever shifting its form, and in its shifting phases even doubling itself. Revelation xii. and xiii. may be taken as its living material image. In xii. we have the old Dragon myth, in xiii. 11-18 the Antichrist legend, in xiii. 1-10 its political application. The three shifting forms of the legend are the three juxtaposed figures of the Dragon, the Beast, and the False Prophet that have been merged in one great eschatological picture !

The Antichrist has in his service a host of devoted ministers. Hippolytus is already able to tell us (chap. vi.) that "the Lord sent His apostles unto all nations, and he [Antichrist] shall likewise send his false apostles." [28] In Adso also we read (1293 C): "Thereafter shall he send his messengers and preachers to the whole world." [29] From these sources the notion found its way into the miracle play of the Antichrist (W. Meyer, 27).

Even more interesting parallels occur, as in the opening of the Homily in Greek Ephrem :

For the shameless one—grasping authority
Sends his demons—unto all the ends of the earth,
To announce unto all—that a great king
Hath appeared in glory—Come hither and behold.[30]

So also in Ephr. Syr., 9 : " The lightnings shall be
his ministers and signify his advent ; the demons shall
constitute his forces, and the princes of the demons
shall be his disciples ; to far-distant lands shall he
send the captains of his bands, who shall impart virtue
and healing." [31]   Philip the Solitary (816 B) : " Verily
the demons shall he send unto the whole world to
preach and commend him, saying, The great king has
risen in Jerusalem. . . . Come ye all unto him." [32]   With
the variants also Adso is familiar (1293 B) : " And the
evil spirits shall be his captains and associates ever
and his counts." [33]   A clear retrospective light is shed
by these passages on Irenæus, V. 28, 2 : " Nor is it to
be wondered at that, the demons and apostate spirits
being his ministers, he shall through them work signs
by which to beguile the dwellers on earth." [34]

Again behind the figure of the Antichrist with his
false apostles there stands the still more powerful
embodiment of a superhuman evil spirit hostile to
God, whose messengers are demons and wicked genii.
And thus the legend again stretches back to New
Testament times, and explains Revelation xvi. 13 :
" And I saw three unclean spirits like frogs *come* out
of the mouth of the dragon. . . . For they are the
spirits of devils, working miracles, *which* go forth unto
the kings of the earth and of the whole world, to

gather them to the battle." With this is to be compared the exposition of Ambrosiaster : " The three unclean spirits signify the disciples of Antichrist, who are to preach him throughout the whole world, who, although they are to be men, they are called unclean spirits and spirits of devils, because demons shall dwell in them and shall speak through their mouths." [35]

CHAPTER XIII.*

ANTICHRIST RULER OF THE WORLD—DROUGHT AND FAMINE
—THE MARK OF ANTICHRIST.

FROM the foregoing passages we see that the Antichrist is not only to seduce the Jews, but also to gather round him the peoples from all the regions of the earth. This is fully described in Ephr. Gr., II. 138 B :

> To conciliate all—he plots craftily
> That he may be loved—soon by the peoples;
> Neither gifts shall he accept—nor speak in anger,
> He shows himself not sullen—but ever cheerful.
> And in all these—well-planned schemes
> He beguileth the world—so long as he shall rule.
> For when the many peoples and nations—shall behold
> Such great virtues—fair deeds and powers,
> All of one mind—shall become
> And with great joy—shall crown (?) him,
> Saying one to another—Surely there is not found
> Such [another] man—so good and just.[1]

An almost literal parallel occurs in pseudo-Hippolytus, chaps. xxiii. and xxiv.; while we read in

---

* For Notes [1] to [25] of this chapter, see Appendix, p. 285.

pseudo-Ephrem : " For towards all shall he be craftily
complaisant, refusing bribes, preferring no one,
pleasant to all, calm in all things, neither seeking
friendly gifts, [but] making show of courtesy towards his neighbours, so that all may bless him,
saying, This is a just man." Chap. vii. : " Then shall
all flock to him in Jerusalem from all quarters." [2]

In Hippolytus, lvi. 28, 24, we already read : " He
therefore having everywhere gathered the people that
had become disobedient," etc. [3]   And in imitation of
Jeremiah xvii. 11* he compares the Antichrist to the
partridge which with crafty voice entices the young
brood that belongs not to her. So in pseudo-Ephrem,
5 : " Who like the partridge gathers to herself the
offspring of confusion, . . . and calleth whom he hath
not begotten." [4]

Ephr. Syr., 10 : " The peoples shall be gathered,
and they shall come that they may see God, and the
crowds of the peoples shall cleave to him, and all
shall deny their own God and invite their fellows to
praise the son of perdition, and one on another they
shall fall and with swords each other destroy."   A
similar notion is presupposed (though here not actually
expressed) in the Apocalypse of Zephaniah. See the
descriptions on p. 128.

Still more important are the following passages,
going back, as they do, to a far older tradition.

---

* So in the Vulgate, " Perdix fovit quæ non peperit " ; *i.e.*,
" The partridge cherisheth the chicks she has not hatched,"
having enticed them, etc. The passage in the English Author-
ised Version makes nonsense.

Hippolytus, xv. 8, 8 : " But saith another prophet also : He shall gather all his power from the rising of the sun to the setting thereof ; whom he hath called and whom he hath not called, they shall go with him. He shall make white the sea with the sails of his ships, and make the plain black with the shields of his heavy-armed, and whoso shall stand up against him in war shall perish by the sword." [5]

Commodian, 891 *et seq.* :

> Again shall arise unto this Nero's destruction
> A king from the East leading four nations thence,
> And summon to himself very many peoples to the city,
> And they shall bring aid, though he be most powerful ;
> And the sea he shall fill with ships many a thousand.
> And whoso shall oppose him shall be slain with the sword.[6]

It has already been pointed out that both of these passages must be referred back to a common source, which is already quoted by Hippolytus as a " prophet." Such a postulated source certainly shows a strong kinship with Daniel, although we cannot yet say that it really derives from him. The conjecture might rather be hazarded that Daniel himself was already drawing on an earlier apocalyptic tradition at the end of chap. xi., where he foretells the fate of Antiochus in language that has hitherto defied all historical explanation.

With the above-quoted passages may be compared 4 Ezra xiii. 5 : "And thereafter I saw, and lo ! there was gathered a multitude of people, of whom there was no number, from the four winds of heaven, that they might war down the man who had come up from the sea." [7]

No explanation has hitherto been offered of the statement in Revelation xi. 9 that "they of the people and kindreds and tongues and nations" of the whole world shall assemble in the vicinity of Jerusalem and take part in the scene there taking place. Such language cannot very well be applied to the Roman legions, who could feel little interest in the final overthrow of the two witnesses by the Antichrist. Hence the reference was originally rather to those multitudes who had been drawn together from all lands and had assembled round the Antichrist. But the greatest confusion has been introduced in the picture by the writer of Revelation xi., who connected the old Antichrist legend with a prediction about the capture of Jerusalem by the Roman army at that time marching on the city (xi. 1, 2).

Thus was the passage xi. 7 still understood by Andreas, who says of the assembled peoples (46, 56) that "they of the Jews and of the Gentiles [were] once prepossessed by the false portents of the Antichrist, having indelibly inscribed on their hearts the abominable name of him." [8]

Elsewhere also Revelation betrays a knowledge of this feature of the tradition, an echo of which is again found in the gathering of the kings and peoples at Armageddon.

Now with this gathering of the peoples about the Antichrist is associated the expectation of the coming of the nations of Gog and Magog. Their appearance is usually made to precede that of the Antichrist, as in Commodian, 809, where they are identified with the Goths, who are represented as coming before the appearance of the first Antichrist.* In nearly all the Jewish apocalypses of the Antichrist Gog and Magog are also the forerunners of Armillus, and it is further stated that the Messiah ben Joseph is to perish before their coming, as has been more fully described farther back.

As the appearance of Gog and Magog is so intimately associated with the Antichrist in all traditions, it may also be conjectured that from these sources was taken Revelation xx. 7-10, where distinctly Jewish characters are betrayed. Only here the Antichrist is brought into direct relation with Gog and Magog, and the whole scene made to come after the millennium.

A long drought together with a terrible famine is with great unanimity described as the chief plague that is to prevail in the Antichrist period.

In the foreground here again stands the series of documents grouped around the same of S. Ephrem. Thus Ephr. Gr., I. :

> The sea is stirred up—[and ?] the land parched ;
> The skies rain not—plants pine away. [9]

* To the Goths reference is also made by Ambrosius in *de Fide ad Gratianum,* ii. 16, with which cf. Jerome, *Proœmium in Ezech.,* xi. (Malvenda, I. 555). See also Ephr. Syr., 6, where the reference is, not to the Goths, but to the Huns ; pseudo-Ephrem, 4 ; Andreas, who also applies Revelation xx. 8 to the Huns ; pseudo-Methodius ; Adso, 1296 ; Bede's Sibyl and Usinger (?) ; Ezra, Syr. Apoc., 12.

139 F : *

> Then the skies no longer rain, the earth
> No longer beareth fruit,
> The springs run out,
> [The] rivers dry up,
> Herbs no longer sprout,
> Grass no longer grows,
> Trees wither from [their roots]
> And no longer put forth fruits,
> The fishes of the sea
> And the monsters therein
> Die out, and thus
> [They say] a fetid stench
> Emits [the] sea
> With fearful roar, that
> Men shall fail and perish
> Through terror. [10]

Then follows in another measure :

And then in dread shall moan and groan—all life alike,
When all shall see—the pitiless distress
That compasseth them—by night and eke by day
And nowhere find—the food wherewith to fill themselves.[11]

Exact parallels occur in pseudo-Hippolytus, xxvii.
109, 9 *et seq.*, 19 *et seq.*

* The edition based on two Greek codices (Vatican, 438 and
562) gives this passage awkwardly appended to the continuous
text, which concludes with 139 D. Here the Latin version
shows the proper connection. In the Greek the interruption
139 D to E 1 γινώσκουσιν should be struck out, being merely a
duplicate of what goes before. Nor does the longer ending
occur in the Munich MSS. collated by W. Meyer. But that is

Pseudo-Ephrem, 8 : " The sky shall withhold its dew, for no rain shall fall on earth, . . . for all the rivers shall dry up and the fountains, . . . the torrents shall run out in their beds because of the intolerable heats, . . . and infants shall waste away at their mothers' breasts, and wives on the knees of their husbands, having no food to eat, . . . for in those days there shall be dearth of bread and water." [12]

Pseudo-Johannine Apocalypse, 6, Cod. E. : " God seeing the unrighteousness of him sendeth from heaven his angel Bauriel, saying, Come away, blow the trump, [they shall ?] control the rain ; and the earth shall be made arid, and the herbage shall languish ; and he shall make the sky brazen, that it yield no moisture to the ground, and hide away the clouds in the bowels of the earth, and curb the horn of the winds, that no wind be gathered on the face of all the land." [13]

Apocalypse of Zephaniah, 128 : " In those days shall the earth fall into unrest, the birds shall fall dead on the ground, the land grow arid, the waters of the sea dry up."

Ephr. Syr., 12 : " The sea shall roar and become dry, and the fishes shall die therein." [14] But here these things are deferred to the day of judgment.

Then we have a much earlier parallel from 4 Ezra

no argument against its authenticity, which is proved to evidence by the parallels following farther on from the Ephremite group of writings. Unfortunately the text of the codices on which the edition is based is so corrupt that I must give up the attempt to restore the rhythmic measure throughout. The Latin version shows great differences.

v. 6, where are enumerated all the signs of the Antichrist times : " The sea of Sodom [the Dead Sea] shall cast up its fishes, and at night utter a voice which many understand not, but all shall hear the voice of it." [15]

Compare also Lactantius, VII. 15, 635, 23 : " For the air shall be infected and become corrupt and pestilent, now by rains, now by baneful drought ; . . . nor shall the earth yield fruits for man, . . . the springs also with the rivers shall become dry ; wherefore shall four-footed creatures fail on the land, and fowls in the air, and fishes in the deep." [16]

On Revelation vi. 5 Victorinus remarks (1252 E) : " But in strictness the saying extends to the times of the Antichrist, since there is to be a great hunger, of which all shall suffer." [17]

Ambrosius on Luke x. 18 : " Then [shall come] the false prophets, then famine, . . . and then . . . thou shalt behold the dryness of the earth, . . . [and] at last the just man in the wilderness and the impious in power." [18]

Armenian Apocalypse of Daniel, 239, 21 : " There shall be a great stress of hunger ; from heaven shall no rain fall, nor the earth yield any green thing."

Greek Apocalypse of Daniel, 103 : " And the waters shall be dried up, and no rain be given to the earth." [19]

Ethiopic Apocalypse of Peter : " In that day shall the Lord God stem the rain from heaven, and the earth shall be without dew or fog ; . . . nor shall the springs yield any welling water, and the sea shall be dried up."

Book of Clement, 82, 30 : " And all his stores shall
be wasted by many, and there shall be a great scarcity
of fruits, and a fierce gale shall prevail." [20]

Another variant, however, is able to tell us that
shortly before the Antichrist's time there is to be an
unusual yield of crops.* This recalls vividly the well-
known statement handed down by Papias, as uttered
by the Lord : " Then the ear of wheat shall yield half
a *choinix* [about three-quarters of a pint], and the
bend of the vine-twig a thousand bunches of grapes,
and the bunch half a jar of wine." [21] Can these
" words of the Lord " have possibly formed part of
the original Antichrist legend ?

A parallel to the above-mentioned tradition is
obviously presented by Revelation xi., and it will be
seen farther on that the tradition here under consideration is more original than that of Revelation xi.

Meanwhile it may here be remarked that the whole
body of tradition in question treats this plague impending on the world quite apart from the appearance
of the two witnesses, to whom in Revelation the
power is given (xi. 6) to ordain this very plague. As
will be seen, the appearance of the two witnesses
acquires in our tradition quite a different significance.

In any case an interesting parallel may here be
quoted from the Bahman Yast, II. 48 : " And a dark
cloud makes the whole sky night, and the hot wind
and the cold wind arrive, . . . and it does not rain,

---

* So in pseudo-Johan. Apoc., 5 ; Dan. Apoc. Gr., 77 *et seq.* ;
Adso, 1296 B ; Bede's Sibyl, with which compare the Sahidic
(Coptic) recension of Zeph. Apoc., p. 124, etc.

and that which rains also rains more noxious creatures than water, and the water of rivers and springs will diminish." Compare also the description given farther on of the effect of the want of rain on the animal kingdom.

In this dire distress the Antichrist through his subordinates beguiles the inhabitants of the earth to accept his mark. Under this condition alone are they allowed to buy bread.

Ephr. Gr., 140 B :

For stern governors of the people—shall be appointed each
     in his place,
And whoso bears with him—the seal of the tyrant
May buy a little food.*

Pseudo-Ephrem, 8 : " And no one can sell or buy of the wheat of decay, except those only who shall have the mark of the Serpent in the forehead and in their hand." [22]

This tradition may now be traced farther.

Lactantius, VII. 17, 639, 9 : " Whosoever shall believe and gather to him shall be marked by him like cattle." [23]

Armenian Apocalypse of Daniel, 239, 18 : " Woe to those that believe in him, and receive his mark. Their right hand shall be bound fast, so that they return not to him in whom they had before put their hope."

* Cf. pseudo-Hippolytus, xxviii. 110, 1, and Phil. Solitarius, 816 D. It should be noted that both add that whoever is marked with the sign of the Beast can no longer receive the sign of the Cross. Cf. Eph. Gr., III. 143 A.

Adso, 1297 A: " And whoso shall believe in him shall receive the mark of his character in their forehead " ;[24] with which compare pseudo-Johannine Apocalypse, 7, Cod. E: " And he brands their right hands that they may dwell with him unto the fire everlasting." [25]

Here, then, fresh light is thrown upon the last-remaining enigmatical trait in Revelation xiii. 16 *et seq.* It was above pointed out that the Antichrist legend lay at the basis of this very passage, and Revelation xiii. 16, 17 is now to be explained as a simple appropriation from this legend, which stands as a parallel tradition independent of the Johannine text. For, in the first place, direct mention is here made of the sealing of the believers by the Antichrist, whereas in Revelation the sealing is done by the second beast in the name of the first. Secondly, the statement that only the sealed shall be allowed to buy (and sell) stands in easy and natural connection with the context, whereas in Revelation it presents a complete puzzle. Obviously the writer borrowed it without more ado from the oral tradition, though in doing so he may have had the imperial currency of Rome in his mind.

Specially important in this connection is the detail in pseudo-Ephrem, who speaks of a " mark of the Serpent." It is such a mark that is branded by the Antichrist on the forehead and hand of his adherents, and thus the Dragon myth is again revived. We thus also understand why Ephrem, III. 143 A, opposes the sign of the Cross to that of Antichrist. When the writer of Revelation xiii. 17 introduces the laboured clause " save he that had the mark, or the name of the beast, or the number of his name," it becomes very probable that it was he who first added the reference to "the name of the beast." And thus the original Antichrist legend is presented to us in Revelation xiii. in almost all its details.

Then follows in the same connection the statement in Ephr. Gr., 141 C,* that with the ever-increasing famine the mark of the Antichrist is of no use to his adherents, who appeal to him in their distress, but are scornfully spurned from his presence, he having himself become helpless. I mention this later picturesque addition, because a striking parallel occurs in the Apocalypse of Zephaniah, p. 128: " Sinners shall lament on earth, and say, What hast thou done unto us, thou son of lawlessness, when thou saidst, I am the Christ, and yet art the devil? Thou canst not rescue thyself, and so rescue us. Thou hast worked signs before us until thou hast alienated us from Christ. Since we have hearkened unto thee, behold now how full we are of misery and distress."

* Also pseudo-Hippolytus, chap. xxxi. 112, 3 ; and Phil. Solitarius, 818 A.

CHAPTER XIV.*

Enoch and Elias—The Flight of the Faithful.

USUALLY the two witnesses, who are also mentioned in Revelation xi., appear before, though often after the incident of the flight of the faithful to the wilderness. With almost absolute unanimity the tradition identifies them with Enoch and Elias, and in this tradition their appearance has quite a different and more significant meaning than in Revelation xi.

Our survey may begin with Ephr. Syr., chap. xi. : " But when the son of perdition shall have attracted the whole world to his cause, Enoch and Elias shall be sent to convict the wicked one by a question full of gentleness." [1] Thereupon they ask him : " If thou art God, tell us what we ask thee " [2]—*i.e.* respecting their own hidden residence, which in patristic literature passed for a great mystery (Malvenda, II. 144). Then they demand of him the test of the raising of the dead, whereupon " the impious one shall be enraged against the saints, and seizing a sword the most nefarious one shall sever the necks of the just "; [3]

* For Notes [1] to [23] of this chapter, see Appendix, p. 288.

after which the prophets are resuscitated by Michael and Gabriel.

Pseudo-Ephrem, 9 : " God, seeing the human race endangered and wavering under the breath of the frightful Dragon, sends them a consoling exhortation through His servants the prophets Enoch and Elias ; and when these just ones shall appear, they shall indeed confound their adversary, the Serpent, with his cunning, and bring back the faithful elect to God, that from his wiles "[4] [gap in the codex]. Then again follows the resuscitation of the prophets.

Ephr. Gr., III. 142 :

But before these things be—the Lord sendeth
Elias (?) the Thesbite—and Enoch [the ?] compassionate,
That they may proclaim—reverence to the race of men,
And openly announce—unto all the knowledge of God,
That they believe not nor obey—the false one through fear
Crying out (?) and saying—A deceiver, O men, is he ;
Let no one believe in him.[5]

Then a few lines farther on :

But few are those—who shall then obey
And believe in the words—of these two prophets.[6]

Then immediately follows an account of the flight of the faithful, without any mention being made of the death of the two prophets ; whereas the parallel passage in pseudo-Hippolytus (xxix. 111, 4) concludes with the statement : " And on that account he shall slay them [not *you*], and with the sword shall smite them." [7]

Pseudo-Johannine Apocalypse, 8 : " And then I shall send Enoch and Elias to convict him, and they shall show him to be a liar and a deceiver, and he shall slay them on the altar." [8] With this is to be compared Philip the Solitary, 816 B.

The fragment of the Syriac Apocalypse of Peter begins : " The accursed Antichrist. And they shall rebuke and denounce him as a liar, and he shall know (?) them by their bodies, and the son of perdition shall speak and say to them, I am the expected Messiah. But they shall convict him of falsehood, and say to him, Thou, a liar art thou, and thou art not the Messiah ; then shall he be enraged against them and kill them, and their bodies shall lie four days in the streets of Jerusalem ; and after that I will command by means of My power, and Enoch and Elias shall again be alive, and rise up with their bodies."

Ethiopic Apocalypse of Peter : " Thereafter shall Enoch and Elias come down ; they shall preach and put to shame that oppressive foe of righteousness, the son of lies. Therefore soon shall they be beheaded, and Michael and Gabriel shall resuscitate them."

Pseudo-Methodius, 99 : " And without delay he shall send his ministers, both Enoch and Elias, and Ioannes [John], son of thunder, who before all the peoples shall convict him of fraud and prove him a liar to all men, and that he hath come for the destruction and deception of the many. But he being sorely convicted and being by all despised in his wrath and fury shall make away with those saints." [9]

Ezra, Syr. Apocalypse, 14: "And then shall the lying Messiah appear and display his destructive power and the onslaught of his wickedness. And he shall drag Enoch and Elias to the altar, and shed their blood on the ground with great suffering."

Bede's Sibyl : "There shall go forth the two most glorious men Enoch and Elias to announce the advent of the Lord, and them shall the Antichrist slay, and after three days shall they be resuscitated." [10]

Adso, 1296 C : "Then shall be sent into the world the two great prophets Elias and Enoch, who shall forearm the faithful with godly weapons against the attack of the Antichrist, and they shall encourage and get them ready for the war. . . . But after they have accomplished their preaching, the Antichrist shall rise up and slay them, and after three days they shall be raised up by the Lord." [11]

The same tradition, quite independent of Revelation xi., occurs also in John of Damascus ; Ambrosiaster on 1 Corinthians iv. 9; Bede, *de Ratione Temporum,* 69; and *Elucidarium.* The distinctive character of this independent tradition lies in the fact that Enoch and Elias do not appear till after the beginning of the Antichrist's sway.

The idea that Elias and Enoch are the two witnesses of the last days is so widespread that it would be superfluous to adduce any more evidence. It may, however, be mentioned that the idea is already known to Irenæus (V. 5, 1), as well as to Hippolytus, xliii. 21, 8, and Tertullian, *de Anima* (and elsewhere) : " Enoch and Elias were translated, nor were they found dead, but their death deferred, though they are reserved to die, that they may extinguish the Antichrist in their blood." [12]

It will suffice to notice the few deviations in the tradition. The original Jewish expectation, as is still to be seen in the Gospels, was for the return of Elias alone (Malachi iv. 1) ; and this seems to have held its ground in the Sibylline literature (cf. Sibyl II. 187). Justin knows only that Elias is to precede the second coming of the Lord.* The influence of this tradition is also seen in Lactantius, VII. 17., who knows of but one witness, which is all the more remarkable since, in other respects, he adheres more closely to Revelation than any of the other authorities hitherto adduced. Commodian, as we have above seen, hesitates between one and two witnesses ; while the later Jewish apocalyptic literature speaks of one only, that is, Elias, except where this prophet is thrust aside by the Messiah ben Joseph—compare, for instance, the History of Daniel. It is noteworthy that in the Old High German poem *Muspilli* there is also mention only of a conflict between Elias and the Antichrist. Of course the patristic writers often speak of the return of Elias alone, but not in their full descriptions of the last days. †

In the Gospel account of the Transfiguration the two witnesses are already introduced, but here identified with Elias and Moses, just as the writer of Revelation xi. may also probably have assumed Elias to be one and Moses the other of his two

* *Dialogus cum Tryph.*, 49.   † Cf. Malvenda, II. 151.

witnesses. Nevertheless, so far as I am aware, this interpretation is expressly found amongst the early authorities only in Hilarius on Matthew xx. 10, although it is somewhat frequently stated that Moses (like Elias) had not yet seen death.* The same exposition occurs in the Commentary of Victorinus, although, strange to say, Victorinus himself elsewhere identifies the two witnesses with Elias and Jeremiah.

The notion that, besides Elias and Enoch, a third witness is also to come in the person of S. John the Baptist occurs, not only in the quoted passage from Methodius, but also in the Commentaries of Andreas and Aretha (on Revelation xi. 3), and in several other authorities.† Then it was adopted by Abbot Joachim in his Exposition of Revelation, and passed to many other writings composed under his influence.

If we now compare with Revelation xi. our independent tradition, and bear in mind its amazing persistence, as set forth in the foregoing pages, we shall discover the following points of difference. 1. In Revelation the two witnesses are probably assumed to be Elias and Moses, whereas in our tradition they are invariably called Elias and Enoch. 2. Elias and Enoch appear after the Antichrist towards the end of his rule, while in Revelation the beast comes up from the bottomless pit after the prophets have completed their testimony. 3. The

* Malvenda, II. 155.
† Ambrosius on Psalm xlv. 10 ; Theophylactus and Euthymius on Revelation xxi. 20 ; pseudo-Hippolytus, xxi. 104, 13 ; Simeon Metaphrastes, *Vita Johannis*, VII. 2.

plague of absolute drought, which in Revelation is brought about by the two witnesses, is in the tradition regarded as a punishment of God for the apostasy to the Antichrist. 4. The prophets appear to take up the conflict against the Antichrist, to instruct the faithful on his true character, and exhort them to rise against him ; whereas in John the witnesses stand in no relation to the Antichrist. In John also the witnesses rise again after three days, and are carried up to heaven. This last trait has found its way only into a few of the above-quoted authorities, and also into Bede's Sibyl, the Syriac Apocalypse of Peter, and Adso. The variant that the witnesses are to be resuscitated by Michael and Gabriel is found in Ephr. Syr., in the Ethiopic Apocalypse of Peter, and pseudo-Ephrem (?); but not Ephr. Gr., pseudo-Hippolytus, the pseudo-Johannine Apocalypse, 8, Philip the Solitary, Ezra's Syriac Apocalypse, pseudo-Methodius, *Elucidarium* (or *Muspilli* ?). As in all the sources the death of the witnesses is immediately followed by the last judgment, this incident has also no place in our tradition.

There can now be no doubt on which side lies the original account. It was above pointed out that in Revelation xi. everything remains obscure and disjointed ; we cannot make out who are the two witnesses, why they threaten the plagues, in what kind of relation they stand to the beast, or why the beast kills them. But all these puzzles are cleared up when we survey the subject in connection with the Antichrist legend. The same legend also supplies an

14

answer to the difficult question, whence the peoples and nations come, and why they rejoice over the death of the witnesses. Nor should this solution any longer appear too hazardous.

We now clearly see how the writer of Revelation set to work in his treatment of chap. xi. The account of the Antichrist, already located in the district of Jerusalem, is by him transferred to the time when this city is being threatened by the Roman legions, in whom he may have recognised the "kindreds and tongues and nations." We are unable, however, to understand why he deviates in certain details; possibly he was himself no longer acquainted with the tradition in its original form. But it is clear that he is personally responsible for the incident about the resurrection of the witnesses after the third day; and from the incident itself it is evident that the writer of Revelation, chap. xi., was a Christian, and in fact a Jewish Christian.

Still, with all this, one point remains unexplained— the origin of the idea of the two witnesses. There can scarcely be a doubt that it cannot have emanated from a Jewish source. Here the return of Elias is expected, while the expectation of the two witnesses would seem to have never been more generally diffused, as is shown by the later Jewish tradition. Hippolytus, who bases all the details respecting the expectation of the return of Elias on the Old Testament, has not a single word on the other witness. Gunkel promises a solution of the riddle, and it is to be hoped he may succeed. Meanwhile what has here been brought together suffices in my opinion to explain the composition of Revelation xi.*

Possibly in its further development the tradition went on to relate that through the preaching of the two witnesses many of the faithful were again converted to God, and had therefore to suffer persecution.

Irenæus is already able to tell us that during the sway of the Antichrist a great persecution is to take place (V. 29, 1). He appeals in support of the statement to the words of the Lord in Matthew xxiv. 31, which words henceforth constantly recur in the descriptions of these last things.† In his exposition (V. 25, 3) of the parable in Luke xviii. 1 *et seq.*, he identifies the unjust judge with the Antichrist and the widow seeking vengeance with the earthly Jerusalem : "The 'afterward' [ver. 4] also means the time of his oppression, in which time the saints shall be put to flight." [13] After him Hippolytus (chaps. lvi. *et seq.*) follows much in the same direction, and gives even fuller details, as in chap. lviii. 30, 6 : "And he, being puffed up by them [the Jews], beginneth to send out missives against the saints, that all refusing to adore and worship him as God are everywhere to be destroyed." [14] Ephrem, Cyril, and others tell us how the

* I may incidentally call attention to the two witnesses Nêriôsang and Srôsh, who in the Bahman Yast precede the Messiah. In the apocalyptic compilation *Onus Ecclesiæ* I find (chap. lxi.) the enigmatic remark, " Sibylla nuncupat eos duo stellas "—that is, " The Sibyl calls them [the witnesses] two stars."

† Cf. Malvenda, II. 145.

Antichrist, who first appeared in the character of a deceiver, throws aside his mask, and assumes the part of a hard and cruel oppressor.

Characteristic is the account of the flight of the faithful in Ephr. Gr., 142 C :

Many therefore of the saints—as many as are then found,
So soon as they shall hear—of the coming of the man of
    corruption,
. . . Shall most speedily flee—to the deserts
And lie hid in the [deserts and mountains]—and in caves
    through fear,
And strew earth and ashes [dust]—on their heads,
Destitute and weeping—both night and day,
With great humility—
And this shall to them be granted—by God the Holy One,
And grace shall lead them—unto the appointed places.[15]

Ephr. Syr., 10 : " But the elect shall flee from the face of him to the tops of the mountains and hills ; some shall fly to the burial-places and hide themselves amid the dead." [16]

Pseudo-Johannine Apocalypse, 7, Cod. B : " But the just shall be hid away, and shall flee to the mountains and caves." [17]

These details may again be followed far beyond the Ephremite legendary writings.

Thus Hippolytus (lxi. 32, 21) applies to the Church the words of Revelation xii. 6 : " And the woman fled into the wilderness, where she hath a place prepared of God."

Lactantius, VII. 17, 639, 21 : " When these things

shall come to pass, then the just and followers of truth shall sever themselves from the wicked, and shall fly to the solitudes." [18]

Commodian, 937 *et seq.* :

> Meanwhile at last he displeaseth the Jews themselves,
> Who murmur together, for that they have been beguiled
>   by fraud ;
> They likewise cry unto heaven with weeping voice,
> That the true God may come to their aid from above.[19]

Apocalypse of Zephaniah, 126 : " They shall take their gold and flee to the rivers, and say, Take us over to the wilderness." With this compare what follows about the protection of the faithful in the desert, and about the renewal of the struggle with the Antichrist, and further the parallel passage in the Jewish Apocalypse of Daniel.

Andreas (li. 51) on Revelation xii. 6 : " And it is probable that the visible desert [shall] save those through the machinations of the apostate and false Christ taking refuge in the mountains and caves and fissures of the ground." [20]

Armenian Apocalypse of Daniel, 239, 26 : " But those alone who dwell on the mountains, in caves, in the clefts and hollows of the ground, shall be able to escape until the second coming of Him who was born of the Holy Virgin."

Here may again be quoted the above restored text of the *Ascensio Jesaiæ*, IV. 13, where special mention is made of the Antichrist's rule : " And he shall hold sway three years and seven months and days twenty

and seven." Then farther on : " And many of the
faithful and of the saints [shall there be], who on
seeing him they expected [not] shall be fugitives
from desert to desert, awaiting the advent of him
[God ?]." The parallel to the tradition, such as we
find it elsewhere in the *Ascensio*, is a fresh confirmation of the correctness of our critical emendation.
The same incident of the flight drawn from such
essentially Jewish sources as those at the disposal of
Lactantius, Commodian, and the *Ascensio* occurs in
all the later Jewish apocalypses mentioned farther
back.

The material so far collected is exceptionally interesting, and gives rise to a series of observations.
To begin with, it is now clear that, as already
conjectured by us, Matthew xxv. 15 *et seq.* is really
a fragment of some apocalypse of the Antichrist. The
" abomination of desolation . . . in the holy place "
is the Antichrist, while the flight to the mountains
foretold to follow thereafter is the flight from the
Antichrist. It has long been recognised that it was
straining the text somewhat violently to apply the
abomination of desolation to the Roman army before
the walls of Jerusalem. Nor are matters much
improved by the present favourite application of the
expression to Caligula (see above, p. 22). On the
other hand, everything becomes easy and natural by
recourse to the Antichrist legend. Even the " catch-
word " borrowed by Matthew xxiv. 21 from Daniel
reappears here in the description of the last tribulation
under the sway of the Antichrist.

Specially important is, moreover, the above-quoted passage from Commodian. It clearly shows that those flying to the desert were originally the faithful Jews, who had discovered the Antichrist's treason. In equally clear language Lactantius (VII. 17) still describes the persecution of the Jews : " Then shall he attempt to raze the Temple of God and persecute the just people ; he also shall entangle the just men with the books of the prophets, and so consume them." [21]

Now this incident, which emanates from a Jewish source, is inextricably interwoven with the eschatological tradition with which we are here concerned. It gives us the explanation of the widespread belief in the conversion of the Jews precisely in the last days of the Antichrist. Christianity adopted the tradition in a form in which Jews and believers had acquired equal importance.

Victorinus remarks on Revelation xii. 6 : " That Catholic Church in which in the last days a hundred and forty-four thousand of the people of Elias shall believe. So also saith the Lord in the Gospel, Then let them which be in Judæa flee into the mountains." [22] The whole context with the incidental remark can have no meaning except on the assumption that amongst the converted and fugitives of the last days Victorinus had the Jews mainly in view.*

* With Malvenda, II. 200, I may refer further to Hilarius on Matthew x. 14, etc. ; Austin, *de Civitate Dei*, XX. 29 ; Gregory on Ezekiel, Homily xii. 7 ; Chrysostom on Matthew, Homily lviii. 1 ; Theodoretus on Daniel xii. 1 and on Malachi iv. 1 ; S. John of Damascus ; Adso.

But most significant is it that we can now understand how Paul (Rom. ix. 26) came to speak of a
conversion of Israel in the last days. This was no
self-invented hope with which to console himself, but
was adopted from the body of the early Jewish tradition.
And thus is cleared up the obscure passage in
Romans xi. 12 : " Now if the fall of them *be* the
riches of the world, and the diminishing of them
the riches of the Gentiles ; how much more their
fulness ? " This is precisely the great benefit that
converted Israel is to confer on the Christian Church
of Gentile origin, that Israel will take the lead in
the opposition to and struggle with the Antichrist.

Revelation vii. 1 *et seq.* also is naturally to be
understood in the same sense. The stereotyped
number 144,000 appears to have formed part of the
original legend. When we are told that 12,000 from
each of the twelve tribes, with the exception of Dan
for the reason above set forth, are to be saved, or to
be " sealed," it might doubtless be inferred from this
very enumeration of the twelve tribes no longer
surviving that the incident itself could not really be
of Jewish origin. But it already occurs in Revelation and in a passage which appears to be obviously
borrowed. And it should be remembered that at a
very early date the expectation of the return of the
twelve tribes was already grafted on to the Antichrist
legend (see above, p. 102). So Victorinus expressly
interprets the passage : " Therefore he also indicates
the very number of the Jews to be converted, and
of the Gentiles ' a great multitude ' (Rev. vii, 9)."

Compare Andreas also on the same passage. Thus at last the 144,000 sealed of God are presented as a natural contrast to those sealed of Antichrist, of whom we are often expressly told that they cannot receive the seal (mark) of God (Christ), because they have accepted that of the Antichrist (see above, pp. 201-2).

From the literary point of view it is also interesting to note that in the Greek Ephrem is met a characteristic account of the distress and of the general flight and disorder of the Antichrist period. Thus II. 223 :

> But all those dwelling—in the east of the earth
> [Shall] fly to the west—through their great fear,
> And again those dwelling—under the setting sun
> Unto its rising—shall fly in trembling.[23]

CHAPTER XV.*

THE SHORTENING OF THE DAYS—THE LAST STRESS—THE DELIVERANCE—THE DOOM OF THE ANTICHRIST.

W E read in Matthew xxiv. 22 : " And except those days should be shortened, there should no flesh be saved : but for the elect's sake those days shall be shortened." A fuller tradition on this subject occurs in the most diverse ramifications of our legend. Lactantius (VII. 17, 636, 17) already tells us that " then shall the year be shortened and the month lessened and the day contracted."[1]

So the Apocalypse of Zephaniah, 128 : " Then shall the shameless one . . . say, Woe unto me, for my time hath passed away. I said, My time shall not pass away, and, lo ! my years have become as the months, my days have fleeted away, like the dust that is wafted away."

The pseudo-Johannine Apocalypse, 8 : " Three years shall be those times, and the three years shall I make as three months, and the three months as three weeks, and the three weeks as three days, and the three

* For Notes [1] to [27] of this chapter, see Appendix, p. 291.

218

days as three hours, and the three hours as three seconds." [2]

Here again we see the fragmentary character of the New Testament tradition. By the " shortening of the days," however, must be understood a definite period of time, which, in fact, is indicated in the parallel tradition as the three and a half years of the Antichrist's sway.

Against those fleeing to the wilderness the Antichrist sends his army. But the faithful in the wilderness are now delivered in a wonderful way, and the power of the Antichrist broken. Thus Lactantius, VII. 17, 640, 2 : " On hearing this the impious one, fired by rage, shall come with a mighty host, and drawing up all his forces shall encompass the mountain on which the just tarry to capture them. But they, seeing themselves hemmed in and enclosed on all sides, shall cry unto God with a loud voice, and implore the heavenly aid ; and God shall hearken unto them and send a great king from heaven, who shall rescue and deliver [them], and disperse all the impious with fire and sword." [3]

This tradition is also known to Victorinus (on Revelation xii. 15 *et seq.*): "The water that the Serpent casts out of his mouth means that by his order the army pursueth her [that is, the faithful fleeing to the wilderness] ; and the earth that opened her mouth and swallowed up the flood [means] the vengence openly taken on those present." [4]

In Zephaniah's Apocalypse the Antichrist calls out :

" Now fly [hasten (?)] to the desert, seize them, . . .
kill them, the saints bring hither." Very characteristic
are the words that follow : " Then shall he take his
fiery wings and fly after the saints, and again contend
with them." According to Zephaniah the deliverance
is brought about by angels, who take the believers on
their wings and bear them to the " holy land."

It is noteworthy that the same tradition is preserved
by pseudo-Hippolytus, who seems here for the first
time to take an independent position ; at least I have
failed to find the incident in any of the Ephremite
writings : " Then to the mountains and caverns and
clefts of the earth shall he send the legions of devils to
spy out those hidden from his eyes, and bring them to
the worship of him, and those obeying to seal with his
seal, and inflict punishment on those refusing to yield."[5]

Similarly Adso, 1297 A : " Then pursuing the rest of
the faithful he shall smite (?) with the sword or make
them apostates, and those who shall believe in him
shall receive his mark on their forehead." [6]

Lastly, Beatus, 541 : " Inaccessible places are there,
whither the saints shall flee and there lie hid, and
Christ shall find them alive in the flesh." [7]

Consequently the believers fleeing to the desert are
there to find their deliverance, for hither is God to
send them the Messiah. Here a clear light is shed
on Matthew xxiv. 26 : " Wherefore if they shall say
unto you, Behold, he is in the desert ; go not forth." *

---

* Allusion may here be made to the historical appearance of
false Messiahs in the wilderness (Acts xxi. 31 ; Josephus, *Arch.*,
XX. viii. 6 ; *Bellum Judaicum*, VII. xi. 1).

Possibly also we have here the solution of the puzzling words that follow : " Behold, he· is in *the secret chambers* ; believe it not." For in Isaiah xxvi. 20 we read : " Come, my people, enter thou into thy chambers, and shut thy doors about thee : hide thyself as it were for a little moment, until the indignation [the wrath of the Lord] be overpast." In some of our sources these very words are referred to the flight of the faithful to the wilderness. Thus the Ethiopic Apocalypse of Peter : " And they shall flee to the mountains, the hollows and the fissures of the ground and hide themselves, as saith the prophet Isaiah, Come, my people, into thine house and hide thee a little while, until the anger of the Lord be overpast." To me it seems not impossible that this interpretation of Isaiah may be very old. If so, we shall have a parallelism between the two expressions " behold he is in the desert " and " behold he is in the secret chambers."

It must now be evident that the second half also of Revelation, chap. xii., comes in contact with our legend. As the text stands at present (compare especially ver. 17), the flight of the woman is no doubt referred to some distinct contemporary event. But, so far at least as the New Testament period is concerned, by the woman pursued by the Serpent was originally understood the Church—in other words, the congregation of Jewish believers in the last days.

Such is the exposition of nearly all patristic writers,* beginning with Hippolytus and Methodius ; only for

* See Malvenda, 147.

them the woman is of course the *Christian* Church. In his interpretation Victorinus also may in some of his details have hit off what the author of the passage may have wished to express by his eschatological imagery.

It is another question (and this affects the special difficulty presented by the exposition of Revelation, chap. xii.) whether, and how far, the several fantastic details are borrowed from the context of an earlier myth. Hitherto Gunkel himself has failed to adduce any convincing parallels or satisfactory explanations. It is no doubt probable enough that the apocalyptic writer borrowed his "local colouring" from the Dragon myth and from the body of legendary matter associated with it. But until the point is proved the possibility remains that the writer who expanded chap. xii. of Revelation described the eschatological conception of the Antichrist's persecution of the faithful in colours harmonising with that first part of the chapter which is really borrowed from the Dragon myth. But even so much I am willing to leave as an assumption, while gladly welcoming further light.

But a still more difficult passage of Revelation has here to be considered. Quite enigmatic is the judgment described in xiv. 14-20. Who is the person that carries out this judgment? Apparently the Messiah, one that like the Son of man is seated on a cloud. But then in ver. 15 there is a question of "another angel"; and in any case he does not execute the judgment alone, but by him stands almost in a superior position this other angel, who likewise sits in judgment.

And, moreover, on whom is judgment held? The reference is only (ver. 20) to much bloodshed " without the city."

Perhaps we may here receive further help from Lactantius, who (VII. 19, 645, 11) describes the overthrow of the host sent by Antichrist to persecute the faithful: " And the power of the angels shall deliver into the hands of the just that multitude which had encompassed the mountain, and *blood shall flow like a torrent,* and the impious one alone shall escape after the destruction of all his forces." [8]   With this is to be compared Victorinus on the same passage : " And blood shall come out 'even unto the horse bridles' [means that] vengeance shall be poured out on the princes of the people—that is, the rulers, whether the devil or *his angels* ; in the last conflict the vengeance of bloodshed shall be poured out." [9]   In pseudo-Hippolytus we are told that the faithful in the wilderness are pursued by demons ; and Commodian writes (983) somewhat obscurely that, as the rebels against God rush forward with their hosts, they are strewn on the ground by the angels in battle.[10]   And the Apocalypse of Zephaniah (128) adds after the above-quoted passage : " The angels shall hearken to it, and come down and fight a battle of many swords with him."

It is highly probable that in Revelation xiv. 14-20 we had originally a description of the battle, which was to be fought by the angels against the hosts of the Antichrist, by whom the faithful are pursued in the wilderness.   This battle takes place without the walls of the city, that is, Jerusalem, headquarters of the Antichrist.

If this be the correct interpretation, then the person seated on the cloud like the Son of man is to be regarded only as an angel. And thus one also understands why at the beginning of chap. xiv. the Lamb appears with the 144,000. These are the steadfast believers who have fled to the wilderness, and who now appear with the Lamb, God having sent the Messiah to them in the wilderness (see Lactantius above). The statement that they dwell on the mountain derives from the same tradition, only the writer seems to have added that this is Mount Zion.

The destruction of the Antichrist by the Saviour is already announced by Paul, who describes his overthrow after Isaiah xi. 4. The Lord slays him by the breath of His mouth, and shall destroy him utterly when he appears on His return.

This idea that Christ Himself is to vanquish the Antichrist continued to be widely diffused,* although in many descriptions the scene almost entirely disappears in the background. It is given in detail by Lactantius (see below) ; by pseudo-Ephrem, 10 ; and many others.† But it is specially remarkable that the

---

* Cf. Ephr. Gr., 143 B ; pseudo-Hippolytus, xxxvii. ; Phil. Solitarius, 818 C ; pseudo-Johannine Apocalypse, xvi. *et seq.* ; D. A. Gr., 116, and Arm., 240.

† Prudentius, *Cathemerinon*, 6, "Qui de furente monstro pulchrum refert trophæum " (" Who gains a glorious triumph over the raging monster ") ; Cyril, xv. 10 ; Jerome, *ad Algasiam*, 11 ; P. A. Syr. ; John of Damascus ; Adso ; Haymo ; *Elucidarium* ;

Messiah, Son of David, kills Armillus by the breath of His mouth in such Jewish sources as the Midrash, the Mysteries of Rabbi Yokhai, and the History of Daniel, although in this last it is not quite clear whether it is Armillus or the Messiah ben Joseph that gets killed. Hence, even on this point, Paul's reference to Isaiah does not seem to be made independently, but to have been handed down to him through the general Jewish tradition.

In later times the idea that the Antichrist is overthrown by the Messiah Himself prevailed to the exclusion of all others. It probably gave rise to an important transformation which the Christian eschatology underwent in mediæval times. In Jerome (on Daniel xii. 11 *et seq.*) the notion is already established that between the destruction of the Antichrist and the last judgment an interval occurs answering to the forty-five days of Daniel xii. 11, 12—that is, the difference between 1290 and 1335.* To me it seems highly probable that the legend had much to do with this application, and that in the Middle Ages people again ventured, against the decision of the Church, to revive millennium theories. Under the influence of Joachim of Fiore hopes began to spread, especially amongst the circles subject to the teachings of the Franciscan friars,

and already in Jewish sources, such as the Testamentum XII. Patr. (Dan v.), the Midrash va-Yosha, the Mysteries of Rabbi Yokhai, and the Jewish History of Daniel. The reference to Isaiah xi. 4 also recurs in pseudo-Ephrem, Cyril, Jerome, John of Damascus, Adso, and Haymo.

* Malvenda, II. 243.

that a golden age was again to come on earth—an age identified with the sway of the Holy Ghost, the reformation of the Church, and the predominance of monastic institutions.

Then we hear in this connection of a second coming of Christ, in contradistinction to His third and final advent at the last judgment.* To be sure this second coming is for the most part treated only in a spiritualistic sense ; nevertheless Christ now overthrows the Antichrist (a conception interpreted in the most diverse ways)—the advent is preceded by Elias and Enoch, two religious orders !—and the conversion of the Jews is now accomplished. In all this the influence of the Antichrist legend is clearly seen. But we should need a separate work to follow up all the points of contact, which can here be indicated only in a general way.

But traces are also perceptible of an earlier form of the saga, in which the Messiah can scarcely have held a clearly defined place.

Thus in *Ascensio* (on Isaiah iv. 14) we read, not of the Messiah, who is here called the Beloved, but of God, that "the Lord shall come with His angels and the powers of the saints from the seventh heaven, with the glory of the seventh heaven, and deliver Berial into Gehenna and his powers also." [11]

So also in Sibyl III. 73 it is said of God that

* Thus Joachim and his numerous followers, Ubertinus de Casalis, the German prophetesses, and apocalyptic writers down to the author of the *Onus Ecclesiæ*.

" He shall Beliar consume and all the overbearing men who shall have put faith in him." [12]

Pseudo-Methodius less clearly : " And then shall appear the sign of the Son of man with much glory, and He shall come on the clouds of the earth, and the Lord shall take him off with the breath of His mouth," [13] where the Latin has, " God shall kill him." [14]

Here the whole account of the Antichrist's end produces a disjointed and abrupt impression. With it may be compared the notion given farther on from Bernardus Senensis, inspired by the mention in Methodius of Michael the Archangel. But the statement is not to be rejected off-hand, because it also occurs in Adso, who is closely connected with pseudo-Methodius. Possibly we no longer possess the concluding part of Methodius in its original form.

But with these references is connected a series of others, in which has been preserved a distinctly earlier tradition. According to this tradition it is the archangel Michael who overcomes the Antichrist, and in these earlier sources the Messiah takes no part in the incident, while God, not Christ, appears as the Judge of the world.

Before giving these references, I may be allowed another general observation.

It would be in every respect extremely interesting to make a connected survey of the speculations indulged in by the later Jewish writers on the subject of Michael the Archangel. We should find, I imagine, that here, if anywhere, Jewish speculation has been the prototype for the development of Christological teachings. In the later Jewish world of thought the archangel Michael takes an amazingly high position precisely as the angel of the people. Even in Daniel xii. 1 *et seq.* Michael is already represented as the great hero of the last days, when he is to champion the cause of his nation. But the most important point is that here his figure already quite thrusts that of the Messiah aside, and even acquires Messianic significance. We should expect that in this, as in all other respects, Daniel's influence must have been much felt in eschatological speculations. Hence in my opinion the dominant place taken by Michael in Revelation xii. is the strongest argument for the Jewish origin of that document. It is he, and not the Child who is yet to be born and who is destined to rule the Gentiles with a brazen sceptre, that overthrows the Dragon when storming the heavens.

Michael's position becomes still more commanding, if it can be assumed that in Revelation xii. was originally described the last and decisive assault of the Dragon on heaven, the revolt of the old Serpent and his final overthrow. In that case Michael would stand out, in the Jewish transformation of this figure, as the vanquisher of the Dragon in the great struggle of the last days.

Now traces of this view still occur in various sources. Thus Ephr. Syr., 12: "Then Gabriel and Michael, captains of the army, starting up shall come down and stir up the saints. But the evil one [Antichrist] with his satellites shall be stricken with shame ; and forthwith the angels shall advance and seize the

accursed one ; whereat the Lord shall cry out from
the heaven and overthrow the accursed one with all
his forces, and forthwith the angels shall thrust him
into Gehenna." [15] Here by "the Lord" is to be understood God, for Christ is afterwards called the "Son."
The conquest of the Antichrist and the destruction
of the world take place without His co-operation.

So also in Codex E. of the pseudo-Johannine Apocalypse another trace is seen of this conception : " When
he hath been captured by Michael the Archangel,
and deprived of his godhead—for I have sent out
from the bosom of my father and have humbled the
polluted one's head, and his eye has been quelled." [16]

Ezra's Apoc., xiii. : " And there shall God send
against them [Gog and Magog] Michael, the fearful
angel, and he shall destroy them without pity." Chap.
xv. : " And angels shall be sent, who thrust the son
of perdition into the Gehenna of fire, and there [then]
is the end."

Bede, *de Ratione Temporum*, 69 : " That son of perdition being smitten either by the Lord Himself or by
Michael the Archangel." [17]

Bede's Sibyl : " And the Antichrist shall be slain
through the virtue of the Lord by Michael the
Archangel, as some teach." [18]

Adso, 1297 B : " The doctors also teach, as saith
Pope Gregory, that Michael the Archangel shall destroy him on Mount Olivet in his pavilion and seat, in
that place whence the Lord ascended into heaven." [19]

Noteworthy also is the passage from Bernardus
Senensis on the Universal Judgment, XI., quoted

by Malvenda, II. 235: "Antichrist by command of Christ shall be thunderstruck through the ministry of Michael the Archangel, who shall also kill him according to Methodius." [20]

So also in the Jewish History of Daniel we read: "Thereupon shall they, Michael and Gabriel, slay him who hath given himself out as the Messiah, and [then] shall God appear from heaven." *

An echo of this tradition is also presented by Ephr. Gr., 143 E:

> And the tyrant is led—bound by the angels
> With all his demons—before the altar. [21]

So also Victorinus on Revelation xv. 1: "These seven bad angels [those having the seven last plagues] he sends to smite the Antichrist." [22]

A parallel pointing to a still earlier period is probably presented by the *Assumption of Moses*, X., where we read: "And then shall His [God's] kingdom appear in [unto] all His creatures, . . . and then Zabulus [the devil] shall come to an end. . . . Then shall be filled the hands of the messenger, who is appointed on high, who forthwith shall avenge them [Israel] on their enemies." [23] There can scarcely be a doubt that here the reference is to the angel Michael. And when we read further, "For the heavenly being shall rise up from the seat of his kingdom," [24] we again find God and Michael standing side by side. in battle, though not with the Antichrist, but against

---

* Theodoretus also shows himself familiar with the whole tradition in his comment on Daniel xii. 1 (Malvenda, II. 181).

the devil. Of course Michael could not originally
have been placed in antagonism to Antichrist, *i.e.* the
false Messiah, but, as here, to the devil, *i.e.* Belial or
the Dragon (Revelation xii. 7).*

Noteworthy is the assumption, apparently derived
from Zechariah, that Antichrist is to meet his end on
Mount Olivet. It would seem, however, that the idea
cannot be with any certainty traced back beyond
Jerome, on Daniel xi. 44 *et seq.* : " Then shall come
the Antichrist to the summit of that mount, . . . that
is, the top of Mount Olivet, . . . and they assert that
there shall Antichrist perish where the Lord ascended to
heaven." [25] In the Jewish History of Daniel also the
Messiah ben David appears on the Mount of Olives.

An earlier parallel is found in the Apocalypse of
Baruch, xl. : " The last captain, who shall survive
after the multitude of his congregations has been
destroyed, shall be bound, and they shall take him
up to Mount Sion, and my Messiah shall convict him
of all his wickedness, and thereafter shall slay him " [26]
(see also 4 Ezra xiii. 34).

A specially archaic variant occurs in Lactantius,
VII. 19, 645, 16 : " Antichrist shall battle with the
truth, and when overcome shall escape, and shall
often renew the war and often be overthrown, until
in the fourth conflict . . . being vanquished and
captured he shall at last pay the penalty of his
crimes " [27] (cf. Commodian, 937 *et seq.*).

* On Michael, the Dragon-slayer, and his analogy to Horus,
vanquisher of Typhon, and to Apollo, the python-killer, see
Dietrich, *Abraxes*, 122 *et seq.*

CHAPTER XVI.*

IN Matthew xxiv. 30 it is foretold that " then shall appear the sign of the Son of man in heaven." What is this sign of the Son of man ? Expositors scarcely ask the question, and yet the point must be raised. In the patristic writings the most diverse fancies are expressed on the subject. Probably the sign of the Son of man is to be conceived as some manifestation in the heavens, perhaps a flaming sword that is to flash before the face of the Messiah descending from heaven. Thus is the tradition presented in Lactantius, VII. 19, 645, 8 : " Suddenly a sword shall fall from heaven, that the just may know that the leader of the holy army is about to descend." [1]

But besides this we find the most varied interpretations. Thus Commodian, 903 : " Then also shall be seen a fiery chariot and a brand streaming through the stars to forewarn the peoples of the fire." [2]

* For Notes [1] to [50] of this chapter, see Appendix, p. 294.

Ephr. Syr., chap. xii. : "Then shall the Lord come down, . . . and between heaven and earth shall His chariot stand still." [3]

Sibyl IV. 172 : "A mighty sign with sword and trump at the rising of the sun." [4]

So also Sibyl V. 158 : "There shall from heaven come a great star down to the dread salt sea, and shall burn up the deep ocean." [5]

And Sibyl XIV. 158 : "And then surely a great sign shall God from heaven display unto speaking mortals with the revolving years, a portent (?) of the evil war impending." [6]

The Book of Clement, 81, 21 : "Then shall be signs in the sky ; a bow shall be seen, and a horn and a brand." [7]

Bede's Sibyl speaks in more general terms : "The sign of the doom ; the earth shall be moist with sweat ; from heaven the king shall come to reign for ever." [8]

The Jewish History of Daniel : "And the banner of the Messiah shall be seen."

On the other hand, the sign of the Son of man is already at a very early period referred to the Cross that is again to appear.* In the pseudo-Methodius (and Usinger's Sibyl) the last Roman emperor lays his crown on the Cross, which is then borne crown and all heavenwards. "It [the Cross] shall appear at the advent before His face unto the conviction of the unbelieving Jews." [9]

---

* Thus pseudo-Ephrem, 10 ; Cyril, xv. 22 ; pseudo-Chrysostom ; pseudo-Hippolytus, xxxvi. 115, 4 ; D. A. Gr. Cod. (see Klostermann, 120, Anmerkung) ; *Elucidarium.*

Less distinct are the statements of Greek Ephrem. In *de Antichristo* the mention of the Cross occurs only in the Latin version. But, on the other hand, a fuller account is found in the description of the Advent, which is extant in five different traditions. Here I give the Recension I.,* where, as I believe, the incident is written in tetrasyllabics, although the text cannot everywhere be restored : " When (?) we behold the sign of the Son of man appearing in the sky, as said the Lord when (?) He was voluntarily nailed to the cross for us ; then all those gazing upwards [shall behold the dread and holy sceptre ?] appear of the great king. [Then] each of us shall recognise [and] remember the word of the Lord foretelling that the sign of the Son of man should appear in the sky and that [thereafter the king shall appear ?]." [10]

With these passages we are plunged into the absolutely fathomless depths of the traditions regarding the Cross. I feel nevertheless compelled to deal briefly with the subject.

The belief in the reappearance of the Cross at the last judgment has, as is well known, played a great part, especially amongst the Eastern Churches. With this belief are also assuredly associated the manifold legends of apparitions of the Cross, of which that mentioned in the Constantine saga is the best known. Others are referred to by Zezschwitz, 56 *et seq.*

But if the Cross was expected to come from heaven, then it must also be supposed to have first gone

* See above, p. 40, after III. 145 and II. 193.

thither. And thus, in this connection, is intruded
upon us the narrative in the Petrine Gospel, which
afterwards became famous, and according to which
the Cross was borne to heaven with Christ at the
Ascension.*

Later this cycle of thought became involved with
another, according to which S. Helena, mother of the
emperor Constantine, was stated to have discovered
the true Cross. In the times when the kingdom of
God was supposed to have begun on earth with the
conversion of the empire to Christianity, the Cross
was naturally no longer expected from heaven, but
was venerated on earth as a holy relic. Thus originated the above-mentioned legend, as we see it in
Methodius (and Usinger's Sibyl). The last Byzantine
emperor at his abdication lays his crown on the Cross,
which is then borne on high with the crown in order
thence to return in the last days. Thus is confirmed
the view above advanced against Zezschwitz (p. 47)
that this relation of Methodius regarding the deposition of the crown is of later date and more
complicated than that occurring in Adso and Bede's
Sibyl.

But quite a special version of the legend survives
in the pseudo-Johannine Apocalypse, chap. xvi.
"And then shall appear the sign of the Son of
man from heaven with power and great glory; and
then the worker of unrighteousness himself shall

---

* The same idea occurs in Sibyl VI. 26-28, and in Chrysostom,
de Cruce et Latrone, Hom. ii. 4 (Zezschwitz, p. 56, and Anmerkung 83, etc.).

behold [it] with his ministers, and he shall gnash his teeth vehemently, and all the foul fiends be put to flight." [11]

Here the Cross, the sign of the Son of man, seems to completely usurp the place of the Son of man Himself. That this is no delusion is shown by a glance at the corresponding material symbolism of early Christendom, for a reference to which I have to thank Dr. Achelis. Here is seen in numerous representations the development of the process by which the Cross, symbol of Christ, takes the place of the Crucified. And in the mosaic of S. Clement's in Rome depicting the scene of the Transfiguration we have the picture that corresponds to the account in the pseudo-Johannine Apocalypse. Nothing is here shown except a cross appearing in the sky (with a medallion of Christ crucified).

Still more eloquent is a passage in the *Elucidarium* (1166), where Christ is made to appear " to the elect in that form which appeared on the mountain, but to the reprobate in that which was suspended on the Cross." [12] But it is to be a luminous cross " brighter than the sun." Compare Meyer's tentative translation of *Völuspâ*, 46 : " The Saviour shineth on that Rood of old renown."

A still more involved picture is lastly presented by the Lower Sahidic recension of the Apocalypse of Zephaniah, 124, which with its parallels has already been discussed (p. 90).

In Michelangelo's *Last Judgment* also we see the Cross borne by the angels by the side of the Judge, where again is made evident the astounding persistence of such eschatological representations.

A definite time for the advent of Christ and the overthrow of the Antichrist is already presented by Lactantius, VII. 19, 644, 8 : " Then shall be opened the mid-heaven in a stormy and dark night, so that in the whole world may appear the light of God descending like a coruscation as the Sibyl hath expressed in these words :

> When He cometh
> There shall be a murky fire at black midnight.

This is the night that it is our privilege to celebrate for the coming of our King and God ; and for this night there is a twofold reason, to wit, that He both regained life when He suffered, and thereafter is to regain the kingdom of the whole world." [13]
Although this expectation appears to be distinctly Christian, the source drawn on by Lactantius is in all probability a Jewish sibyl. Hence it is that Lactantius continues to declare with such strong emphasis that " He is the Liberator and Judge and King and God whom we call Christ." [14]
On the other hand, it may probably have been a Jewish expectation that, in the night when once the people of Israel were liberated from the land of Egypt, in the same night would come to pass the great deliverance from Antichrist. In the *Elucidarium*, III. 12, we further read : " At midnight in the hour when the angel made Egypt desolate, and when the

Lord despoiled hell, in the same hour He shall deliver His elect from this world." [15]   In the Jewish Book of Zorobabel we are likewise told that Menakhem, son of Ammiel, shall suddenly appear on Mount Nisan.

A trace of this old expectation of Christ's return on Easter eve (Holy Saturday) still survives in a popular custom.   In the Church of the Holy Sepulchre in Jerusalem the Easter fire still annually appears, not indeed at the hour of midnight, but for practical reasons * at noon, as my colleague Dr. Achelis informs me.

God or Christ, surrounded by the angelic hosts, comes to sit in judgment, and before Him rushes a fierce, fiery storm which burns up the world.

Ephr. Syr., chap. ii. : " Then shall the Lord come down from on high in the dread glory of His angels, . . . the sea shall roar and be dried up, . . . the heavens and the earth shall be dissolved, and darkness and smoke shall prevail.   Against the earth shall the Lord send fire, which lasting forty days shall cleanse it from wickedness and the stains of sin." [16]

Ephrem III. 145 (text restored from the five recensions, but substantially that of III. 145) :

> How may we then endure—my beloved brethren,
> When we shall see the fiery—river coming out
> In fury like the wild—seething ocean,
> And the hills and the valleys—consuming, and all
> The world and the works—therein ; then, beloved,

---

* To stop the unseemly scenes formerly witnessed at these midnight celebrations.

With that fire (?)—the rivers shall fail,
The springs shall vanish—the sea dry up,
The air be agitated—the stars (?) shall fall out,
From the sky the sun—shall be consumed, the moon
Pass away, the heavens—rolled up like a scroll.[17]

Ephr. Gr., III. 143 B :

In the end like the lightning—flashing from heaven
Shall come God, our King—and deathless Bridegroom,
In the clouds with glory—unimaginable (?),
And before His glory shall run—the serried hosts
Of angels and archangels—(all breathing fiery flames ?)
And a river full of fire—with frightful crash (?).[18]

Pseudo-Ephrem, 10 : " And the Lord coming forth shall appear with great power and much majesty ; with all the powers of the heavens, and the universal choir of saints." [19]

Pseudo-Johannine Apocalypse, 14 : " Then shall I send My angels before the face of all the earth, and they shall consume the earth cubits eight thousand and five hundred, and they shall consume the lofty mountains, and all the rocks shall be fused, . . . and all plants and all cattle shall be burnt," etc.[20]

Pseudo-Johannine Apocalypse, 18 : " [Then] shall fall the stars from heaven, . . . the moon shall be hid and no light be in it, . . . the light of the sun shall be suppressed (?), . . . half of the sea shall fail, . . . Hades shall be disclosed." [21]

Cyril, xv. 10 : " [He shall come] attended by myriads of angels " ; xv. 21 : " A river of fire rushing on, searching [the hearts] of men (?)." [22]

Pseudo-Chrysostom : " A river of fire filled with a restless worm." [23]

This tradition goes far back.   Thus Sibyl III. 71 :

But when the threats of the great God shall draw
	nigh,
And the fiery power shall come with overflow (?) on
	the earth,
		Then surely the universal elements
Of the world shall be dissolved, when God dwelling in
	the firmament
Shall roll up the heaven, [which] like a scroll shall be
	put away (?),
And all the many-shaped vault of heaven shall fall on
	the vast earth,
And on the deep shall flow a ceaseless torrent of glow-
	ing fire,
And shall consume the earth, consume the sea,
And the pole of heaven, the nights, the days, and e'en
	the creation,
And fuse all in one and set apart unto purification—
And no longer [shall bide] the buoyant spheres of the
	luminaries,
Neither night nor dawn, nor the many days of sorrow,
Neither spring nor winter, nor yet summer nor the
	harvest-tide.[24]

Sibyl II. 197 :

[The fire] from heaven shall flow and all consume,
The earth, the great ocean and pale green sea,
Lakes and rivers, both springs and pitiless Hades,
And the vault of heaven ; but the heavenly lights
Shall run together in one all-desolate form.

206 :

> Then shall all elements of the Cosmos fail,
> Air, earth, sea, light, the pole, days and nights.[25]

Greek Apocalypse of Peter (Macarius, IV. 7) : " And all the power of heaven shall melt away, and all the stars shall fall as the leaves falleth off from the vine, and as a falling fig from the fig tree." [26]

Lactantius, VII. 19, 645, 10 : " And He shall come down to mid-earth with His attendant angels, and an unquenchable flame shall go before Him." [27]

Commodian, 1005 :

> At the given sign the plague shall fall from all the ether,
> With a crash of thunder the raging fire shall descend.[28]

Ascensio Jesaiœ, IV. 1 *et seq.* : " God shall come with His angels and with the powers of His saints " ; IV. 18 : " Then in wrath shall the voice of the Beloved rebuke this heaven and this dry [land], and the mountains and the hills, the cities and the desert, . . . and from it shall the Beloved cause fire to rise, and [it] shall consume all the wicked." [29]

Apocalypse of Zephaniah, 129 : " On that day it shall come to pass that the Lord shall hear it, and in great wrath the heaven and the earth shall be commanded, and they shall cast forth fire, and the flame shall encompass of the earth seventy and two ells, and the sinners devour and the devils like stubble."

Greek Apocalypse of Daniel, 109 : " But after fulfilment of the three times and one half God shall rain

16

down fire on the earth, and the earth shall be consumed thirty cubits ; then shall the earth cry unto
God, I am a virgin, O Lord, before Thy face." [30]

Ezra (Tischendorf, xxix.) : " Then shall I burn the
heaven eighty cubits and the earth eight hundred
cubits." [31]

Armenian Apocalypse of Daniel, 240, 13 : " Then
shall the sun be darkened and the moon changed to
blood. The stars shall fall down like leaves, and heaven
shall be rolled up like a scroll, . . . and all things
shall be scorched and parched by the wind. Fiery
angels shall come down from heaven, and fire shall
flare up throughout the whole world."

Syriac Apocalypse of Peter : " And fire shall eat
into the earth from above, and the ocean and the great
sea round the globe shall become dry. The light of
sun and moon shall grow dark, the stars be scattered
and fall down, and the heaven rolled up like a sheet of
paper."

Ethiopic Apocalypse of Peter : " And the sun shall
suffer eclipse and the moon become blood, and the
stars fall from heaven through the greatness of God's
wrath over mankind and the Messiah."

Bede's Sibyl :

Fire shall burn up earth and sea and heaven, . . .
The springs shall fail (?), and the everlasting flame con-
    sume ; . . .
[He] shall cast down the hills, and raise up valleys from the
    depths, . . .
From the heavens shall fall both fire and a sulphur
    stream ! [32]

Elucidarium: "With all the hierarchies of the angels shall He come, . . . all the elements shall be stirred by the mingled storm of fire and frost raging on all sides." [33]

Muspilli : " When the blood of Elias—drippeth on the ground—then shall the mountains burn—no tree stand on all the earth—The waters shall grow dry— the meres be sucked up—slowly glows the heaven aflame—The moon falls and burns up the mid-earth— no stone stands firm—then cometh the day of vengeance on the land—cometh with fire men to search —Then can none of kin each other help—before the world's doom—when the broad rain shall all consume —and fire and air sweep all away." [34]

A strong position is held in our tradition by the brief account of the last days in Isaiah xxxiv. 4 : " And all the host of heaven shall be dissolved, and the heavens shall be rolled together as a scroll : and all their host shall fall down, as the leaf falleth off from the vine, and as a falling fig from the fig tree." The passage is found imbedded in a connected tradition of the Antichrist in Sibyl III. 82 *et seq.*, and in the earlier Petrine Apocalypse, and also occurs in later sources, where, however, it is referred to the forewarnings of the end of the world,* and is similarly treated in Revelation vi. 12 *et seq.* It need, I suppose, scarcely here be assumed that Revelation vi. formed itself the concluding part of a shorter eschatological document. But at all events it may be rightly inferred that, in his description of the earthquake, the

* Cf. Ephr. Gr., D. A. Arm., P. A. Syr., P. A. Æth.

apocalyptic writer borrowed from the current tradition imagery which belonged originally to a description ot the end of the world. The fact that we meet with the same description in Matthew xxiv. 29 *et seq.* merely affords another proof that in this chapter the writer has made use of the Antichrist legend.

Characteristic is the final conflagration which is found constantly associated with the same tradition. No doubt the idea that a fiery tempest is to be let loose by God emanates from Daniel vii. 10. Nevertheless the distinctly expressed view that the world is to perish by fire seems to have been originally drawn from our tradition both by Jewish and Christian writers. But I will not venture to decide whether the idea itself derives from the Stoic school, or was developed under Oriental influences in late Jewish times. Such a question cannot be settled off-hand, without first exploring the ground inch by inch. It is significant that, although the idea already prevailed, the Book of Revelation does not speak of a destruction of the world by fire. In fact this belief, which was afterwards universally accepted, is mentioned in the New Testament once only—that is, in the Second Epistle of Peter iii. 6, 7: " Whereby the world that then was, being overflowed with water, perished : but the heavens and the earth, which are now, by the same word are kept in store, reserved unto fire against the day of judgment and perdition of ungodly men."

Even here we again see how little the whole body of the New Testament writings, compared with our single tradition, has contributed to determine the eschatological views of Christendom. The account of the last conflagration has been handed down from age to age with wonderful persistency, so that it stands out clearly in all its fulness in the Sibylline literature as well as in the Old High German *Muspilli* lay.

It is indeed surprising how we are everywhere told with the fullest details that the last fire is to consume the ocean, the rivers, and the springs ; while the words " and there was no more sea " are the only echo of all these details found in Revelation (xxi. 1). May it be assumed that in the mention of these particulars a lingering reminiscence survives of the belief that the old Serpent who revolts in the last days was originally the marine monster, who contends with the God of creation ?

In one of our earliest sources, the Syriac Ephrem, we still read how " God shall rebuke the sea and it shall dry up." And we are further told that at the end of time the sea shall utter a frightful roar.*

When again the description of the end is compared with the sketch in Revelation, it becomes extremely surprising that in the whole tradition not a trace is anywhere to be found of the idea of a millennium. From this it may be inferred that the common source of the Jewish and Christian tradition of our saga goes back to a time when, in the Jewish eschatology, there was not yet developed this further detail of the system, as it occurs about the close of the first century in 4 Ezra, Baruch, and Revelation. There was a time in the Christian Church also when the

* Cf. Ephr. Gr., 4 Ezra, Book of Clement.

millennium view was dominant, thanks to the influence
of Revelation. Justin, Irenæus, Lactantius, Tertul-
ian, Victorinus, were all believers in a millennium.
But then it is difficult to understand how, despite
Revelation and the patristic tradition, the millennium
theory came at last to be rejected as a Jewish super-
stition. The difficulty, however, may in a measure be
cleared up by remembering that Christendom had at
its disposal an early eschatological tradition which
knew nothing of a golden age to last for a thousand
years.

The essentially Jewish character of these views, and
consequently also of the parts of Revelation dealing
with them, is seen in the consideration that in the
Jewish sources of the Antichrist legend the idea of the
interregnum suddenly reappears (compare especially
the History of Daniel), while the usual description of
the end of the world is thrust aside.

A special trait in the description of the end is the
letting loose of the winds for the purifying of the
world. This last echo of a myth, which has already all
but disappeared from Daniel (vii. 1, etc.), occurs in the
pseudo-Johannine Apocalypse, 15 (Gunkel, 323 *et seq.*):
"Then shall I throw open the four parts of the east,
and there shall issue forth four great winds, and they
shall thoroughly winnow the face of all the earth, . . .
and the Lord shall scatter sin like chaff from the earth,
and the earth shall be made white as snow, . . . and
she shall cry unto Me, saying, I am [as] a maid
before Thee." [35]

Syriac Apocalypse of Peter : " Thereupon shall I order the four winds, and they shall be let loose one in the direction of the other."

Armenian Apocalypse of Daniel : " From heaven storms shall hither come."

Pseudo-Hippolytus, viii. 97, 1 : " Fierce gales of wind shall agitate the earth and the sea without measure." [36]

The same idea is also prevalent in the Sibylline literature, as in Sibyl VIII. 203 :

And the sun shall appear darkling by night,
And the stars quit the sky, and with great fury a hurricane
Shall lay waste the earth, and [then] shall be the resur-
    rection of the dead.[37]

This wide diffusion of the tradition leaves no doubt that the enigmatic fragment of Revelation vii. 1 *et seq.* was taken from this very source by the apocalyptic writer, who draws from the same authority his previous description of the incidents that follow the opening of the sixth seal (vi. 12-17).

In 1 Thessalonians iv. 16 Paul is able to tell us that " the Lord Himself shall descend from heaven with a shout, with the voice of the archangel, and with the trump of God." He shows his dependence on the same apocalyptic tradition as in 2 Thessalonians, and by the expression " the word of the Lord " in ver. 15 Paul does not mean any particular utterance of the Lord, but rather has in mind this old and vener-ated tradition. The great day of judgment is ushered in with " the voice of the archangel," which is to be taken as a perfect equivalent to " the trump of God." This sounding of the trump by Michael the Archangel, which proclaims the divine judgment, is a constant feature of our tradition, a faint echo of which lingers in Matthew xxiv. 31.

Lactantius (VII. 16, 637, 1) expressly quotes a sibyl as saying that " a trumpet blast shall send forth from heaven a sound of much wailing." [38]

Bede's Sibyl : " But from on high a trump sends down a moaning sound." [39] This literal parallelism shows how old is the tradition in this document.

Commodian, 901 : " Meanwhile the trump suddenly gives out a fearful blast from heaven, and lo ! it rings harsh through the firmament, everywhere with reverberating note." [40]

Ethiopic Apocalypse of Peter : " And thrice shall the horn be sounded by Michael the Archangel. . . . At the third blast of the horn shall the dead instantly rise up."

Pseudo-Chrysostom : " And before His face Michael the Archangel sounds the trump, and awakens those slumbering from Adam unto the consummation of all time." [41]

Pseudo-Johannine Apocalypse, 9 : " And Michael and Gabriel shall come out from heaven and sound the trump." [42]

That there should also be frequent mention of several angelic trumpeters was naturally to be expected from Matthew xxiv. 31. But the sounding of the trumpet by Michael the Archangel, as already

known to Paul, is peculiar to our tradition, and has
been preserved with it.

It is no longer possible to state in quite clear
language how the Antichrist legend concluded.   But
in any case we should apparently reject the description of the last judgment which is given under
the influence of Matthew xxv. 41-46 in greatest
detail by Greek Ephrem ; in Hippolytus, lxiv. ; in
the parallel part of pseudo-Hippolytus (39 *et seq.*);
and elsewhere.*   Here we have probably an interpolation, which was evidently based on Matthew,
and which is perhaps not earlier than Ephrem.   At
the same time it is not altogether impossible that in
Matthew xxv. itself we have some older eschatological
material.

But with the account drawn from Matthew another
is connected, which is even more widespread and persistent.   Here we read how in a vast hall of justice
all the generations of men from Adam are gathered
before God—the various nations, Jews as well as
Gentiles, the diverse ranks and classes of the peoples.
Such is the form taken by the legend in Greek Ephrem,
in pseudo-Hippolytus, and in the pseudo-Johannine
Apocalypse, where it is seen in its most genuine
aspect.   Lactantius also (VII. 20 and 24) appeals to
Sibylline authority, where a similar scene seems to
occur.   Compare the line : " They shall all of them

* Cf. Cyril, xv. 24 ; P. A. Æth. and Syr. ; Eterianus, xxv.
217 D ; and the *Elucidarium* ; traces also occur in D. A. Gr. and
J. A. 25.

come unto the altar of God the King." [43]   With all
this should also be compared the great judgment
scene in the opening of the Talmudic document Abodah
Sarah translated by Ewald (4 *et seq.*).   Widely
diffused is the introduction to this scene, where we
are told how all generations since Adam appear
before God.

Thus in the Johannine Apocalypse, 10 : " Those, O
Lord, who have died since Adam unto this day, and
the dwellers in Hades from all time, . . . whence shall
they rise again ? " [44]

Ephr. Syr., 12 : " Thereupon the angels going forth
shall gather the sons of Adam." [45]

Syriac pseudo-Apocalypse : " And all the children of
Adam shall appear before Me, trembling with fear."

Pseudo-Chrysostom : " Awakening those who had
fallen asleep from Adam unto the end of time." [46]

Another trait constantly recurring in this tradition
is the description drawn from Daniel xii. 3, respecting the appearance of the righteous and of the
unrighteous on the last day.   Thus pseudo-Johannine
Apocalypse, 23 : " For the just shall shine as asters
and as the sun, and the sinners stood wrapped in
gloom." [47]

Pseudo-Hippolytus, xxxix. 116, 21 : " Then the just
shall shine as the sun, but the sinners shall appear
abashed and sullen." [48]

Syriac Apocalypse of Peter : " Hail to him whose
works are good, for his face shall beam and he shall
rejoice and be glad.   But woe to him whose works are
evil, for he shall be sad and his face black."

Hildegard, *Scivias*, III. 12 : " The good shining in brightness, and the bad appearing in blackness." [49]

Lactantius, VII. 26 : " And God shall change men to the likeness of angels, and they shall be white as snow." [50]

Perhaps we have here an eschatological tradition connected with Matthew xiii. 43, for Daniel xii. 3 is not quite parallel.

That in the pitiless doom of God the mutual supplications of the next akin shall avail naught is already insisted upon in 4 Ezra vii. 41 *et seq.* Compare also Commodian, 1035 *et seq.*, and the allied passage in the Syriac Apocalypse of Peter.

In conclusion, without attempting to deal with the influence of the Antichrist legend on the Germanic peoples in the mediæval times, I may here refer to an interesting fragment of the old (Continental) Saxon Genesis, to which my attention has been directed by Herr Lueken. The passage (vers. 136-150) has reference to Enoch's translation and return to earth, concluding with the fate of the Antichrist :

" Him [Enoch] heaven's ruler took up and placed him where he must ever dwell in bliss until He [God] send him again into the world, heaven's high warden to the children of men, unto the teaching of the peoples. Then cometh also the evil one, the Antichrist, [and] destroyeth all nations, when he with the sword shall be the murderer of Enoch with sharp cutting. By the strength of his [the Antichrist's] hands wanders the soul [of Enoch] the ghost on the good way, and God's angel cometh and on him the malefactor wreaks vengeance. Of his life shall the Antichrist be bereft, the foe felled, [and] the people led to God's kingdom, the throng of men a long while. And thereafter ariseth the new earth, the sound land."

AN OLD ARMENIAN FORM OF THE ANTICHRIST SAGA.*

BUT after this the liberation of all the lands of Christendom from the Aryan hosts shall be wrought by the Romans. And then the earth shall repose in goodly paths for long epochs, and shall become like a garden full of all things. But the lawless shall be repulsed, and shall fall under the yoke of slavery to the Romans. And men will lament the past, and the goods which then failed them. After that shall be manifested the son of perdition, the Antichrist.†

Whilst then I ‡ am still in the flesh I declare unto you

---

* Translated by Mr. F. C. Conybeare, from a Life of S. Nerses published in 1853 at San Lazaro, Venice, as Vol. VI. of the Sopherk series, from four MSS. of the twelfth and thirteenth centuries. The Life of S. Nerses was compiled soon after the Frankish conquest of Jerusalem, mostly from materials as old as the fifth century. Mr. Conybeare remarks that "these predictions about the Antichrist are put into the mouth of the dying saint. For the Temple at Jerusalem the compiler substitutes the Christian Church, and introduces some other Christian touches. But on the whole he presents us with a fairly primitive and complete form of the legend so confirming what Bousset says as to the stability of the myth in its main outlines, no matter how fluctuating the events which men sought to explain by means of it " (*Academy,* October 19th, 1895).

† The Armenian equivalent for Antichrist (*nerhn*) can be nothing else but a transliteration of νέρων.

‡ *I.e.* Nerses Parthevi, a patriarch of the Armenians in the fourth century.

[him], whose advent is by the inspiration of Satan. But he ruleth not over Turks or Persians or Gentiles, but over the votaries of the all-victorious cross. For he is very son of perdition of those who fell from their glory. But yonder abomination shall be for the refutation of the Jews, since they it is who give ear to the deceiver. But do ye instruct your children, and your children their children; and let them write it down and keep the record until the approach of the abomination, in order that they may be ready against the snare and may not be swallowed up in his snare. . . .

The sign then of the manifestation of the Antichrist is this. When the earth shall be filled with tumult, after the good time, and the sovereignty be taken away from the Romans; as was made known to Daniel concerning the four beasts: the he-lion, that is the Kingdom of the Medes; and the bear, which is that of the Babylonians; and the leopard, which is that of the Persians; and the fourth, which was manifested terrible and wondrous, which devoured and brake in pieces the earth, which is the Kingdom of the Romans. For as at the coming of Christ the rule of Israel was destroyed, so likewise the manifesting of the abomination will destroy the rule of the Romans. But three kingdoms were annihilated, and the fourth stood firm, which is the Kingdom of the Romans, which is destroyed by the Antichrist.

To begin with, cruelty shall flourish, and love be dried up, and droughts occur and earthquakes and plagues. Brother shall betray brother unto death and father son. This was declared by the Lord, as ye know. And the earth shall be overshadowed. For that which they will sow, they shall not reap; and that which they shall have planted, they shall not eat; and many presages shall there be of the manifestation of the Antichrist. Think ye not however that he is Satan, or a devil from among his hosts. No, but a man lost in mind and soul of the tribe of Dan,

and he is born in Chorazin, a village of the people of
Israel; and his name is Hrômelay, and his mother's name
Nerlimine.* And her name is Hrasim. And he is born
of virgins and goeth unto Byzantium and is great in name
according to the greatness of the Greeks.

Then the kingdom of the Greeks is divided into ten
sceptres; and Antichrist himself shall be one of the kings;
and he shall slay the three kings, and bring the rest into
subjection unto himself, and himself be lord over all. He
shall reign for three times and a half of times; and he
destroyeth the earth in his wrath, and he beareth in himself
the entire livery of Satan, and his coming is at the inspiration of Satan. And he will work signs and wonders during
a thousand and two hundred and sixty days. But blessed
is he who shall endure and arrive at the days of our Lord
Jesus Christ and be saved. Then if there be grinding two
in one mill, the one shall be taken and the other left. And
there shall shoot forth the leaf of the fig tree, which is the
Antichrist. The branches shooting up are his ministers.
The mill is this life, and the taking is the discrimination
of good from evil.

The Son of Perdition therefore shall sit in the church of
God, and shall begin to blaspheme God. And he demands
that worship should be paid him as if to God; and showeth
himself off as God, and boasteth in pride over all so-called
gods. But he will permit himself alone to be reverenced in
place of God, filling the earth with evils and with foulness.

Then sendeth God the two prophets, Enoch and Elias,
for the salvation of men; and they warn the faithful and

* So the most complete twelfth-century MS.; but two other uncial
sources have the one Melitene and the other Nelitene—cf. *Sibyll.*,
III. 63 (cited by Bousset): ἐκ δὲ Σεβαστηνῶν ἥξει Βελίαρ μετοπίσθεν.
I render the Armenian as it stands; but we should evidently read:
"But his mother is of Melitene, and her name is Hrasim." Romelay
= Romulus.

turn again the hearts of the fathers unto their children, even as the Lord also declared, saying, Elias cometh and shall prepare my way. As then in the first coming John was the forerunner of Christ, so also in the second coming Elias is reserved to be forerunner along with Enoch. They shall therefore both come and say : Believe ye not in the abomination which is in the holy place ; for he is the great dragon and crafty serpent. With his guile he tricks you and with his false miracles. Go ye not nigh unto him, but flee unto the mountains ; and be patient yet a little while. He is a false Christ, and by means of false prophets would fain deceive the worshippers of the cross. He is the in- spiration of many a madness. But pray ye day and night, since the time of trouble is short, but the bliss unending.

Christ of a verity is not on earth, but in heaven in unspeakable glory ; and he shall consign him yonder to outer darkness and pitiless tortures. Nor doth Christ come before Pilate for judgment, but himself judgeth the earth.

This and the like thereto do Enoch and Elias preach unto men. Then the earth waxeth foul and fetid with the stench of the dead ; and it is contaminated on all sides, and all the faces of men are sick with the stress of famine and of thirst for water. Gold and silver and all sorts of raiment are thrown down,* but no one desireth them in the peril which is imminent in the evilness of the time. Then do men remember their outrageous deeds, the mul- titude namely, that accepted on their brows the foul sign of madness, " Give us aid in our straits, for we perish all together." But he will not succour them, but only tricks them with vain hope. Even then Enoch and Elias are taken by his hand, and that abomination tortureth them with terrible blows and blasphemeth God with many words. But when the holy prophets yield not to his chicanery and

* *I.e.* in would-be payment for meat and drink.

false signs, he will slay Enoch and Elias before the eyes of many. And there is rejoicing among the false prophets, when they behold the death of the true prophets.

Then doth the great dragon himself, the son of perdition, cry aloud in the hearing of all, and say: Behold ye my mighty power. Since for many a year they had been immortal, and no others can be rescued from my hands.* And no one hath been able to overcome my might. And yet more doth his wickedness flame up in the land, whom the Lord Jesus shall utterly destroy with the breath of his mouth. And he multiplies his blasphemies against the most high in the hearing of many. But even while he continueth to speak in such wise, on a sudden in the twinkling of an eye there cometh a shock of terrible thunder; and at the selfsame moment the ministers of the foul Antichrist are consumed and melt away.

Then doth appear in brilliancy the royal sign unto the strengthening of those that took refuge in him unto the glory of the just ones, for that they bound themselves in his love. The parts of the all-victorious cross flash with light, and the hosts of holy church, and [or also] take their full growth along with the Lord's cross; and full of light they are [yet] eclipsed by its light.† Let the nations mourn, for he cometh to judge them that were not sealed therewith, them that knew it not, the sign of the Lord.

Then there cometh from heaven in unspeakable glory the king of glory. The heavens are shrivelled up and are consumed like wax before the fire. Rivers running free and full of gloom pour down from on high, purifying the earth from all lawlessness and foul deeds. There are heard the voices of the army of light. There stir the hosts of heaven, and the great trumpet sounds among the tombs. Arise ye

* This sentence is obscure.

† The punctuation of the Armenian text seems to be wrong.
? Remove comma after " church."

17

dead, to meet the bridegroom ! For he is here, he is come
in his father's glory. Arise, just ones and sinners, and
receive your reward !

Then with grief inconsolable shall mourn the creation
that is not ready [*or* creatures that are not]. And in haste
they don their bodies that are indestructible. Then the
sinners appear in sombre and shadow-like bodies, for they
are tinged with the works of their wickedness. Foremost
walk in person the elect in resplendent bodies; they are
lifted up from earth in clouds of light to meet Christ, and
the heavenly ones wonder at them and say : What have
they done upon earth, for they come in a crowd unto the
Lord full of joy ? The Lord will make answer and say to
them : These are my good soldiers, who denied themselves,
and renounced the earth and crucified themselves along
with their passions and desires for their love of me. Now
therefore I will give them joy unending. And when the
angels shall hear this, they will say : Ye are blessed by the
Lord ; rejoice ye therefore in your gladness.

Then the king of glory shall sit down on his throne; and
angels with awe minister unto him. And first of all Satan
is bound without inquisition, and is dispatched into the
abyss of Tartarus. And with cruel torments are bound his
hosts on the left hand, for they taught men evil works.
They do not deserve to be brought to judgment, since they
have no defence to make before his tribunal. And without
delay they are removed out of his sight. But the just shall
stand on his right hand in hope of the good reward. The
sinners also stand there in great shame, each for retribution
for his deeds. The assize is met and the books are opened;
they are bound together in sheaves like the tares and are
cast into the unquenchable fire. But unto some also are
shut the doors of the blissful wedding, so that they cannot
see and look upon the heavenly bridegroom ; and because
they have not lit the torches of pity, he saith unto them :

I know you not, get ye out of my sight. But before this the king bestoweth the heavenly crown upon the worthy, saying unto them : Come ye blessed ones of my Father, and inherit the kingdom made ready for you from the beginning of the world.

The heavens are made new, the earth is made new; it is green and puts forth leaves in gladness. And the kingdom is thirtyfold, as also the garden sixtyfold, and the heavens hundredfold. And there shall not be on earth any toil or sweat ; no crafty serpent nor beguiling woman ; but there shall be trees that fade not with their fruit, and all pain and sorrow shall be removed, and there shall be only joy and delight. And to some he will give a kingdom upon earth ; but for the martyrs there gleam scarlet crowns and robes and glory. With them are the virgins, who polluted not themselves on this earth ; along with the virgin Mary shall they receive the adornment of the crown of glory, transfigured. Like the sun among the stars, even so shall excel the glory of the virgins amidst the wedded ones.

And do ye, my children, take note of all this, that ye may be saved from the meshes of the pursuer. . . .

APPENDIX.

APPENDIX.

GREEK AND LATIN TEXTS.

CHAPTER II.

[1] Τὸ δὲ οὐχ ἅμα πάντες ἴσασιν, οὐ γὰρ πάντων πάντα.

[2] Forte quoniam apud Judæos erant quidam sive per scripturas profitentes de temporibus consummationis se scire *sive de secretis*, ideo hæc scribit docens discipulos suos ut nemini credant talia profitenti.

[3] De quo pauca tamen suggero quæ legi secreta.

CHAPTER III.

[1] Et in his omnibus bella Persarum sunt—in illis diebus veniunt [venient?] ad regnum Romanum duo fratres et uno quidem animo præsunt (?), sed quoniam unus præcedit alium, fiet inter eos scidium.

[2] Λόγος εἰς τὴν παρουσίαν τοῦ κυρίου καὶ περὶ συντελείας τοῦ κόσμου καὶ εἰς τὴν παρουσίαν τοῦ 'Αντιχρίστου.

[3] Περὶ τῆς συντελείας τοῦ κόσμου καὶ περὶ τοῦ 'Αντιχρίστου.

[4] Τοῦ ἁγίου 'Εφραὶμ λόγος εἰς τὸν 'Αντίχριστον.

[5] Λόγος περὶ τοῦ σταυροῦ.

[6] Λόγος εἰς τὴν δευτέραν παρουσίαν τοῦ Χριστοῦ.

[7] 'Ερωτήσεις καὶ ἀποκρίσεις.

[8] Περὶ τοῦ σημείου τοῦ σταυροῦ.

⁹ Λόγος εἰς τὸν τίμιον καὶ ζωοποιὸν σταυρὸν καὶ εἰς τὴν δευτέραν παρουσίαν καὶ περὶ ἀγάπης καὶ ἐλεημοσύνης.

¹⁰ εἰς τὴν δευτέραν παρουσίαν τοῦ κ. ἡ. Ἰ. Χρ.

¹¹ Ἐρωτήσεις καὶ ἀποκρίσεις.

¹² Περὶ τῆς κοινῆς ἀναστάσεως καὶ μετανοίας καὶ ἀγάπης.

¹³ Περὶ ἀποταγῆς ἐρωτήσεις.

¹⁴ Περὶ μετανοίας καὶ κρίσεως καὶ εἰς τὴν δευτέραν παρουσίαν.

¹⁵ Μακαρισμοὶ ἕτεροι.

¹⁶ Περὶ τῆς συντελείας τοῦ κόσμου καὶ περὶ τοῦ Ἀντιχρίστου καὶ εἰς τὴν δευτέραν παρουσίαν τοῦ κυρίου ἡμῶν Ἰησοῦ Χριστοῦ.

¹⁷ Εἰς τὴν δευτέραν παρουσίαν τοῦ κυρίου ἡμῶν Ἰ. Χρ. καὶ περὶ ἐλεημοσύνης.

CHAPTER IV.

¹ De illo tunc debet rex procedere de Bizantio Romanorum et Græcorum habens scriptum in fronte, ut vindicet regnum Christianorum, qui subiciet filios Hismahel et vincet eos et eruet regnum Christianorum de jugo pessimo Sarracenorum. In illis diebus nemo poterit sub cœlo regnum superare Christianorum. Postea gens Sarracenorum ascendet per 7 tempora et facient universa mala in toto orbe terrarum perimentque pene omnes Christianos. Post hæc surget regnum Romanorum et percutiet eos, et erit post hæc pax et regnum Christianorum usque ad tempus Antichristi.

² Sib. Beda.	² Adso.
Et tunc exsurget rex nomine et animo constans. Ille idem constans erit rex Romanorum et Græcorum.	Tempore prædicti regis, cuius nomen erit C., rex Romanorum totius imperii. . . .
³ Et ipse rex scripturam habebit ante oculos dicentem :	Hic semper habebit præ oculis scripturam ita dicentem :

Rex Romanorum omne sibi vindicet [vindicat] regnum

terrarum [Christianorum]. Omnes ergo insulas et civitates [paganorum] devastabit et universa idolorum templa destruet et omnes paganos ad baptismum convocabit, et per omnia templa crux Christi [Jesu] erigetur.

⁴ [Et postea rex] veniet [in] Jerusalem et ibi deposito [capitis] diademate [et omni habitu regali] relinquet Deo patri et filio eius Chr. J. regnum Christianorum [regnum Christianorum Deo patri relinquet et filio eius J. Chr.]. Adso adds the words, *et erit sepulcrum eius gloriosum.*

⁵ Καὶ μετ᾽ αὐτὸν βασιλεύσει ἕτερος ἐξ αὐτοῦ ἔτη ιβ΄. καὶ οὗτος προιδὼν τὸν θάνατον αὐτοῦ πορευθῇ εἰς τὰ Ἱεροσόλυμα, ἵνα παραδώσῃ τὴν βασιλείαν αὐτοῦ τῷ Θεῷ (Klostermann, *Analecta,* 116, 81).

⁶ Καὶ ὁ μέγας Φίλιππος μετὰ γλωσσῶν δεκαοκτὼ καὶ συναχθήσονται ἐν τῇ Ἑπταλόφῳ καὶ συγκροτήσουσι πόλεμον.

⁷ Τότε βοῦς βοήσει καὶ Ξηρόλοφος θρηνήσει. On Ξηρόλοφος, see Gutschmid, 153.

⁸ Τότε αἰφνίδιον ἐπαναστήσεται βασιλεὺς Ἑλλήνων ἤτοι Ῥωμαίων, καθάπερ ἄνθρωπος ἀπὸ ὕπνου πιὼν οἶνον.

⁹ Et jam regnum Romanorum tollitur de medio et *Christianorum imperium traditur Deo et Patri* et tunc venit consummatio, cum' cœperit consummari Romanorum regnum et expleti fuerint omnes principatus et potestates. The introduction of this passage from 1 Corinthians, chap. xv., occurs also in the pseudo-Methodius (cf. Zezschwitz, 56).

¹⁰ EPHREM, III. 190.

Porro sicut Nilus—crescendo inundat regionem, accingent se regiones contra imperium Romanum, et bellabunt gentes cum gentibus et regnum cum regno et ex una regione in alteram transibunt Romani veluti in fuga.

¹⁰ PSEUDO-EPHREM, I.

In illis diebus multi consurgent contra regnum Romanum . . . erunt enim commotiones gentium.

11 Εἶναι δὲ τὸν Γὼγ καὶ Μαγώγ τινες μὲν Σκυθικὰ ἔθνη νομίζουσιν ὑπερβορεῖα, ἅπερ καλοῦμεν οὐννικὰ πάσης ἐπιγείου βασιλείας πολυανθρωπότερα καὶ πολεμικώτερα.

12 Extollent vocem sancti, et ascendet clamor eorum in cœlum, exietque e deserto populus Hagaræ Saræ ancillæ filius, qui accepit fœdus Abrahæ mariti Saræ et Hagar, et movebit se, ut in nomine deserti veniat tamquam legatus filii perditionis.

13 Et surget in huius gentis loco regnum Romanorum, quod subjiciet terram usque ad fines eius, et nemo erit qui resistet ei. Postquam autem multiplicata fuerit iniquitas in terra . . . tunc exsurget justitia divina et funditus delebit populum, et ex perditione egressus veniet super terram vir iniquus.

14 Eriget se contra fideles tribus modis i. e. terrore, muneribus et miraculis; dabit credentibus in se auri atque argenti copias; quos autem muneribus corrumpere non poterit, terrore superabit; quos autem terrore non poterit vincere, signis et miraculis seducere tentabit.

15 Minis blanditiis et omnibus modis seducet.

16 Antichristus quoque multa deceptis munera largietur et terram suo exercitui dividet, quosque terrore non quieverit, subjugabit avaritia. The Spanish priest Beatus follows Jerome in his Commentary (Florence, p. 442).

CHAPTER V.

1 37. Οἱ δὲ υἱοὶ τῆς ἀπωλείας στηρίξαντες δώσουσι τὰ πρόσωπα αὐτῶν ἐπὶ τὴν δύσιν τοῦ ἥλιου.

28. Οὐαί σοι Ἑπτάλοφε ἐκ τῆς τοιαύτης ὀργῆς, ὅταν κυκλωθῇς ὑπὸ στρατοπέδου πολλοῦ . . . καὶ κρατήσει [to be read instead of πατήσει] τὸ μειράκιον ἐπί σε ἐλεεινῇ.

2 Καὶ ἐν τῷ μὴ εἶναι ἄνδρα χρήσιμον βασιλεύσει γυνὴ μιαρὰ ἐν τῇ ἑπταλόφῳ καὶ μιάνῃ τὰ ἅγια τοῦ Θεοῦ θυσιαστήρια καὶ σταθεῖσα ἐν μέσῳ τῆς ἑπταλόφου βοήσει φωνῇ μεγάλῃ λέγουσα·

τίς Θεὸς πλὴν ἐμοῦ καὶ τίς δύναται ἀντιστῆναι τὴν ἐμὴν βασιλείαν; καὶ εὐθὺς σεισθήσεται ἡ ἑπτάλοφος καὶ καταποντισθήσεται σύμψυχος ἐν βυθῷ.

³ Καὶ τότε δὴ πᾶς κόσμος ὑπαὶ παλάμῃσι γυναικὸς—ἔσσεται ἀρχόμενος καὶ πειθόμενος περὶ παντός.—ἔνθ' ὁπότ' ἂν κόσμου παντὸς χήρη βασιλεύσῃ—καὶ ῥίψῃ χρυσόν τε καὶ ἄργυρον εἰς ἅλα δῖαν—χαλκόν τ' ἠδὲ σίδηρον ἐφημερίων ἀνθρώπων—ἐς πόντον ῥίψῃ, τότε δὴ στοιχεῖα πρόπαντα—χηρεύσει κόσμου ὁπότ' ἂν Θεὸς αἰθέρι ναίων—οὐρανὸν εἰλίξῃ.

⁴ Ἡ τελευταία ὅρασις τοῦ μεγάλου προφήτου Δανιήλ, ἥτις διὰ τοῦ ἐν ἁγίοις πατρὸς ἡμῶν Μεθοδίου Πατάρων ἐφανερώθη ἡμῖν (*Cod. Pseudepigr. Vet. Test.,* I. 1140).

⁵ De egressu filii Dan maledicti, qui est Antichristus et de descensu Eliæ et Enoch, quodque hos ille interfecturus est et prodigia magna ac miracula multa editurus.

CHAPTER VI.

¹ Exsurget iterum in istius clade Neronis
Rex ab oriente[m] cum quattuor gentibus inde
Invitatque sibi quam multas gentes ad urbem,
Qui ferant auxilium, licet sit fortissimus ipse,
Implebitque mare navibus cum milia multa ;
Et si quis occurrerit illi, mactabitur ense ;
Captivatque prius Tyrum et Sidona subactas.

² Τὸ δὲ ὅρμημα αὐτοῦ πρῶτον ἔσται ἐπὶ Τύρον καὶ Βήρυτον.

³ Ipsum denique Neronem ab Antichristo esse perimendum.

⁴ Βιβλίον Κλήμεντος πρῶτον τὸ καλούμενον διαθήκη τοῦ κυρίου ἡμῶν Ἰησοῦ Χριστοῦ.

⁵ Ἐγερθήσεται δὲ καὶ ἐν τῇ δύσει βασιλεὺς ἀλλόφυλος, ἄρχων μηχανῆς πολλῆς ἄθεος ἀνθρωποκτόνος πλάνος . . . μισῶν τοὺς πιστούς, διώκτης. Then (82, 40): Πότε ἐλεύσεται ὁ υἱὸς τῆς ἀπωλείας ὁ ἀντίπαλος καὶ ὑψούμενος καὶ ἐπαιρόμενος, etc.

⁶ Ἐγερθήσεται δὲ καὶ ἐν τῇ δύσει βασιλεὺς ἀλλόφυλος . . . μισῶν τοὺς πιστούς, διώκτης· κυριεύσει δὲ καὶ ἐθνῶν βαρβάρων καὶ ἐκχυνεῖ αἵματα πολλά . . . ἔσται δὲ ἐν πάσῃ πόλει καὶ ἐν παντὶ τόπῳ ἁρπαγὴ καὶ ἐπιδρομὴ λῃστῶν καὶ ἐκχύσεις αἱμάτων.

⁷ Et sonus et vox et maris bullitio.

Et in terra erunt monstrua... draconum generatio de homines similiter et serpentium.

Et mox nubserit femina, pariet filios dicentes sermones perfectos.

⁷ Ezra v. 7. Mare Sodomiticum ... dabit vocem noctu.

v. 8. Et bestiæ agrestes transmigrabunt regionem suam, et mulieres menstruatæ parient monstra.

vi. 21. Et anniculi infantes loquentur vocibus suis, et prægnantes immaturos parient infantes trium et quattuor mensium.

CHAPTER VIII.

¹ Αὐτὰρ ἐπεὶ Ῥώμη καὶ Αἰγύπτου βασιλεύσει.

² Ἀλλὰ τὰ μὲν δεκάτῃ γενεῇ μάλα πάντα τελεῖται· νῦν δ' ὃς ἀπὸ πρώτης γενεῆς ἔσται τάδε λέξω.

³ Ἀλλ' ὁπότ' ἂν δεκάτη γενεή δόμον Ἄιδος εἴσω.

⁴ Ἔνθ' ὁπότ' ἂν κόσμου παντὸς χήρη βασιλεύσῃ.

⁵ Θηλυτέρης μετέπειτα μέγα κράτος· ἦ κακὰ πολλά αὐξήσει Θεὸς αὐτός, ὅτ' ἂν βασιληίδα τιμὴν στεψαμένη τετύχῃ.

⁶ Ἠδὲ γυναικὸς ἀδουλώτου ἐπὶ κῦμα πεσούσης.

⁷ Sunt autem Judæi trans Persida flumine clausi,
Quos usque in finem voluit Deus ibi morari.

⁸ Alexander Gog et Magog æternaliter conclusit. Undecim tribus Hebræorum montibus æternaliter circumcinxit. More on this point may be seen in Malvenda, II. 571.

CHAPTER IX.

[1] Et amici omnes semet ipsos expugnabunt.

[2] Et erit in illo tempore, debellabunt amici amicos ut inimicos.

[3] Et erit incomposito vestigio, quam nunc vides regnare regionem et videbunt eam desertam. Si autem tibi dederit altissimus vivere et videbis [quæ] post tertiam turbatam (Hilgenfeld). The Greek runs, Τὴν μετὰ τὴν τρίτην θορυβουμένην.

[4] Est et alia major necessitas nobis orandi pro imperatoribus etiam pro omni statu imperii rebusque Romanis, qui vim maximam universo orbi imminentem ipsamque clausulam sæculi acerbitates horrendas comminantem *Romani imperii commeatu scimus retardari,* itaque nolumus experiri et dum precamur differri Romanæ diuturnitati favemus. And *ad Scapulam,* 2 : Christianus nullius est hostis, nedum imperatoris, quem . . . salvum velit cum toto Romano imperio, quousque sæculum stabit. Tamdiu enim stabit. Cf. also his exposition of 2 Thessalonians ii., Resurr. Carnis., 24, and Jerome on the same passage in his epistle to Algasia and in his Commentary on Jeremiah, 25, 26; the exegesis of Chrysostom in the *Ambrosiaster*; Pelagius (in Jerome) ; Sedulius ; Primasius ; Theophylactus ; Œcumenius.

[5] *Sibyllæ* tamen aperte interituram esse Romam loquuntur. . . . Hystaspes quoque, qui fuit Medorum rex antiquissimus . . . sublatuiri ex orbe imperium nomenque Romanum multo ante præfatus est. 16 (635, 1) : Quomodo autem id futurum sit ostendam. In primis multiplicabitur regnum et summa rerum potestas per plurimos dissipata et concisa minuetur . . . donec reges decem pariter existant, . . . hi . . . disperdent omnia et comminuent et vorabunt. VII. 25 (664, 18) : Etiam res ipsa declarat lapsum ruinamque

rerum brevi fore, nisi quod incolumi urbe Roma nihil istius
videtur esse metuendum. At vero cum caput illud orbis
occiderit et ῥύμη esse cœperit, quod Sibyllæ fore aiunt,
quis dubitet venisse jam finem . . .? Illa est civitas, quæ
adhuc sustentat omnia, precandusque nobis et adorandus est
deus cæli, si tamen statuta eius et placita differri possunt,
ne citius quam putamus Tyrannus ille abominandus veniat.
For the above allusion to the Sibyls, see Sibyl III. 364 ;
VIII. 165.

⁶ Et cum cœperit regnum Romanorum gladio consummari adest adventus mali . . . in expletione enim Romani
regni necesse est sæculum consummari. . . . 5 : Et jam
régnum Romanorum tollìtur de medio *et Christianorum
imperium traditur Deo et patri,* et tunc veniet consummatio
cum cœperit consummari Romanorum regnum.

⁷ Ἄνθρωπον μάγον . . . ἁρπάζοντα μὲν ἑαυτῷ τῆς Ῥωμαίων
βασιλείας τὴν ἐξουσίαν . . . ἔρχεται δὲ ὁ προειρημένος Ἀντίχριστος οὗτος, ὅταν πληρωθῶσιν οἱ καιροὶ τῆς Ῥωμαίων βασιλείας.

⁸ Jam illud imperium ad eos pertinere, qui Latini
dicuntur, spiritus . . . declaravit et docuit per Hippolytum
in eo libro, quo Johannis Theologi apocalypsin interpre-
tatur. Here may also be compared the other passages
quoted above from Adso, the Sibyls in Bede and pseudo-
Methodius.

⁹ Quidam putant hoc de imperio dictum fuisse Romano.

CHAPTER X.

¹ Ἐν περιτομῇ ὁ σωτὴρ ἦλθεν εἰς τὸν κόσμον, καὶ αὐτὸς
ὁμοίως ἐλεύσεται.

² Hunc ergo suscitatum Deus mittet regem dignum
dignis et Christum qualem meruerunt Judæi. Et quoniam
aliud nomen allaturus est, aliam etiam vitam instituturus,
ut sic eum tamquam Christum excipiant Judæi, ait [enim]

Daniel (xi. 37): desideria mulierum non cognoscet, cum prius fuerit impurissimus et nullum Deum patrum cognoscet. Non enim seducere populum poterit circumcisionis nisi legis vindicator.

[3] Nostri autem et melius interpretantur et rectius, quod in fine mundi hæc sit facturus Antichristus, qui consurgere habet de modica gente i. e. de populo Judæorum.

[4] Alter rex orietur ex Syria.

[5] Exsurget iterum . . . rex ab orientem. Here *ab* (" from ") is surely to be retained and not replaced with the latest editor by *ad* (" to "), for the king as a matter of fact is to come *from* the East (cf. 905 *et seq.* of Commodian). The ungrammatical *ab* orient*em* may be due to the ignorance of the scribe at a time when the accusative was everywhere tending to absorb all the other oblique cases.

[6] Nobis Nero factus Antichristus, ille Judæis.

[7] Καὶ ἀνατελεῖ ὑμῖν ἐκ τῆς φυλῆς Ἰούδα καὶ Λευὶ τὸ σωτήριον κυρίου καὶ αὐτὸς ποιήσει πρὸς τὸν Βελίαρ πόλεμον.

[8] Καὶ Βελίαρ θ' ἥξει καὶ σήματα πολλὰ ποιήσει ἀνθρώποις.

[9] Ἐκ δὲ Σεβαστηνῶν ἥξει Βελίαρ μετοπίσθεν.

[10] Descendet Beliar angelus magnus rex huius mundi . . . in specie hominis.

[11] Ille . . . veniet . . . quasi apostata et iniquus et homicida ; quasi latro.

[12] Tunc apparebit ille nequissimus et abominabilis draco, ille quem appellavit Moyses in Deuteronomio dicens : Dan catulus leonis accubans et exiliens ex Basan. Accubat enim, ut rapiat et perdat et mactet. Catulus leonis vero non sicut leo de tribu Dan sed propter iram rugiens ut devoret.

[13] Ἐπειδὴ γὰρ ὁ κλέπτης   καὶ ἀλάστωρ καὶ ἀπηνὴς
πρῶτος μέλλει ἔρχεσθαι   ἐν τοῖς ἰδίοις καιροῖς
βουλόμενος κλέψαι καὶ   θῦσαι καὶ ἀπολέσαι.

[14] Τότε φανήσεται ὁ ἀρνητὴς καὶ ἐξορισμένος ἐν τῇ σκοτίᾳ ὁ λεγόμενος Ἀντίχριστος.

[15] Καὶ κρατήσει ὁ τρισκαταρότατος δαίμων.

¹⁶ Et regnabit quem non sperant qui inhabitant super terram.

¹⁷ Qui de improviso advenerit regnum sibi vindicans.

¹⁸ Et multi fideles et sancti, quum viderunt eum quem ipsi + non sperabant, [suspensum Jesum Dominum Christum, postquam ego Jesaias vidi eum qui suspensus est et accendit, et credentes quoque in eum, ex iis pauci in illis diebus reliqui erunt servi eius] fugient[es] ex eremo in eremum præstolantes eius (domini) adventum.

¹⁹ Ne eum [Antichristum] putemus . . . diabolum esse vel dæmonem sed *unum de hominibus* in quo totus Satanas habitaturus sit corporaliter.

²⁰ Τίς δὲ οὗτός ἐστιν; ἆρα ὁ σατανᾶς; οὐδαμῶς· ἀλλ' ἄν-θρωπος τις πᾶσαν αὐτοῦ δεχόμενος τὴν ἐνέργειαν.

²¹ Ἐν σχήματι ἀνθρώπου ἐφάνη ὁ σωτὴρ καὶ αὐτὸς ἐν σχή-ματι ἀνθρώπου ἐλεύσεται.

²² Γενηθήτω Δὰν ὄφις. . . . ὄφις οὖν τίς ἀλλ' ἢ ὁ ἀπ' ἀρχῆς πλάνος ὁ ἐν τῇ γενέσει εἰρημένος ὁ πλανήσας τὴν Εὖαν καὶ πτερνίσας τὸν Ἀδάμ;

²³ Ἐπειδὴ ὁ σωτὴρ τοῦ κόσμου βουλόμενος τὸ γένος τῶν ἀνθρώπων σῶσαι, ἐκ τῆς ἀχράντου καὶ παρθένου Μαρίας ἐτέχθη καὶ ἐν σχήματι σαρκὸς τὸν ἐχθρὸν κατεπάτησεν ἐν ἰδίᾳ δυνάμει τῆς αὐτοῦ θεότητος, τὸν αὐτὸν τρόπον καὶ ὁ διάβολος ἐκ μιαρᾶς γυναικὸς ἐξελεύσεται ἐπὶ τῆς γῆς, τίκτεται δὲ ἐν πλάνῃ ἐκ παρθένου, ὁ γὰρ Θεὸς ἡμῶν σαρκικῶς ἡμῖν ἐπεδήμησε . . . ὁ δὲ διάβολος εἰ καὶ σάρκα ἀναλάβοι ἀλλὰ ταῦτα ἐν δοκήσει. So also Philippus Solitarius in Dioptra, III. 10, p. 815 D: Itaque nascetur ex muliere libidinosa opinione quidem incarnatus sed non etiam re ipsa.

²⁴ Διδαχθῶμεν ὦ φίλοι,   ὁποίῳ τῷ σχήματι
ἐλεύσεται ἐπὶ γῆς   ὁ ἀναίσχυντος ὄφις.
ἐπειδήπερ ὁ σωτὴρ   τοῦ σῶσαι βουλόμενος
τὸ γένος τῶν ἀνθρώπων   ἐκ παρθένου ἐτέχθη
καὶ σχήματι ἀνθρώπου   ἐπάτησε τὸν ἐχθρὸν
ἐν ἁγίᾳ δυνάμει   τῆς αὐτοῦ θεότητος.

APPENDIX. 273

137 E:

Μαθὼν τοῦτο ὁ ἐχθρὸς,   ὅτι πάλιν ἔρχεται
ἐξ οὐρανοῦ (ὁ) κύριος   ἐν δόξῃ θεότητος,
ἐλογίσατο οὕτως   ἀναλαβεῖν τὸ σχῆμα
τῆς αὐτοῦ παρουσίας   καὶ ἀπατῆσαι πάντας.

A few lines farther on:

Τίκτεται δὲ ἀκριβῶς   ἐκ γυναικὸς μιαρᾶς
τὸ ἐκείνου ὄργανον,   οὐκ αὐτὸς δὲ σαρκοῦται.

[25] Ephr. Gr. is recalled by Cyril, xv. 14 : Ὁ σατανᾶς ὀργάνῳ κέχρηται ἐκείνῳ αὐτοπροσώπως δι' αὐτοῦ ἐνεργῶν.

[26] Μιμεῖται γὰρ ὁ τῶν ἀνθρώπων ἀλάστωρ τοῦ Θεοῦ καὶ σωτῆρος ἡμῶν τὴν ἐνανθρώπησιν, καὶ ὥσπερ αὐτὸς ἀνθρωπείαν φύσιν ἀναλαβὼν τὴν ἡμετέραν ἐπραγματεύσατο σωτηρίαν, οὕτως ἐκεῖνος ἄνθρωπον ἐκλεξάμενος πᾶσαν αὐτοῦ δέξασθαι δυνάμενον τὴν ἐνέργειαν . . . ἀνθρώπους πειράσεται.

[27] Sicut e contrario angelus sanctus in Tobiæ libro speciem et similitudinem . . . Azariæ suscepit.

[28] Lactantius, VII. 17 (I. 638, 14): Malo spiritu genitus.

[29] Sulpicius Severus, Dial., II. 14: Malo spiritu conceptus. Cf. also Andreas, who assumes in the Antichrist an ἀγγελικὴ οὐσία, an "angelic substance" (50, 13), with which cf. 51, 45 : ὁ ἐν τῷ Ἀντιχρίστῳ ἐνεργῶν διάβολος ("the devil operating in the Antichrist"). Cf. further the following passages :

Pseudo-Ephrem, 6 : Ex semine viri et ex immunda vel turpissima virgine malo spiritu vel nequissimo mixto concipitur.

Adso, 1292 B : Nascetur autem ex patris et matris copulatione, sicut et alii homines, non ut quidam fabulantur de sola virgine. . . . In ipso vero . . . germinationis suæ primordio diabolus simul intrabit in uterum matris suæ.

Jacob Edess. Ephr. Syr., I. 192 D : Coluber Antichristus Danitica matre nascetur patre Latino, qui clam nec amore

18

legitimo *quasi lubricus anguis* ad ejus feminæ concubitum prorepet.

Elucidarium: De meretrice generis Dan nascetur. In matris utero diabolo replebitur.

Birgitta Revel., VI. 67 : Antichristus nascetur de maledicta femina et de maledicto homine, de quorum seminibus diabolus formabit corpus suum.

30 Καὶ περὶ τοῦ δράκοντος τοῦ ἀναιδεστάτου καὶ δεινοῦ τοῦ μέλλοντος ταράσσειν πᾶσαν τὴν ὑπούρανον.

31 Ἐγερθήσεται ὁ ὄφις ὁ κοιμώμενος.

32 Δεινὸν τὸ θηρίον δράκων μέγας ἀνθρώποις ἀκαταγώνιστος.

33 Draconi natura doloso et callido . . . eum comparat.

34 Μέγας ἀγὼν ἀδελφοὶ   ἐν τοῖς καιροῖς ἐκείνοις
ἐπὶ πᾶσιν ἀνθρώποις   μάλιστα δὲ (τοῖς) πιστοῖς,
ὅτ᾽ ἂν ἐπιτελοῦνται   σημεῖα καὶ τέρατα
ὑπ᾽ αὐτοῦ τοῦ δράκοντος   ἐν πολλῇ ἐξουσίᾳ
ὅτ᾽ ἂν πάλιν ἑαυτὸν   δείκνυσιν ὥσπερ Θεὸν
ἐν φαντάσμασι φοβεροῖς   ἀέρει ἱπτάμενος
καὶ πάντας τοὺς δαίμονας   ἐν σχήματι ἀγγέλων
ἱπταμένους ἐν φόβῳ   ἔμπροσθεν τοῦ τυράννου,
βοᾷ γὰρ ἐν ἰσχύι   ἀλλάσσων καὶ τὰς μορφὰς
ἐκφοβῆσαι ἀμέτρως   ἅπαντας τοὺς ἀνθρώπους.

35 Τοὺς γὰρ δαίμονας αὐτοῦ ἀποδείξει ὡς ἀγγέλους φωτεινοὺς καὶ στρατιὰς ἀσωμάτων παρεισάξει, ὧν οὐκ ἔστιν ἀριθμὸς, καὶ ἔμπροσθεν πάντων ἀναδεικνύει αὐτὸν εἰς τὸν οὐρανὸν ἀναλαμβανόμενον μετὰ σαλπίγγων καὶ ἤχων καὶ κραυγῆς ἰσχυρᾶς εὐφημούντων αὐτὸν ἀδιηγήτοις ὕμνοις, καὶ ἐκλάμπων ὥσπερ φῶς ὁ τῆς σκοτίας κληρονόμος, καὶ ποτε μὲν εἰς οὐρανοὺς ἀνιπτάμενος, ποτὲ δὲ ἐπὶ τῆς γῆς κατερχόμενος ἐν δόξῃ μεγάλῃ, ποτὲ δὲ καὶ ὡς ἀγγέλους τοὺς δαίμονας ἐπιτάσσων τοῦ ποιεῖν τὰ θελήματα αὐτοῦ μετὰ πολλοῦ φόβου καὶ τρόμου.

36 Dioptra, III. 10, 816 C : In sublime volans ut angelus [imo ut dæmon] et terrores ac prodigia ad deceptionem effingens.

37 Nam cum omnem voluntatem seductoris diaboli com-

pleverit, ita quod justo judicio Dei amplius tantam
potestatem iniquitatis et crudelitatis suæ habere omnino
non permittetur, omnem cohortem suam congregabit et sibi
credentibus dicet, quia ad cœlos ire velit—et ecce velut
ictus tonitrui repente veniens caput ipsum tanta fortitudine
percutit, quod et de monte illo dejicitur et quod spiritum
suum in mortem emittit.

38 Ἤρξατο αἰφνιδίως μορφὰς ἐναλάσσειν ὥστε γενέσθαι αὐτὸν
ἐξαίφνης παιδίον καὶ μετ᾽ ὀλίγον γέροντα ἄλλοτε δὲ καὶ νεανίσκον
. . . καὶ ἐβάκχευεν ὑπουργὸν ἔχων τὸν διάβολον. Cf. also
chap. xxii.: εἰς τοῦτον δὲ τὸν Σίμωνα δύο οὐσίαι εἰσιν ἀνθρώπου
καὶ διαβόλου (" in this Simon are two beings, [those] of man
and the devil ").

39 Quin et figurarum et colorum conversionibus omnino
instar Protei alius ex alio . in sublime volans ut angelus
[imo ut dæmon] et terrores ac prodigia ad deceptionem
effingens.

40 Καὶ παιδίον γίνεται καὶ γέρων, καὶ μηδεὶς αὐτῷ πιστεύει,
ὅτι ἐστὶν ὁ υἱός μου ὁ ἀγαπητός.

41 Μύρεο καὶ σύ Κόρινθε τὸν ἐν σοὶ λυγρὸν ὄλεθρον,
ἡνίκα γὰρ στρεπταῖσι μίτοις Μοῖραι τριάδελφοι
κλωσάμεναι φεύγοντα δόλῳ ἰσθμοῖο παρ᾽ ὀμφὴν
ἄξουσιν μετέωρον, ἕως ἐσίδωσιν ἅπαντες.

42 Πυρφόρος ὄσσε δράκων ὁπότ᾽ ἂν ἐπὶ κύμασιν ἔλθῃ
γαστέρι πλῆθος ἔχων καὶ θλίψῃ σεῖο τὰ τέκνα
ἐσσομένου λιμοῦ τε καὶ ἐμφύλου πολέμοιο,
ἐγγὺς μὲν κόσμοιο τέλος καὶ ἔσχατον ἦμαρ.

43 Κωμάζει (?) βουλῇσι τὸν ἐγκρυφίῃσι λοχείαις·
Ἀσίδος ἐκ γαίης ἐπὶ Τρωικὸν ἅρμ᾽ ἐπιβάντα
θυμὸν ἔχοντ᾽ αἴθωνος· ὅτ᾽ ἂν δ᾽ ἰσθμὸν διακόψῃ
παπταίνων ἐπὶ πάντας ἰὼν πέλαγος διαμείψας,
καὶ τότε θῆρα μέγαν μετελεύσεται αἷμα κελαινόν.

44 Πεντήκοντα δ᾽ ὅ τις κεραίην λάχε, κοίρανος ἔσται
δεινὸς ὄφις φυσῶν πόλεμον βαρὺν . . .
καὶ τμήξει τὸ δίκυμον ὅρος λύθρῳ τε παλάξει,

ἀλλ' ἔσται καὶ ἄιστος ὁ λοίγιος. εἶτ' ἀνακάμψει
ἰσάζων Θεῷ αὐτὸν, ἐλέγξει δ' οὔ μιν ἐόντα.

45 Ὁ Ἀντίχριστος ὁ ἐκ τῶν σκοτεινῶν καὶ βυθίου τῆς γῆς
χωρίων ἐξιὼν, ἐν οἷς ὁ διάβολος καταδεδίκασται.

46 . . . Et po-tquam consummatum est, descendet Berial
angilus magnus rex huius murdi, cui dominatur ex quo
exstat, et descendet e firmamento suo [in specie hominis
regis iniquitatis matricidæ . hic est rex huius mundi] . . .
hic angelus Berial [in specie istius regni] veniet, et venient
cum eo omnes potestates huius mundi et audient eum in
omnibus quæ voluerit.

47 Πνεύματα τοῦ Βελίαρ.

48 Καὶ αὐτὸς ποιήσει πρὸς τὸν Βελίαρ πόλεμον καὶ τὴν
ἐκδίκησιν τοῦ νίκους δώσει πέρασιν ὑμῶν.

49 Et ascendimus in firmamentum, ego et ille, et ibi vidi
Sammaelem eiusque potestates, et erat magna pugna in eo
et sermones Satanici, et alius cum alio rixabatur . . . et
dixi[t] angelo: quæ est hæc rixa? Et dixit mihi: ita est,
ex quo hic mundus existit, usque nunc, et hæc pugna donec
veniet is, quem tu visurus es, eumque delebit.

50 Τὸ εἶδος τοῦ προσώπου αὐτοῦ ὡσεὶ ἀγροῦ. ὁ ὀφθαλμὸς
αὐτοῦ ὁ δεξιὸς ὡς ἀστὴρ τὸ πρωὶ ἀνατέλλων καὶ ὁ ἕτερος ἀσά-
λευτος, τὸ στόμα αὐτοῦ πῆχυς μία, οἱ ὀδοντες αὐτοῦ σπιθαμιαῖοι,
οἱ δάκτυλοι αὐτοῦ ὡς δρέπανα, τὸ ἴχνος τῶν ποδῶν αὐτοῦ σπιθα-
μῶν δύο καὶ εἰς τὸ μέτωπον αὐτοῦ ἡ γραφὴ Ἀντίχριστος.

CHAPTER XI.

1 Ἀνορθοῦται δὲ εὐθὺς   ἐκείνου βασιλεία,
     καὶ πατάξει ἐν θυμῷ   τρεῖς βασιλεῖς μεγάλους.

2 Et ibunt illi tres Cæsares resistere contra ;
     Quos ille mactatos volucribus donat in escam.

3 Et idola quidem seponens ad suadendum quod ipse sit
Deus, se autem extollens unum idolum.

⁴ Ἆρξε ὑψοῦσθαι τῇ καρδίᾳ καὶ ἐπαίρεσθαι κατὰ τοῦ Θεοῦ πάσης τῆς οἰκουμένης κρατῶν.

⁵ Ἰσάζων Θεῷ αὐτὸν, ἐλέγξει δ' οὔ μιν ἐόντα.

⁶ Qui ingressus in eo [templo] sedebit ut Deus et jubet se adorari ab omnibus gentibus.

⁷ Καὶ παραδεικνύει αὐτὸν ὡς Θεὸν καὶ στήσει τὸν τόπον αὐτοῦ εἰς τὸν τόπον τοῦ κρανίου.

⁸ Et dicet ego sum Deus O. M. et ante me non fuit quisquam. IV. 11 : Et statuet simulacrum suum ante faciem suam in omnibus urbibus.

⁹ Faciet etiam, ut imago aurea Antichristo in templo Hierosolymis ponatur, et intret angelus refuga et inde voces et sortes reddat.

¹⁰ Ἀνέστησεν ὁ σωτὴρ καὶ ἔδειξεν τὴν ἁγίαν σάρκα ὡς ναὸν καὶ αὐτὸς ἀναστήσει ἐν Ἱεροσολύμοις τὸν λίθινον ναόν. So also Pseudo-Hippolytus, chap. xx. 104, 3, with which compare the parallel in Ephr. Gr.; S. Martin of Tours: Ab illo urbem et templum esse reparandum ("that by him the city and temple are to be restored"); Ephr. Syr., 8 : Ædificabit et constituet Sion et Deum se faciet ("He shall build up Zion and make himself God"); and pseudo-Ephrem, chap. vii. : Jubet sibi ræædificari templum Dei, quod est in Hierusalem ("He command the temple of God that is in Jerusalem to be rebuilt for himself").

¹¹ Ὅθεν καὶ ὡς προτιμῶν   τὸν τόπον καὶ τὸν ναὸν
δείκνυσιν πᾶσιν αὐτοῖς   πρόνοιαν ποιούμενος.

¹² Ἵνα αὐτοὺς [sc. Ἰουδαίους] μειζόνως ἀπατήσῃ περισπού-δαστον ποιεῖται τὸν ναὸν ὑποψίαν διδοὺς, ὅτι αὐτός ἐστιν ὁ ἐκ γένους Δαβίδ. See also pseudo-Johannine Apoc., 7, Cod. E : Ὅθεν καὶ ὡς πρότιμον (!) δείκνυσιν αὐτὸν τοῦ τόπου καὶ τοῦ ναοῦ πρόνοιαν ποιούμενος.

¹³ Καὶ μεγαλύνει τοὺς Ἰουδαίους καὶ τὸν κατεσκαμμένον ναὸν κατοικήσει.

¹⁴ Ἐν τῷ ναῷ καθεδεῖσθαι ... ὑπ' αὐτοῦ ἀνορθοῦσθαι προσ-δοκωμένῳ τοῖς θεομάχοις Ἰουδαίοις.

15 Templum etiam destructum, quod Salomon Deo paravit, ædificabit et in statum suum restaurabit.

16 Et reædificabunt templum, quod est destitutum a Romanis, sedebitque ibi.

17 Antichristus antiquam Jerusalem reædificabit, in qua se ut Deum coli jubebit.

18 Tunc eruere templum Dei conabitur et justum populum persequetur.

19 Συνήγαγε τὰ διασκορπισμένα πρόβατα ὁ σωτὴρ, καὶ αὐτὸς ὁμοίως ἐπισυνάξει τὸν διεσκορπισμένον λαόν.

20 Αὐτὸς γὰρ προσκαλέσεται πάντα τὸν λαὸν πρὸς ἑαυτὸν ἐκ πάσης χώρας τῆς διασπορᾶς ἰδιοποιούμενος ὡς τέκνα ἴδια ἐπαγγελόμενος ἀποκαταστήσειν τὴν χώραν καὶ ἀναστήσειν αὐτῶν τὴν βασιλείαν.

21 Ad quem fugit vidua oblita Dei i. e. terrena Hierusalem ad ulciscendum de inimico. The same application is made by Hippolytus, lvi. 28, 27. Cf. also Irenæus V., 30, 3 : Ad ostentationem quandam continet ultionis et vindictam inferentis, quod ille simulat se male tractatos vindicare.

22 Hunc ergo suscitatum Deus mittet regem dignum dignis et Christum, qualem meruerunt Judæi.

23 Inde tamen pergit victor in terra Judæa,
. . . Multa signa facit ut illi credere possint,
Ad seducendos eos quoniam est missus iniquus.
. . . Nobis Nero factus Antichristus, ille Judæis.

24 Gloriabuntur autem in eo Judæi et accingent se, ut veniant ad eum. Ille vero blasphemabit dicens : ego sum pater et filius, etc.

25 Τιμῶν μετ' ὑπερβολῆς τὸ γένος τῶν Ἰουδαίων.
αὐτοὶ γὰρ προσδοκῶσι τὴν ἐκείνου ἔλευσιν.
πλείονα δὲ ὁ δῆμος ὁ φονευτὴς [τῶν] Ἰουδαίων
τιμῶσι καὶ χαίρονται τῇ αὐτοῦ βασιλείᾳ.

26 Καὶ διὰ μὲν τῆς τοῦ Χριστοῦ προσηγορίας Ἰουδαίους τοὺς τὸν Ἠλειμμένον προσδοκῶντας ἀπατῶντα.

²⁷ Tunc gratulabuntur [ei] Judæi, quod eis reddiderit usum prioris testamenti.

²⁸ Καὶ συναχθήσονται ἄγνωστοι καὶ ἀγραμμάτιστοι λέγοντες πρὸς ἀλλήλους· μὴ ἄρα εὑρίσκομεν αὐτὸν δίκαιον; ἔστιν ἐπιστηρίζων (?) ὁ δῆμος τῶν φονευτῶν Ἰουδαίων.

²⁹ Καὶ πράξει θαυμαστὰ καὶ παράδοξα πράγματα καὶ μεγαλυνεῖ τοὺς Ἰουδαίους.

³⁰ Nostri autem et melius interpretantur et rectius, quod in fine mundi hæc sit facturus Antichristus, qui consurgere habet de "modica gente," i. e. de populo Judæorum. Cf. also Victorinus, 1247 D : Synagoga sunt Satanæ quoniam ab Antichristo colliguntur ("The synagogues are Satan's since they are gathered together by him ").

³¹ Tunc ad eum concurrent [omnes Judæi] et existimantes se recipere Christum recipient diabolum. Cf. Haymo on 2 Thessalonians ii. : "Then shall all the Jews flock to him"; *Elucidarium* : Tunc Judæi ex toto orbe venientes summo voto suscipient ("Him the Jews coming from the whole world shall receive with loud applause "). Even in the Arabic tradition the Antichrist is king of the Jews (see above).

³² Ἐν περιτομῇ ὁ σωτὴρ ἦλθεν εἰς τὸν κόσμον, καὶ αὐτὸς ὁμοίως ἐλεύσεται.

³³ "Desideria mulierum non cognoscet, cum prius fuerit impurissimus et nullum Deum patrum cognoscet," non enim seducere populum poterit circumcisionis nisi legis vindicator.

³⁴ Tum complebitur illud eloquium Danielis prophetæ : et deum patrum suorum nescibit neque desideria mulierum cognoscet.

³⁵ Nova consilia in pectore suo volutabit ut . . . denique immutato nomine atque imperii sede translata confusio ac perturbatio humani generis persequetur.

³⁶ Et circumcidet se et filium Dei omnipotentis se esse mentietur; and elsewhere, 1296 A : Hierusalem veniens circumcidet se dicens Judæis : ego sum Christus vobis

repromissus, qui ad salutem vestram veni, ut vos qui dispersi estis congregem et defendam.

³⁷ Et cum venerit Hierosolymam, circumcidet se dicens Judæis: ego sum Christus vobis promissus.

³⁸ Denique et sanctos non ad idola colenda revocaturus est, sed ad circumcisionem colendam, et si quos potuerit seducere, ita demum faciet, ut Christus ab eis appelletur. Cf. also S. Martin of Tours, 444: Antichristus enim cum venerit legem priscam et circumcisionem annuntiabit; and 445: ipse enim Antichristus, cum impurissimus sit, castitatem et sobrietatem prædicaturus est; quia neque potator vini erit neque ullum genus mulierum ad eum accessum—habebit.

³⁹ Νερὼν εἶπεν: οὐκοῦν καὶ Σίμων περιετμήθη; Πέτρος εἶπεν· οὐδὲ γὰρ ἄλλως ἠδύνατο ἀπατῆσαι ψυχάς, εἰ μὴ Ἰουδαῖον εἶναι ἑαυτὸν ὑπεκρίνετο καὶ τὸν τοῦ Θεοῦ νόμον διδάξαι ἐπεδείκνυτο.

⁴⁰ Ἐν σχήματι δὲ τούτου   ἥξει ὁ παμμιαρὸς
ὡς κλέπτης ψευδευλαβής,   ἀπατῆσαι σύμπαντα,
ταπεινὸς καὶ ἥσυχος,   μισῶν φησιν ἀδίκων,
ἀποστρέφων εἴδωλα,   προτιμῶν εὐσέβειαν,
ἀγαθὸς φιλόπτωχος,   εὐειδὴς ὑπερβολῇ,
πάνυ εὐκατάστατος,   ἱλαρὸς πρὸς ἅπαντας.

⁴¹ Sed nefandus ille corruptor potius animarum quam corporum, dumque adulescens subdolus draco sub specie justitiæ videtur versari, antequam sumat imperium.

⁴² Καὶ ἄρχεται τὸ κρῖναι μετὰ πραότητος καὶ ἐλεημοσύνης πολλῆς καὶ συγχωρήσεως ἁμαρτωλῶν καὶ ὥς φησί συγχωρεῖ ἁμαρτήματα.

⁴³ Τὰ πρῶτα μὲν ἐπιεικείαν ὡσανεὶ λόγιος τὶς καὶ συνετὸς σωφροσύνην τε καὶ φιλανθρωπίαν ὑποκρίνεται.

⁴⁴ Καὶ ἐν προοιμίοις τῆς βασιλείας αὐτοῦ ὑποκρίνεται ἀγαθοσύνην. Cf. the Ethiopic Apocalypse of Peter: "In all his doings he studies courtesy."

⁴⁵ Et propter hoc non annumeratur tribus hæc in Apocalypsi cum his quæ salvantur. The same remark is made by

Andreas, Aretha, Bede, and others quoted by Malvenda, I. 155.

[46] Nostri autem secundum superiorem sensum interpretantur omnia de Antichristo, qui nasciturus est de populo Judæorum et de Babylone venturus. So also Andreas and Aretha on Revelation, chap. ix. 14; Bede on Revelation xvii.; Haymo on 2 Thessalonians ii.; Strabo; Adso; *Elucidarium*; Rupertus Tuitiensis on Revelation xiii.; Anselmus Laudunensis on Daniel xi. 37.

[47] Εἰκὸς δὲ καὶ τὸν Ἀντίχριστον ἐκ τῶν ἀνατολικῶν μερῶν τῆς Περσικῆς γῆς, ἔνθα ἡ φυλὴ τοῦ Δὰν, ἐκ ῥίζης Ἑβραίων ἐξερχόμενον.

[48] Alter rex orietur ex Syria.

[49] De Persida homo immortalem esse se dicit.

[50] Οὗτος γεννᾶται ἐν Χωραζῇ, διότι διέτριψεν ἐν αὐτοῖς ὁ κύριος, καὶ Βηθσαιδὰ (?), διότι ἐν αὐτῇ ἀνετράφη. So also in *Quæstiones ad Antiochum* (Migne, XXVIII.) 109 : Ἐκ τῆς Γαλιλαίας, ὅθεν ὁ Χριστὸς ἐξῆλθεν, ἐξέρχεται ("From Galilee whence Christ came, he [also] cometh").

[51] Καὶ ἀνατελεῖ ὑμῖν ἐκ τῆς φυλῆς Ἰούδα καὶ τοῦ Λευὶ τὸ σωτήριον κυρίου· καὶ αὐτὸς ποιήσει πρὸς τὸν Βελίαρ πόλεμον.

[52] Ἀνέγνων γὰρ ἐν βίβλῳ Ἐνὼχ τοῦ δικαίου, ὅτι ὁ ἄρχων ὑμῶν ἐστιν ὁ Σατανᾶς, καὶ ὅτι πάντα τὰ πνεύματα τῆς πορνείας καὶ ὑπερηφανίας τῷ Λευὶ ὑπακούσονται, τοῦ παρεδρεύειν τοῖς υἱοῖς Λευὶ, τοῦ ποιεῖν αὐτοὺς ἐξαμαρτάνειν ἐνώπιον κυρίου.

CHAPTER XII.

[1] Καὶ στήσει ὄρεων ὕψος, στήσει δὲ θάλασσαν,
Ἥλιον πυρόεντα μέγαν λαμπράν τε σελήνην.

[2] Et eius verbo orietur sol noctu, et luna quoque ut sexta hora appareat, efficiat.

[3] Et relucescet subito sol noctu et luna interdiu.

[4] Jubebit ignem descendere a cœlo et solem a suis cursibus stare.

⁵ Tunc incipiet ostendere signa mendacia in cœlo et in terra, in mari et in arida, advocabit pluviam et illa descendet.

⁶ Μεταστρέψει τὸν ἥλιον εἰς σκότος καὶ τὴν σελήνην εἰς αἷμα.

⁷ Ποιήσει τὴν ἡμέραν σκότος καὶ τὴν νύκτα ἡμέραν, τὸν ἥλιον μεταστρέψει ὅπου βούλεται, καὶ ἁπαξαπλῶς πάντα τὰ στοιχεῖα τῆς γῆς καὶ τῆς θαλάσσης ἐν δυνάμει τῆς φαντασίας αὐτοῦ ἐνώπιον τῶν θεωρούντων ἀναδείξει ὑπήκοα.

⁸ Καὶ νέκυας στήσει καὶ σήματα πολλὰ ποιήσει
ἀνθρώποις· ἀλλὰ οὐχὶ τελεσφόρα ἔσσετ᾽ ἐν αὐτῷ,
ἀλλὰ πλάνα, καὶ δὴ μέροπας πολλούς τε πλανήσει.

⁹ Μετὰ δὲ τούτων ἁπάντων σημεῖα ἐπιτελέσει . . . ἀλλ᾽ οὐκ ἀληθῆ, ἀλλ᾽ ἐν πλάνῃ, ὅπως πλανήσῃ τοὺς ὁμοίους αὐτῷ ἀσεβεῖς. 24 : λεπροὺς καθαρίζων, παραλύτους ἐγείρων, δαίμονας ἀπελαύνων . . . νεκροὺς ἀνιστῶν.

¹⁰ Increpabit leprosos et purificabuntur, cæcos et videbunt lumen, vocabit surdos et audient, mutos et loquentur.

¹¹ Τυφλοὶ ἀναβλέψουσιν, χωλοὶ περιπατήσουσι, δαίμονες ἰαθήσονται . . . καὶ ἐν τοῖς αὐτοῦ ψευδοσημείοις καὶ φαντασιώδεσι τέρασιν. . . .

¹² Δι᾽ οὗ [sc. τοῦ διαβόλου] καὶ νεκροὺς ἐγείρειν καὶ σημεῖα ἐπιτελεῖν τοῖς πεπηρωμένοις τὰ τῆς διανοίας ὄμματα φανήσεται.

¹³ Faciet enim tam stupenda miracula, ut jubeat ignem de cœlo descendere . . . et mortuos resurgere. The deceptive nature of the Antichrist's wonders is also dwelt upon by Irenæus, V. 28, 2 ; Cyril, xv. 10 ; Jerome, *ad Algasiam*, 11 ; Chrysostom on 2 Thessalonians ii. ; John of Damascus ; Bede's Sibyl.

¹⁴ Faciet nempe omnia signa, quæ fecit Dominus noster in mundo, defunctos autem non suscitabit, quia non habet potestatem in spiritus.

¹⁵ Aver diu zeichen, diu er tut,
Diu ne sint niemen gut ;
Er ne kuchet niht den toten.

¹⁶ Λέγουσί τινες, ὅτι οὐ δύναται ὁ Ἀντίχριστος νεκρὸν ἄνθρωπον ἀναστῆσαι, ἐπεὶ πάντα τὰ λοιπὰ σημεῖα ποιεῖ.

¹⁷ Ὁ γὰρ πατὴρ τοῦ ψεύδους τὰ τοῦ ψεύδους ἔργα φαντασιοσκοπεῖ, ἵνα τὰ πλήθη νομίσῃ θεωρεῖν νεκρὸν ἐγειρόμενον τὸν μὴ ἐγειρόμενον.

¹⁸ Mortuos scilicet in conspectu hominum resuscitari . . . [sed et mendacia erunt et a veritate aliena].

¹⁹ Suscitabit mortuos non vere, sed diabolus . . . corpus alicuius intrabit . . . et in illo loquetur, ut quasi vivum videatur.

²⁰ Si tu es Deus, voca defunctos et resurgent . scriptum est enim in libris prophetarum et etiam ab apostolis, quod Christus quando apparebit, mortuos a sepulcturis suscitabit.

²¹

Μεγαλύνων σημεῖα	πληθύνων τὰ φόβητρα,
ψεῦδος καὶ οὐκ ἀλήθειαν	ταῦτα ἐνδεικνύμενος.
τοιούτῳ δὲ τρόπῳ	μεθιστᾷ ὁ τύραννος
τὰ ὄρη, φαντάζει [δε?]	ψευδῶς καὶ οὐκ ἀληθείᾳ
τῶν πληθῶν παρεστώτων	λαῶν πολλῶν καὶ δήμων
καὶ εὐφημούντων αὐτὸν	διὰ τὰς φαντασίας.

Cf. Philippus Solit., 816 C : Terrores ac prodigia ad deceptionem effingens, ut inconsideratis mentibus montes transferre videatur ("Portents and prodigies simulating unto deception, so that to thoughtless minds he may seem to remove mountains").

²²

Πάλιν αὐτὸς ὁ δράκων	ὑφαπλώννει τὰς χεῖρας
καὶ συνάγει τὸ πλῆθος	ἑρπετῶν καὶ πετεινῶν·
ὁμοίως δ' ἐπιβαίνει	ἐπάνω τῆς ἀβύσσου
καὶ ὥσπερ ἐπὶ ξηρᾷ	περιπατεῖ ἐπ' αὐτῇ.
φαντάζει τὰ σύμπαντα.	

²³ Ὄρη καὶ βούνους μετακινήσει καὶ διανεύσει τῆς μεμιασμένης χειρὸς αὐτοῦ· δεῦτε πρός με πάντες καὶ διὰ φαντάσματα καὶ πλάνης (!) συνάγονται ἐν τῷ ἰδίῳ τόπῳ.

²⁴ Ego per aerem volavi, igni commixtus unum corpus effectus sum, statuas moveri feci, animavi exanima, lapides

panes feci, de monte in montem volavi, transmeavi manibus angelorum sustentatus, ad terras descendi.

²⁵ Ἀνδριάντας ποιεῖ περιπατεῖν καὶ ἐπὶ πῦρ κυλιόμενος οὐ καίεται, ἐνίοτε δὲ καὶ πέταται, καὶ ἐκ λίθων ἄρτους ποιεῖ, ὄφις γίνεται, εἰς αἶγα μεταμορφοῦται, διπρόσωπος γίνεται. 33 : ποι-οῦντα θαυμάσια πρὸς κατάπληξιν καὶ ἀπάτην, οὐ σημεῖα ἰατικὰ πρὸς ἐπιστροφὴν καὶ σωτηρίαν.

²⁶ Magica enim arte homines eludet et phantasia, ut Simon Magus fecisse credendus est, qui quod non faciebat, facere videbatur.

²⁷ Per magicam artem et phantasiam deludet homines, sicut et Simon Magus illusit illum, qui putans occidere eum arietem occidit pro eo. This legend is fully related in the *Martyrium Petri et Pauli* (Lipsius and Bonnet, 118 *et seq*), chap. xxxi., as elsewhere.

²⁸ Ἀπέστειλεν ὁ κύριος ἀποστόλους εἰς πάντα τὰ ἔθνη καὶ αὐτὸς ὁμοίως πέμψει ψευδαποστόλους. From Hippolytus the pseudo-Hippolytus borrows the relation in xxii. 106, 12.

²⁹ Deinde per universum mundum nuntios mittet et praedicatores suos.

³⁰ Λαβὼν γὰρ ὁ ἀναιδὴς	τότε τὴν ἐξουσίαν
δαίμονας ἀποστέλλει	εἰς πάντα τὰ πέρατα,
ὥστε κηρύξαι πᾶσιν,	ὅτι βασιλεὺς μέγας
ἐφάνη μετὰ δόξης.	δεῦτε καὶ θεάσασθε.

³¹ Fulgura ministri eius erunt et signum dabunt adventus eius, daemones constituent eius copias et principes daemonio-rum erunt eius discipuli ; mittet duces agminum suorum in regiones procul dissitas et dabunt virtutes ac sanitatem.

³² Daemones utique se praedicatum et commendatum per orbem terrarum mittet, surrexit, dicent, magnus rex Hiero-solymis . . . omnes ad eum accedite.

³³ Et maligni spiritus erunt duces eius et socii semper et comites indivisi.

³⁴ Et non est mirandum si daemoniis et apostaticis spiritibus ministrantibus ei per eos faciat signa, in quibus seducat habitantes super terram.

[35] Spiritus tres immundi discipulos designant Antichristi, qui eum per universum orbem prædicaturi sunt, qui quamvis homines sint futuri, spiritus immundi et spiritus dæmoniorum vocantur, quia dæmones in ipsis habitabunt et per ora eorum loquentur.

CHAPTER XIII.

[1] Ἀρέσαι δὲ ἅπασι
ὅπως ἂν ἀγαπηθῇ
δῶρα δὲ οὐ λήψεται,
κατηφὴς οὐ δείκνυται,
ἐν ἅπασι δὲ τούτοις
ἐξαπατᾷ τὸν κόσμον,
ὅταν γὰρ θεάσονται
τηλικαύτας ἀρετὰς
πάντες ἐπὶ τὸ αὐτὸ
καὶ ἐν χαρᾷ μεγίστῃ
λέγοντες πρὸς ἀλλήλους·
τηλικοῦτος ἄνθρωπος

τεχνάζεται δολίως,
ἐν τάχει ὑπὸ λαῶν,
μετ᾽ ὀργῆς οὐ λαλήσει,
ἀλλὰ ἱλαρὸς ἀεί.
σχήμασιν εὐταξίας
ἕως οὗ βασιλεύσει.
λαοὶ πολλοὶ καὶ δῆμοι
κάλλη τε καὶ δυνάμεις,
μιᾷ γνώμῃ γίνονται,
βασιλεύουσιν αὐτὸν
μὴ ἄρα εὑρίσκεται
ἀγαθὸς καὶ δίκαιος.᾽

[2] Erit enim omnibus subdole placidus, munera non suscipiens, personam non præponens, amabilis omnibus, quietus universis, xenia non appetens, affabilis apparens in proximos, ita ut beatificent eum homines dicentes: justus homo hic est. Chap. vii. : Tunc confluent ad eum in civitatem Hierusalem undique omnes.

[3] Οὗτος οὖν ἐπισυνάξας πρὸς ἑαυτὸν τὸν πάντοτε ἀπειθῆ λαὸν γεγεννημένον.

[4] Qui sicut perdix colliget sibi filios confusionis . . . et vocat quos non genuit. Cf. Caspari, 215, Anmerkung 7.

[5] Λέγει δὲ καὶ ἕτερος προφήτης· ξυνάξει πᾶσαν δύναμιν αὐτοῦ ἀφ᾽ ἡλίου ἀνατολῶν ἄχρις ἡλίου δυσμῶν· οὓς κεκλήκοι καὶ οὓς οὐ κεκλήκοι πορευθήσονται μετ᾽ αὐτοῦ. λευκανεῖ τὴν θάλασσαν ἀπὸ τῶν ἱστίων τῶν πλοίων καὶ μελανεῖ τὸ πεδίον ἀπὸ τῶν θυρεῶν τῶν ὅπλων, καὶ πᾶς ὃς ἂν συναντήσῃ αὐτῷ ἐν πολέμῳ μαχαίρᾳ πεσεῖται. In chap. liv. 27, 30 et seq. Hippolytus

refers the same passage wrongly to the Antichrist's gathering of the διασπορά (scattered tribes) of Israel.

6 Exsurget iterum in istius clade Neronis
Rex ab orientem cum quattuor gentibus inde,
Invitatque sibi quam multas gentes ad urbem,
Quæ ferunt auxilium, licet sit fortissimus ipse :
Implebitque mare navibus cum milia multa,
Et si quis occurrerit illi mactabitur ense.

7 Et vidi post hæc, et ecce congregabatur multitudo hominum, quorum non erat numerus, de quatuor ventis cœli, ut debellarent hominem, qui ascenderat de mari.

8 Οἱ ἅπαξ προκατειλημμένοι τοῖς ψεύδεσι τοῦ Ἀντιχρίστου τέρασι καὶ τὸ θεοστυγὲς αὐτοῦ ὄνομα ἀνεξαλείπτως ἐν ταῖς καρδίαις ἐγγράψαντες ἔκ τε Ἰουδαίων ἔκ τε ἐθνῶν.

9 Θάλασσα ταράσσεται,　　　　[καὶ?] ἡ γῆ ξηραίνεται,
οὐρανοὶ οὐ βρέχουσι,　　　　τὰ φυτὰ μαραίνονται.

10 Τότε οἱ οὐρανοὶ οὐκέτι βρέχουσιν, ἡ γῆ
οὐκέτι καρποφορεῖ,
αἱ πηγαὶ ἐκλείπουσιν,
[οἱ] ποταμοὶ ξηραίνονται,
βοτάνη οὐ[κέτι] φύεται,
χλόη οὐκ[έτι] ἀνατέλλει,
[τὰ] δένδρα ἀπὸ [ῥιζῶν] ψύχονται
καὶ οὐκέτι βλαστάνουσιν.
οἱ ἰχθύες πῆς θαλάσσης
καὶ τὰ κήτη ἐν αὐτῇ
τελευτῶσιν, καὶ οὕτως
[φησιν] δυσωδίαν λιμινὴν
ἀναπέμπει [ἡ] θάλασσα
καὶ ἦχον φοβερὸν ὥστε ἐκλείπειν καὶ ἀποθνήσκειν
[τοὺς] ἀνθρώπους ἀπὸ [τοῦ] φόβου.

11 Τότε θρηνεῖ δεινῶς ὁμοῦ　　　πᾶσα ψυχὴ καὶ στενάζει,
ὅτ᾽ ἂν πάντες θεάσονται　　　θλίψιν ἀπαραμύθητον
τὴν περιέχουσαν αὐτοὺς　　　νύκτωρ τε καὶ μεθ᾽ ἡμέραν
καὶ οὐδαμοῦ εὑρίσκοντες　　　ἐμπλησθῆναι τῶν βρωμάτων.

¹² Suspendet cœlum rorem suum, pluvia enim super terram non erit . . . siccabunt enim universa flumina magna et fontes . . . torrentes aridabunt venas suas propter intolerabilem æstum . . . et tabescent filii in sinu matrum suarum et conjuges super genua virorum suorum non habentibus escas ad comedendum . erit enim illis diebus penuria panis et aquæ.

¹³ Θεωρῶν ὁ θεὸς τὴν ἀδικίαν αὐτοῦ ἀποστέλλει ἄγγελον ἐξ οὐρανοῦ τὸν Βαυριὴλ λέγων· ἀπέλθατε σαλπίσατε [ἀέρος ἃς?] κρατήσουσιν τὸν ὑετόν· καὶ ἡ γῆ ξηρανθήσεται, καὶ αἱ βοτάναι ψυγήσονται, καὶ ποιήσει τὸν οὐρανὸν χαλκοῦν, ἵνα δρόσον μὴ δώσῃ ἐπὶ τὴν γῆν, καὶ κρύψῃ τὰς νεφέλας εἰς τὰ ἔγκατα τῆς γῆς καὶ καταστείλῃ κέρας τῶν ἀνέμων, ἵνα μὴ ἄνεμος συστῇ ἐπὶ προσώπου πάσης τῆς γῆς.

¹⁴ Increpabit mare et desiccabitur, piscesque morientur in medio ejus.

¹⁵ Mare Sodomiticum pisces rejiciet et dabit vocem noctu, quam non noverant multi, omnes autem audient vocem eius.

¹⁶ Aer enim vitiabitur et corruptus ac pestilens fiet modo importunis imbribus, modo inutili siccitate . . . nec terra homini dabit fructum . . . fontes quoque cum fluminibus arescent . . . propter hæc deficient et in terra quadrupedes et in aere volucres et in mari pisces.

¹⁷ Proprie autem extenditur verbum usque ad Antichristi tempora, quoniam magna fames est futura quaque omnes lædentur.

¹⁸ Tunc pseudoprophetæ tunc fames . . . et invenies . . . tunc ariditatem terræ . . . denique justus in deserto, iniquus in regno est.

¹⁹ Καὶ τὰ ὕδατα ἀποφρύξουσι, καὶ ὑετὸς ἐπὶ γῆς οὐ δοθήσεται.

²⁰ Καὶ πᾶν τὸ κτῆμα αὐτοῦ ἀπολεῖται ἀπὸ πολλῶν, καὶ ἀπορία καρπῶν ἔσται μεγάλη, καὶ χειμὼν ἐπιταθήσεται κρατερός.

²¹ Τότε ὁ στάχυς τοῦ σίτου ἐκφυεῖ ἡμιχοίνικον, καὶ ὁ ἀγκὼν τοῦ κλήματος ἐκφυεῖ χιλίους βότρυας, καὶ ὁ βότρυς ἐκφυεῖ ἡμίσταμνον οἶνον.

²² Et nemo potest venundare vel emere de frumento caducitatis, nisi qui serpentinum signum in fronte aut in manu habuerint.

²³ Quicunque crediderint atque accesserint ei, signabuntur ab eo tamquam pecudes.

²⁴ Et qui in eum crediderint signum characteris eius in fronte suscipient.

²⁵ Καὶ γράφει αὐτῶν τὰς χεῖρας τὰς δεξιὰς, ἵνα καθέζονται μετ' αὐτοῦ εἰς τὸ πῦρ τὸ αἰώνιον.

CHAPTER XIV.

¹ Quum autem in suum propositum filius perditionis attraxerit totum mundum, mittentur Henoch et Elias, ut iniquum coarguant quæstione plena mansuetudinis.

² Si tu es Deus—ostende nobis, quod a te petimus.

³ Irascetur eo momento iniquus contra sanctos et arrepto gladio scelestissimus abscindet colla justorum.

⁴ Tunc—aspiciens Deus humanum genus periclitantes et afflatu draconis horribilis fluctuantes mittit eis consolatoriam prædicationem per famulos suos prophetas Enoch at Eliam. —cumque justi apparuerint, illi confundunt quidem adversarium serpentem cum eius calliditate et revocant advocatos fideles ad Deum, ut ab eius seductione . . .

⁵ Πρὶν ἢ δὲ ταῦτα γενέσθαι   ἀποστέλλει ὁ κύριος
Ἡλίαν (?) τὸν Θεσβίτην   καὶ τὸν Ἐνὼχ ὡς εὔσπλαγχνος,
ὅπως αὐτοὶ γνωρίσωσιν   εὐσέβειαν γένει βροτῶν,
καὶ κηρύξαι παρρησίᾳ   ἅπασι θεογνωσίαν,
μὴ πιστεῦσαι καὶ πειθαρχεῖν   φόβου ἕνεκεν τῷ ψεύδει,
κράζοντες (?) καὶ λέγοντες·   πλάνος ἔστιν ὦ ἄνθρωποι,
μηδεὶς αὐτῷ πιστεύσειεν.

⁶ Πλὴν ὀλίγοι εἰσί τότε   οἱ ἔχοντες ὑπακοῦσαι
καὶ πιστεύειν τοῖς ῥήμασιν   ἀμφοτέρων τῶν προφητῶν.

⁷ Καὶ διὰ τοῦτο αὐτοὺς [not ὑμᾶς] ἀποκτενεῖ καὶ ἐν ῥομφαίᾳ πατάξει αὐτούς.

⁸ Καὶ τότε ἀποστελῶ Ἐνώχ καὶ Ἡλίαν πρὸς ἔλεγχον αὐτοῦ καὶ ἀποδείξουσιν αὐτὸν ψευστὴν καὶ πλάνον καὶ ἀνελεῖ αὐτοὺς ἐπὶ τὸ θυσιαστήριον.

⁹ Καὶ ἀποστελεῖ ἐν συντομῇ τοὺς αὐτοῦ θεράποντας τόν. τε Ἐνώχ καὶ τὸν Ἡλίαν καὶ τὸν υἱὸν τῆς βροντῆς Ἰωάννην, οἵτινες ἐνώπιον πάντων τῶν ἐθνῶν ἐλέγξουσιν αὐτοῦ τὴν πλάνην καὶ δείξουσιν αὐτὸν ψευστὴν ἐπὶ παντὸς ἀνθρώπου, καὶ ὅτι δι᾽ ἀπώλειαν καὶ πλάνην τῶν πολλῶν ἐξελήλυθεν. ὁ δ᾽ ἐκεῖνος ὑπ᾽ αὐτῶν δεινῶς ἐλεγχόμενος καὶ ὑπὸ πάντων περιφρονούμενος ἐν θυμῷ καὶ ὀργῇ ἀνελεῖ τοὺς ἁγίους ἐκείνους.

¹⁰ Egredientur duo clarissimi viri Enoch et Elias ad annuntiandum adventum Domini, et Antichristus occidet eos, et post dies tres a Domino resuscitabuntur.

¹¹ Tunc mittentur in mundum duo magni prophetæ Elias et Henoch, qui contra impetum Antichristi fideles divinis armis præmunient et instruent eos et confortabunt et præparabunt ad bellum. . . . Postquam vero impleverint prædicationem suam, insurget Antichristus in eos et inter-ficiet, ipsi vero occisi post tres dies a Domino suscitabuntur.

¹² Translatus est Henoch et Elias, nec mors eorum reperta est, dilata scilicet, ceterum morituri reservantur, ut Antichristum sanguine suo extinguant. So also pseudo-Cyprianus, *de Montibus*, Sina et Sion, 5; Evang. Nicodemi, 25; Arabic History of Joseph, chap. xxxii.; Apocalypse of Paul (Tischendorf, p. 50, 68); and other passages in Malvenda, 142, 151, 158. This interpretation prevails in all Commentaries not influenced by the spiritualising exegesis of Ticonius.

¹³ Deinde et tempus tyrannidis eius significat, in quo tempore fugabuntur sancti.

¹⁴ Ὃς φυσιωθεὶς ὑπ᾽ αὐτῶν [sc. Ἰουδαίων] ἄρχεται βίβλους κατὰ τῶν ἁγίων ἐκπέμπειν τοῦ πάντας πανταχοῦ ἀναιρεῖσθαι τοὺς μὴ θέλοντας αὐτὸν σεβάζειν καὶ προσκυνεῖν ὡς θεόν. A perse-cution is also spoken of by Victorinus, on Revelation xii. 6; Jerome, on Daniel xi. 32; Book of Clement, 80, 15;

Prosper, *Dim. Temp.*, 10; Methodius, Adso (Malvenda, II. 149), and most expositors of Revelation xii. (Malvenda, II. 147). See also Ephr. Gr., III. 138 D; pseudo-Hippolytus, xxv. 108; Cyril, xv. 15; Phil. Solitarius, 816 B.

¹⁵ Πολλοὶ μὲν οὖν τῶν ἁγίων,   ὅσοι τότε εὑρίσκονται,
ἅμα εὐθὺς ἀκούσωσι   τὴν ἔλευσιν τοῦ μιαροῦ,
. . . καὶ φεύγουσι μετὰ   τῆς μεγίστης ἐν ἐρήμοις
σπουδῆς
καὶ κρύβονται ἐν [ἐρήμοις   καὶ σπηλαίοις μετὰ φόβου
καὶ] ὄρεσι
καὶ πάσσουσι γῆν καὶ   ἐπὶ τὴν κεφαλὴν αὐτῶν
σποδὸν
μετὰ κλαυθμοῦ δεόμενοι   νύκτωρ τε καὶ μεθ' ἡμέραν
ἐν πολλῇ ταπεινώσει.
καὶ δωρεῖται αὐτοῖς τοῦτο   παρὰ θεοῦ τοῦ ἁγίου,
καὶ ὁδηγεῖ αὐτοὺς ἡ χάρις   εἰς τόπους τοὺς ὡρισμένους.

With this compare pseudo-Hippolytus, chap. xxxii. 112, 26.

¹⁶ Fugient autem electi a facie ejus ad vertices montium et collium, fugient aliqui in sepulchra et occultabunt se inter mortuos.

¹⁷ Οἱ δὲ δίκαιοι κρυβήσονται καὶ φύγωσιν ἐν ὄρεσι καὶ σπηλαίοις.

¹⁸ Cum hæc facta erunt, tum justi et sectatores veritatis segregabunt se a malis et fugient in solitudines.

¹⁹ Displicet interea jam sero Judæis et ipsis,
Susurrantque simul, quoniam sunt fraude decepti,
Exclamant pariter ad cælum voce deflentes,
Ut deus illis subveniat verus ab alto.

²⁰ Εἰκὸς δὲ καὶ τὴν αἰσθητὴν ἔρημον σώζειν τοὺς ἐν ὄρεσι καὶ σπηλαίοις καὶ ταῖς ὀπαῖς τῆς γῆς διὰ τὴν τοῦ ἀποστάτου καὶ ψευδοχρίστου ἐπιβουλὴν φεύγοντας.

²¹ Tunc eruere templum Dei conabitur et justum populum persequetur. Idem justos homines obvolvet libris prophetarum atque ita cremabit.

²² Ecclesiam illam catholicam, ex qua in novissimo tem-

pore credituri sunt centum quadraginta quattuor milia hominum Eliæ, sed et ceterum populum inveniri in adventu Domini hic dicit. Sic et Dominus in evangelio ait: tunc qui in Judæa sunt, etc.

²³ Ἅπαντες δὲ οἱ ὄντες   ἐπὶ γῆς ἀνατολῶν
ἐπὶ δυσμὰς φεύγουσιν   ἐκ τῆς πολλῆς δειλίας,
καὶ πάλιν δὲ οἱ ὄντες   ἐπὶ δυσμῶν ἡλίου
ἐπὶ τὴν ἀνατολὴν   φεύγουσι μετὰ τρόμου.

Quite a similar account occurs in pseudo-Ephrem, chap. iv.; pseudo-Hippolytus, xxxiii. 113, 8; Dan. Apoc. Arm., 239, 24; pseudo-Methodius, xcix.; Adso, 1293 C; Philippus Solitarius, 817 A, and the Arabic tradition in Tabari (see above, p. 116).

CHAPTER XV.

¹ Tunc annus breviabitur, et mensis minuetur, et dies in angustum coarctabitur.

² Τρία ἔτη ἔσονται οἱ καιροὶ ἐκεῖνοι, καὶ ποιήσω τὰ τρία ἔτη ὡς τρεῖς μῆνας καὶ τοὺς τρεῖς μῆνας ὡς τρεῖς ἑβδομάδας καὶ τὰς τρεῖς ἑβδομάδας ὡς τρεῖς ἡμέρας καὶ τὰς τρεῖς ἡμέρας ὡς τρεῖς ὥρας καὶ τὰς τρεῖς ὥρας ὡς τρεῖς στιγμάς. This trait is given in quite a similar way in the Greek Apocalypse of Daniel, 106; in Apocalypse of Ezra, 13 and 14; in Bede's Sibyl; Adso, 1294 C; the Jewish History of Daniel; and more summarily in pseudo-Hippolytus, cxiv. 13, and the Ethiopic Apocalypse of Peter. The *Elucidarium* also seems to be acquainted with the incident, but rejects it.

³ Quo audito inpius inflammatus ira veniet cum exercitu magno et admotis omnibus copiis circumdabit montem, in quo justi morabuntur, ut eos comprehendat . illi vero ubi se clausos undique atque obsessos viderint, exclamabunt ad Deum voce magna et auxilium cœleste implorabunt, et

exaudiet eos Deus et mittet regem magnum de cœlo, qui eos
eripiat ac liberet omnesque inpios ferro ignique disperdat.

⁴ Aquam quam emisit de ore suo serpens: jussu suo
exercitum eam sequi significat, aperuisse terram os suum et
devorare aquas : vindictam de præsentibus manifestam.

⁵ Τότε ἀποστελεῖ ἐν ὄρεσι καὶ σπηλαίοις καὶ ταῖς ὀπαῖς
τῆς γῆς τῶν δαιμόνων τὰς φάλαγγας πρὸς τὸ ἐρευνῆσαι τοὺς
ἀποκρυβέντας ἐκ τῶν ὀφθαλμῶν αὐτοῦ καὶ προσαγαγεῖν αὐτοὺς
εἰς προσκύνησιν αὐτοῦ καὶ τοὺς μὲν πειθομένους αὐτῷ σφραγίσει
τῇ σφραγίδι αὐτοῦ. τοὺς δὲ μὴ βουλομένους αὐτῷ ὑπακοῦσαι
τιμωρίας . . . ἀναλώσει.

⁶ Post ceteros fideles persequens reddet gladio aut
apostatas faciet, et qui in eum crediderint, signum characteris eius in fronte suscipient.

⁷ Loca sunt ibi inaccessibilia ; ibi sancti confugient et
ibi latitabunt, quos Christus in carne vivos invenerit.

⁸ Et virtus angelorum tradet in manus justorum mul-
titudinem illam, quæ montem circumsederint *et fluet san-*
guis more torrentis; deletisque omnibus copiis impius solus
effugiet.

⁹ Et exiet sanguis usque ad frenos equorum : exiet ultio
usque ad principes populorum i. e. rectores sive diabolum
sive angelos eius, novissimo certamine exiet ultio sanguinis
effusi.

¹⁰ Quum properant autem exercitu Dei rebelles,
    Sternunturque solo ab angelis prœlio facto.

¹¹ Veniet dominus cum angelis suis et cum potestatibus
sanctorum e septimo cœlo cum gloria septimi cœli et trahet
Berialem in Gehennam et potestates quoque eius.

¹² Καὶ Βελίαρ φλέξει καὶ ὑπερφιάλους ἀνθρώπους
    πάντας, ὅσοι τούτῳ πίστιν ἐνεποιήσαντο.

¹³ Καὶ τότε φανήσεται τὸ σημεῖον τοῦ υἱοῦ τοῦ ἀνθρώπου
μετὰ δόξης πολλῆς καὶ ἥξεται ἐπὶ τῶν νεφελῶν τῆς γῆς, καὶ
ἀνελεῖ αὐτὸν ὁ κύριος τῷ πνεύματι τοῦ στόματος αὐτοῦ.

¹⁴ Interficiet eum Deus.

¹⁵ Tunc exsilientes Gabriel et Michael duces exercitus descendent et suscitabunt sanctos; pudore autem afficietur malus [Antichristus] cum suis satellitibus; angeli porro accedentes apprehendent maledictum; simul clamabit Dominus de cœlo et subvertet maledictum cum omnibus suis copiis, et illico angeli detrudent eum in geennam.

¹⁶ Ὅτε αἰχμαλωτεύθη ὑπὸ τοῦ ἀρχαγγέλου Μιχαὴλ καὶ ἦρεν ἐξ αὐτοῦ τὴν θεότητα (καὶ ἀπεστάλην ἐγὼ ἐκ τῶν κόλπων τοῦ πατρός μου καὶ συνέστειλα τὴν κεφαλὴν αὐτοῦ τοῦ μεμιαμένου, καὶ ἐσβέσθη ὁ ὀφθαλμὸς αὐτοῦ). Cf. also chap. ix., where Michael and Gabriel bring about the resurrection of the dead; and also P. A. Æth. Here Michael and Gabriel awaken Elias and Enoch.

¹⁷ Percusso autem illo perditionis filio sive ab ipso Domino sive Michaele archangelo.

¹⁸ Et occidetur virtute Domini Antichristus a Michaele archangelo ut quidam docent.

¹⁹ Tradunt quoque doctores, ut ait Gregorius Papa, quod Michael archangelus perimet illum in monte Oliveti in papilione et solio suo, in loco illo de quo Dominus ascendit ad cœlos. This according to Adso and Haymo on 2 Thessalonians ii.

²⁰ Antichristus de mandato Christi fulminabitur per ministerium archangeli Michael, qui etiam interficiet eum *secundum Methodium.*

²¹ Καὶ ἄγεται ὁ τύραννος   δεδεμένος ὑπ' ἀγγέλων
σὺν ἅπασι τοῖς δαίμοσιν   ἐνώπιον τοῦ βήματος.

²² Hos angelos malos septem ad percutiendum Antichristum mittit.

²³ Et tunc parebit regnum illius [sc. dei] in omni creatura illius . . . et tunc Zabulus [diabolus] finem habebit. . . . Tunc implebuntur manus nuntii, qui est in summo constitutus, qui protinus vindicabit illos [sc. Israel] ab inimicis eorum.

²⁴ Exsurget enim Cœlestis a sede regni sui.

25 Tunc veniet Antichristus usque ad summitatem montis eius . . . id est verticem montis Oliveti . . . et asserunt ibi Antichristum esse periturum, unde Dominus ascendit ad cœlos. Beatus (542), Adso, and the *Elucidarium* make the same statement, but on the authority of Jerome; so also Theodoretus in his Commentary on the same passage in Daniel.

26 Dux ultimus qui tunc reliquus erit vivus, cum vastabuntur multitudo congregationum eius, et vincietur, et adducent eum super montem Sion, et Messias meus arguet eum de omnibus impietatibus eius.—et postea interficiet eum.

27 Antichristus . . . contra verum dimicabit et victus effugiet et bellum sæpe renovabit et sæpe vincetur, donec quarto prœlio . . . debellatus et captus tandem scelerum suorum luat pœnas.

CHAPTER XVI.

1 Cadet repente gladius e cœlo, ut sciant justi ducem sanctæ militiæ descensurum.

2 Videbitur et tunc ignea quadriga per astra
Et facula currens, nuntiet ut gentibus ignem.

3 Tunc descendet Dominus . . . et consistet currus eius inter cœlum et terram.

4 . . . σῆμα μέγιστον
ῥομφαίῃ σάλπιγγι θ' ἅμ' ἠελίῳ ἀνιόντι.

5 Ἥξει δ' οὐρανόθεν
ἀστὴρ μέγας εἰς ἅλα δεινὴν καὶ φλέξει
πόντον τε βαθύν. . . .

6 Καὶ τότε δὴ μέγα σῆμα Θεὸς μερόπεσσι βροτοῖσιν
οὐρανόθεν δείξει περιτελλομένοις ἐνιαυτοῖς
φάλκην ἐσσομένοιο τέρας πολέμοιο κακοῖο.

7 Τότε ἔσται ἐν τῷ οὐρανῷ σημεῖα· τόξον ὀφθήσεται καὶ κέρας καὶ λαμπὰς.

⁸ Judicii *signum*, tellus sudore madescet,
E cœlo rex adveniet per sæcla futurus.

⁹ Αὐτὸς μέλλει φαίνεσθαι ἐν τῇ παρουσίᾳ ἔμπροσθεν αὐτοῦ εἰς ἔλεγχον τῶν ἀπίστων Ἰουδαίων.

¹⁰ Ὅταν (?) ἴδωμεν τὸ σημεῖον τοῦ υἱοῦ τοῦ ἀνθρώπου ἐν τῷ οὐρανῷ φανὲν, κάθως εἶπεν ὁ κύ-ριος, ἐν ᾧ προσηλώθη ἑκουσίως ὑπὲρ ἡμῶν. τότε πάντες θεωροῦντες ἐν τῷ ὕψει φάνεν τὸ φοβερὸν καὶ ἅγιον (?) σκῆπτρον τοῦ μεγάλου βασιλέως. ἐπιγινώσκει ἕκαστος καὶ (?) μνημονεύει τοῦ λόγου τοῦ κυρίου προ- εἰρήκοτος. φανήσεται τὸ σημεῖον τοῦ υἱοῦ τοῦ ἀνθρώπου ἐν τῷ οὐρανῷ καὶ ἐν πληρο- (!) φορίᾳ γί-νονται πάντες, ὅτι ὀπίσω αὐτοῦ μέλλει ἀναφαίνεσ- θαι ὁ βασιλεύς.

¹¹ Καὶ τότε φανήσεται τὸ σημεῖον τοῦ υἱοῦ τοῦ ἀνθρώπου ἀπὸ τοῦ οὐρανοῦ μετὰ δυνάμεως καὶ δόξης πολλῆς. καὶ τότε θεωρήσει αὐτὸς ὁ τῆς ἀδικίας ἐργάτης μετὰ τῶν ὑπηρετῶν αὐτοῦ καὶ βρύξει μεγάλα, καὶ πάντα τὰ ἀκάθαρτα πνεύματα εἰς φυγὴν τραπήσονται.

¹² Electis in ea forma quæ in monte apparuit, reprobis vero in ea quæ in cruce pependit. Cf. pseudo-Hippolytus, xxxix. 117, 23 ; and Meyer, *Völuspâ*, p. 190.

¹³ Tunc aperietur cœlum medium intempesta et tenebrosa nocte, ut in orbe toto lumen descendentis dei tamquam fulgur appareat ; quod Sibylla his versibus locuta est :

ὁππότ' ἂν ἔλθῃ
πῦρ ἔσται ψολόεν τι μέσῃ ἐνὶ νυκτὶ μελαίνῃ.

Hæc est nox, quæ a nobis propter adventum regis ac dei nostri pervigilio celebratur : cuius noctis duplex est ratio, quod in ea et vitam tum recepit, cum passus est, et postea regnum orbis terræ recepturus est.

¹⁴ Hic est enim liberator et judex et ultor et rex et Deus, quem nos Christum vocamus.

¹⁵ Media nocte, qua hora angelus Ægyptum devastavit, et Dominus infernum spoliavit, ea hora electos suos de hoc mundo liberabit.

¹⁶ Tunc descendet Dominus ex alto in formidanda angelorum gloria . . . increpabit mare et desiccabitur . . . solventur cœli et terræ, et fient tenebræ ac caligo. Mittet Dominus in terram ignem, qui eam per quadraginta dies obtinens purificabit ab iniquitate et a sordibus peccatorum. For the notion that the earth is to be cleansed by fire, cf. the false Johannine Apocalypse, 16 ; D. A. Gr., III. ; *Muspilli*, for which see below.

¹⁷ Πῶς ὑπενεγκῶμεν τότε
ὅτ᾽ ἴδωμεν τὸν πύρινον
μετὰ θυμοῦ ὡσ[περ] ἀγρίαν
καὶ τὰ ὄρη καὶ τὰς νάπας
οἰκουμένην καὶ τὰ ἐν αὐτῇ
ἐκ τοῦ πυρὸς (?) ἐκείνου
αἱ πηγαὶ ἀφανίζονται,
ὁ ἀὴρ συγκλονίζεται,
ἐκ τοῦ οὐρανοῦ ὁ ἥλιος
παρέρχεται, ὁ οὐρανὸς,
¹⁸ Ἥξει λοιπὸν ὡς ἀστραπὴ
Θεὸς ἡμῶν βασιλεὺς
ἐν νεφέλαις μετὰ δόξης
προτρεχόντων ἐνώπιον
ἀγγέλων καὶ ἀρχαγγέλων
καὶ ποταμὸς πλήρης πυρὸς

ἀδελφοί μου ἀγαπητοὶ,
ποταμὸν ἐξερχόμενον
θάλασσαν κατεσθίοντα
καὶ κατακαίοντα πᾶσαν
ἔργα, τότε ἀγαπητοὶ
οἱ ποταμοὶ ἐκλείψουσιν,
ἡ θάλασσα ξηραίνεται,
(?) τὰ ἄστρα ἐκπεσοῦσιν,
σβεσθήσεται, ἡ σελήνη
ἑλίσσεται ὡς βιβλίον.
ἀστράπτουσα ἐξ οὐρανοῦ
καὶ νύμφιος ἀθάνατος
ἀνεικάστου (?)
δόξης αὐτοῦ τῶν ταγμάτων
ὄντες πάντες φλόγες πυρὸς.
ἐν φοβερῷ ῥυζήματι.

¹⁹ Et prodiens apparebit Dominus cum virtute magna et majestate multa—nec non et omnibus virtutibus cœlorum cum universo choro sanctorum.

²⁰ Τότε ἀποστελῶ τοὺς ἀγγέλους μου ἐπὶ προσώπου πάσης τῆς γῆς καὶ κατακαύσουσι τὴν γῆν πήχας ὀκτακισχιλίας πεντακοσίας, καὶ κατακαήσονται τὰ ὄρη τὰ μεγάλα, καὶ αἱ πέτραι πᾶσαι χωνευθήσονται . . . καὶ κατακαήσονται πᾶν δένδρον καὶ πᾶν κτῆνος κ. τ. α.

²¹ Πεσοῦνται οἱ ἀστέρες τοῦ οὐρανοῦ . . . κρυβήσεται ἡ σελήνη
καὶ οὐκ ἔσται ἐν αὐτῇ φῶς . . . κατασταλήσεται τοῦ ἡλίου τὸ
φῶς . . . λυθήσονται οἱ οὐρανοὶ . . . ἐκλείψει τὸ δίμοιρον τῆς
θαλάσσης . . . ἀποσκεπασθήσεται ὁ Ἅιδης.

²² [Ἐλεύσεται] ὑπὸ μυριάδων ἀγγέλων δορυφορούμενος.   xv.
21 : ποταμοῦ πυρὸς ἕλκοντος δοκιμαστικοῦ τῶν ἀνθρώπων.

²³ Ποταμὸς πυρὸς γέμων τε σκώληκος ἀκοιμήτου.

²⁴ Ἀλλ' ὁπότ' ἂν μεγάλοιο Θεοῦ πελάσωσιν ἀπειλαὶ
    καὶ δύναμις φλογόεσσα δι' οἴδματος ἐς γαῖαν ἥξει
80 :   τότε δὴ στοιχεῖα πρόπαντα
    χηρεύσει κόσμου, ὁπότ' ἂν Θεὸς αἰθέρι ναίων
    οὐρανὸν εἰλίξῃ, καθ' ἅπερ βιβλίον εἰλεῖται.
    καὶ πέσεται πολυμόρφος ὅλος πόλος ἐν χθονὶ δίῃ
    καὶ πελάγει· ῥεύσει δὲ πυρὸς μαλεροῦ καταράκτης
    ἀκάματος, φλέξει δὲ γαῖαν, φλέξει δὲ θάλασσαν
    καὶ πόλον οὐράνιον νύκτ' ἤματα καὶ κτίσιν αὐτήν,
    εἰς ἓν χωνεύσει καὶ εἰς καθαρὸν διαλέξει.
    κοὐκ ἔτι φωστήρων σφαιρώματα καγχαλόωντα,
    οὐ νὺξ οὐκ ἠὼς οὐκ ἤματα πολλὰ μερίμνης
    οὐκ ἔαρ οὐ χειμὼν οὔτ' ἄρ θέρος οὐ μετόπωρον.

²⁵ Ῥεύσει ἀπ' οὐρανόθεν καὶ πάντα τόπον δαπανήσει
    γαῖαν τ' ὠκεανόν τε μέγαν γλαυκήν τε θάλασσαν,
    λίμνας καὶ ποταμοὺς, πηγὰς καὶ ἀμείλιχον Ἅιδην
    καὶ πόλον οὐράνιον . ἀτὰρ οὐράνιοι φωστῆρες
    εἰς ἓν συρρήξουσι καὶ εἰς μορφὴν πανέρημον.
206 : καὶ τότε χηρεύσει κόσμου στοιχεῖα πρόμαντα
    ἀὴρ γαῖα θάλασσα φάος πόλος ἤματα νύκτες·
212 : ἀλλ' ἅμα πάντα
    εἰς ἓν χωνεύσει καὶ εἰς καθαρὸν διαλέξει.
Cf. also Sibyl IV. 172 *et seq.*; V. 155 *et seq.*

²⁶ Καὶ τακήσεται πᾶσα δύναμις οὐρανοῦ καὶ πάντα τὰ ἄστρα
πεσεῖται, ὡς φύλλα ἐξ ἀμπέλου, καὶ ὡς πίπτει φύλλα ἀπὸ συκῆς.
Cf. Hippolytus, lxiv. 34, 7 : Ὃς ἐπάξει τὴν ἐκπύρωσιν ("Who
shall bring about the conflagration"). ἐκπύρωσις is doubtless
a term of Stoic origin (Dietrich, *Nekyia*, 199).

²⁷ Et descendet comitantibus angelis in medium terræ, et antecedet eum flamma inextinguibilis.

²⁸ Cuius signo dato pestis ruet æthere toto,
Cum strepitu tonitrui descendet impetus ignis.

²⁹ Veniet Deus cum angelis suis et cum potestatibus sanctorum e septimo cœlo. IV. 18, tunc vox Dilecti increpabit in ira hoc cœlum et hanc aridam [terram] et montes et colles et urbes et desertum . . . et Dilectus surgere faciet ignem ex ipso et consumet omnes impios. Cf. Sibyl III. 73, and the description of the end of the world in *Assumptio Mosis*, 10.

³⁰ Μετὰ δὲ τὴν συμπλήρωσιν τῶν τριῶν καὶ ἥμισυ χρόνων βρέξει ὁ Θεὸς πῦρ ἐπὶ τὴν γῆν καὶ κατακαήσεται ἡ γῆ πήχεις τριάκοντα . τότε βοήσει ἡ γῆ πρὸς τὸν Θεὸν· παρθένος εἰμί, κύριε, ἐνώπιόν σου.

³¹ Τότε τὸν οὐρανὸν καύσω πήχας ὀγδοήκοντα καὶ τὴν γῆν πήχας ὀκτακοσίας.

³² Exuret terras ignis pontumque polumque . . .
Tradentur fontes, æternaque flamma cremabit . . .
Dejiciet colles, valles extollet ab imo . . .
Recidet e cœlis ignisque et sulphuris amnis.

³³ Cum ordinibus omnibus angelorum ad judicium veniet . . . omnia elementa turbabuntur tempestate ignis et frigoris mixtim undique furente.

³⁴ sô daz Eliases pluot   in erda kitriufit,
sô inprinnant die pergâ,   poum ni kistentit,
ênihc in erdu,   ahâ artruknênt,
muor varsuuilhit sih,   suilizôt lougiu der himil,
mâno vallit   prinnit mittilagart,
stên ni kistentit.   verit denne stûatago in lant,
verit mit diu vuiru   viriho uuîsôn,
dar ni mac denne mâk andremo   helfan vora demo
      mûspille.
denne daz preita uuasal   allaz varprennit,
enti vuir enti luft   iz allaz arfurpit.

³⁵ Τότε ἀποσκεπάσω τὰ τέσσαρα μέρη τῆς ἀνατολῆς, καὶ ἐξέλθωσιν τέσσαρες ἄνεμοι μεγάλοι καὶ ἐκλικμήσουσι πᾶν τὸ πρόσωπον τῆς γῆς . . . καὶ ἐκλικμήσει κύριος τὴν ἁμαρτίαν ἀπὸ τῆς γῆς, καὶ λευκανθήσεται ἡ γῆ ὥσπερ χιών . . . καὶ βοήσει πρός με λέγουσα· παρθένος εἰμὶ ἐνώπιόν σου κύριος.

³⁶ Καταιγίδες ἀνέμων τὴν γῆν καὶ τὴν θάλασσαν ἀμέτρως ἐκταράσσουσαι. Cf. also E. A., 8 : "And then shall the four winds of the heaven be stirred up " ; and pseudo-Chrysostom : Ἀλλαγήσονται τοίνυν οἱ οὐρανοὶ καὶ ἡ γῆ κενὴ γενήσεται ("Therefore shall the heavens be changed and the earth made void ").

³⁷ Ἥλιος μὲν ἀμαυρὰ βλέπων νύκτωρ ἀναφαίνει,
λείψει δ᾽ ἄστρα πόλον· πολλῇ δέ τε λαίλαπι τυφὼν
γαῖαν ἐρημώσει, νεκρῶν δὲ ἀνάστασις ἔσται.

³⁸ Σάλπιγξ οὐρανόθεν φωνὴν πολύθρηνον ἀφήσει.

³⁹ Sed tuba per sonitum tristem demittit ab alto.

⁴⁰ Interea fremitum dat tuba de cœlo repente.

Ecce canit cœlo rauca sed ubique resultans.

⁴¹ Καὶ ἔμπροσθεν αὐτοῦ σαλπίζων Μιχαὴλ ὁ ἀρχάγγελος καὶ ἐξυπνίζων τοὺς κεκοιμημένους ἀπὸ Ἀδὰμ ἕως τῆς συντελείας τοῦ αἰῶνος.

⁴² Καὶ ἐξέλθωσιν ἔξω τοῦ οὐρανοῦ καὶ σαλπίσουσι Μιχαὴλ καὶ Γαβριήλ. Cf. also the Othoth of the Messiah, where Michael sounds the trump and awakens the dead ; the History of Daniel, where Elias is the trumpeter ; *Völuspá* (47), where Heimdall blows the horn before the great conflagration.

⁴³ Ἥξουσι δ᾽ ἐπὶ βῆμα Θεοῦ βασιλῆος ἅπαντες. Cf. also Commodian, 1026 *et seq.*, and 4 Ezra vi. 32.

⁴⁴ Κύριε οἱ ἀποθανόντες ἀπὸ τοῦ Ἀδὰμ μεχρὶ τῆς σήμερον καὶ οἱ κατοικοῦντες ἐν τῷ Ἅιδῃ ἀπὸ τοῦ αἰῶνος . . . ποταποὶ ἀναστήσονται ;

⁴⁵ Exeuntes illico angeli congregabunt filios Adam.

⁴⁶ Καὶ ἐξυπνίζων τοὺς κεκοιμημένους ἀπὸ Ἀδὰμ ἕως τῆς συντελείας τοῦ αἰῶνος.

[47] Οἱ γὰρ δίκαιοι λάμψουσιν ὡς φωστῆρες καὶ ὡς ὁ ἥλιος, οἱ δὲ ἁμαρτωλοὶ ἔστωσαν ζοφώδεις.

[48] Τότε οἱ δίκαιοι ἐκλάμψουσιν ὡς ὁ ἥλιος, οἱ δὲ ἁμαρτωλοὶ κατηφεῖς καὶ σκύθρωποι ἀναδειχθήσονται.

[49] Boni in claritate fulgentes et mali in nigredine apparentes.

[50] Et transformabit Deus homines in similitudinem angelorum et erunt candidi sicut nix.

INDEX.

A

Abaddon, meaning of the term, 152, 153

Abassides, apocalyptic references to, 73

Adso, his Sibylline document, 47; relations to pseudo-Methodius, 54; its source, 62

Advent of Christ, 226; cometh in the night, 237

Agog. See "Gog and Magog"

Alexander legend, its relation to Antichrist, 63

Alexandre, on Sibyl III., 95

Ambrosiaster, Commentaries, 92, 142

Ambrosius, Commentaries, 92

Andreas, his Apocalyptic Commentaries, 58 note, 92

"Another prophet" quoted by Hippolytus, 28, 193

Antichrist, referred to in Rev. xi., 21; is the "son of perdition" of 2 Thess. ii., 22; his appearance in Jerusalem, 24; is of the tribe of Dan, 26; is the second beast with the two horns, 26; his first exploits, 28; his temptations, 64; his double form, 84; is the Nero redivivus of Victorinus, 84; is the emperor Decius in the *Visio Jesaiæ*, 85; is the Dragon of Babylonia, 99; is Armillus,

105; is the Dajjat of Tabari, 116, 117; forewarnings of his Advent, 121 *et seq.*; Jewish origin of, 133; his name, 136; his relations to the devil, 138-145; to the Babylonian Dragon, 144, 145, 146; to Simon Magus, 147-149; described as a human monster, 156, 157; his first victories, 158-160; is seated in the Temple, 160-162; rebuilds the Temple, 162, 163 : is the false Messiah; 166-169; his kingdom, 167; claims to be the Son of God, 168-170; comes from the tribe of Dan, 171-174; his signs and wonders, 175-181; rises from the dead. 181; his ministers, 188-190; simulates virtue to deceive, 191; ruler of the world, 192, 193; his mark, 201, 202; persecutes the faithful, 211-214; his hosts overthrown by the angels, 223; is destroyed by Christ, 224, 225; and also by Michael and Gabriel, 227-231; seated on Olivet and Sion, 231

Antichrist legend, its significance, 5; its persistence, 7; its relation to the Dragon myth, 13; Slavonic text, 44; its varied aspects in later times, 131, 143; general survey, 182-188

D

Dajjat, the Antichrist in Tabari's Chronicle, 116, 117
Damascus, destroyed in the last days, 73, 76
Dan, tribe of, Antichrist comes from, 26, 171, 172; Testament of, 101, 173
Daniel vii. and xi., connected with Rev. xvii., 28
Daniel, Armenian Apocalypse of, 156
Daniel, Greek Apocalypse of, 51, 63, 66
Daniel, Persian History of, 109, 110, 111
Decius, Roman emperor, the Antichrist, 85
Demons, ministers of Antichrist, 189
Devil, the, relations to Antichrist, 138-146
Diemer, *Deutsche Gedichte*, 178
Dietrich, on Jewish and Christian eschatology, 16, 117 note
Dragon myth, Babylonian, traced back to primitive man, Prologue, *passim*; source of the Antichrist legend, 13; its influence on Rev., 13-14; its relations to Antichrist, 144, 145, 150, 164, 165, 183-185, 223
Drought and famine in the last days, 195-200

E

Ebert, on Commodian, 79
Edda, E. H. Meyer, on its mythology, 16. See also "Völuspâ"
Eisenmenger, on the Othoth ha-Mashiakh and the Book of Zorobabel, 106
Elias, one of the two witnesses, 27, 58; Apocalypse of, 90, 108; his return in the last days, 203-208
Enoch, one of the two witnesses, 27, 58; reappears in the last days, 203-208,

Ephrem, S., his apocalyptic writings tabulated, 37-39; his metrical system, 37; relations to Rev., 40; his hymns and discourses, 56; his Syriac Discourse, 59; its date, 61; reference to Antichrist as Satan, 141; and as the Dragon, 146
Epiphanius, reputed author of the *Vitæ Prophetarum*, 71 note
Eschatological literature, Gunkel on its persistence, 7; is independent of New Testament, 129; its varied aspects, 131
Esoteric oral tradition, 7, 31
Ethiopic Apocalypse of Peter, 72
Eucherius, Commentaries, 92
Euthymius, Commentaries, 92
Ezra, Syriac Apocalypse of, 59, 75
Ezra, 4, reference to Heraclius and Chosroes, 77; relation to Book of Clement, 86; its eschatological predictions, 101, 102

F

Fabricius, Last Vision of Daniel, 72
Faithful, the, persecuted by Antichrist, 211; fly to the desert, 212, 213; their delivery, 219, 220
False Messiah, the Antichrist, 166, 169, 182, 206
Famine and drought in the last days, 195-200
Fathers of the Church, their teaching on Antichrist and Rome, 27; references to Antichrist as the devil, 139-142
Firmicus Maternus, on the devil and Antichrist, 140
Flight of the faithful, 212, 213; of the woman in Rev. xii., 221
Forewarnings of the last days, 121 *et seq.*
Friedlieb, on the Sibyls, 98

G

Gabriel, S., resuscitates the two witnesses, 205 ; slays the Antichrist, 223, 224

Genesis xlix., reference to Dan, 26

Godfrey of Viterbo, his *Pantheon*, 45, 63 ; on Gog and Magog, 103

Gog and Magog, referred to by Adso and Bede, 48 ; by pseudo-Methodius, 50, 54 ; by Jerome, 55 ; identified as the Huns, 57, 92 ; relations to the Antichrist, 195

Graetz, on the Mysteries of Simon ben Yokhai, 105, 106

Gunkel, his *Schöpfung und Chaos*, 5 ; his laws of interpretation, 6 ; on Rev. and Babylonian myths, 8 ; on Rev. and historic events, 10 ; on Rev. and the Dragon myth, 13 ; his traditional method of exegesis, 14 ; his theory of the Antichrist legend, 143, 144

Gutschmid, on Adso and Bede, 49 ; on pseudo-Methodius, 50

H

Haymo, on 2 Thess., 139 note

Heraclius saga, 55, 77

Hildegard, S., Predictions, 93 ; on the death of Antichrist, 149

Hippolytus, his work on the Antichrist, 25 ; identifies Antichrist, not with Rome, but with the two-horned beast, 26 ; quotes "another prophet" on the Antichrist, 28 ; on esoteric teaching, 31 ; on the Little Daniel, 71 ; on the devil and Antichrist, 140

Honorius of Autun, *Elucidarium*, 93 ; its relation to the *Völuspâ*, 112

Hugo Eterianus, *de Regressu, etc.*, 93

Huns, identified as Gog and Magog, 55, 59, 60

I

Irenæus, *Adv. Hæreses*, 92 ; on the last days, 123, 124

Isaiah xxvi. 20 explained, 221

Islám, apocalyptic references to, 72-78

Isolin, on Rev. and the Syriac Apocalypse of Ezra, 3

Israel, ten tribes of, 102 ; reference to. in the Sibyls and in Commodian, 102, 103 ; relation to the Gog and Magog myth, 103

J

Jacob of Edessa, on the last days, 125

Jellinek, on Jewish apocalyptic writings, 106

Jeremiah one of the two witnesses, 208

Jerome, *ad Oceanum*, 55 ; on Dan. xi., 64 ; *ad Algasiam*, 92 ; on the devil and Antichrist, 140

Jerusalem, referred to in Rev. xi., 20

Jewish apocalyptic literature, 96

Jews, converted in the last days, 215-217

Joachim, Abbot, on the third witness, 208

John of Damascus, "Εκθεσις, 93, 139 note

John the Baptist, a third witness, 208

John the Theologian, his contention with Antichrist, 70

Judas Iscariot, reference to, by Papias, 157

Judgment, the last, 249

Justin, on Zech. xii., 103

K

Kalemkiar, his Armenian Vision of Daniel, 66

0177

Printed in the United States
17650LVS00005B/104

9 780788 505416